Mothers without Custody

MOTHERS WITHOUT CUSTODY

by

GEOFFREY L. GREIF

MARY S. PABST

Lexington Books

D.C. Heath and Company · Lexington, Massachusetts · Toronto

The material in this book does not represent an implied endorsement from the members of the organization Mothers Without Custody.

—Geoffrey Greif

Library of Congress Cataloging-in-Publication Data

Greif, Geoffrey L.
Mothers without custody.

Bibliography: p.
Includes index.
1. Absentee mothers—United States. 2. Custody of children—United States. I. Pabst, Mary S. II. Title.
HQ759.G76 1988   306.8′9   86-45006
ISBN 0–669–13024–9 (alk. paper)

Published simultaneously in Canada
Printed in the United States of America
Casebound International Standard Book Number: 0–669–13024–9
Library of Congress Catalog Card Number: 86–45006

The paper used in this publication meets
the minimum requirements of American National Standard
for Information Sciences—Permanence of Paper
for Printed Library Materials, ANSI Z39.48–1984.
∞™

ISBN 0–669–13024–9

88 89 90 91 92 8 7 6 5 4 3 2 1

We dedicate this book to
MAUREEN, JENNIFER, ALISSA, BRIAN, AND ALEXANDER.

Contents

Preface

W HEN Chuck Berry picked up his guitar in the 1950s and wrote his classic rock and roll song "Memphis," he was describing the pain of being separated from his 6-year-old daughter, Marie. The only information we are given is that the singer and Marie's mother did not agree, and thus a once-happy home was torn apart. Who would have guessed that thirty years later, Chuck could have considered writing the song from the perspective of a mother living apart from her children? Yet increasingly, especially following a divorce, mothers are assuming the noncustodial role.

This book is about mothers who are living apart from their children. In a way, it is an outgrowth of work that I began in 1982, when I surveyed more than 1,100 single fathers with custody. As I was going through the data, I realized that I was getting only one side of the story. I decided to survey noncustodial mothers so that I could get the other perspective on how these custodial arrangements evolve, the kinds of relationships that develop between the family members, and how the mothers adapt to living away from their children. Whereas I found that custodial fathers were viewed dichotomously—praised, on the one hand, for being nurturing and responsible fathers but insulted, on the other, because people assume that they are incompetent and need help to parent—a different impression emerged of the mothers. They are viewed unidimensionally—and that view is usually negative. Yet despite this negative view, I found that many of the mothers—one-third—are doing quite well, a third have mixed feelings about many aspects of their situation, and a third have not adjusted well. Neither sinners nor saints, these mothers are ordinary women who, for a variety of reasons—

from the noble to the questionable—are not the parent who spends the most time with the children.

Thus, there is no monolithic "mother without custody" who can readily be dismissed or blamed as uncaring or as incompetent to parent. The situation is more complicated; most of these mothers are noncustodial for other reasons. The vast majority maintain contact with their children. A common thread, though, is the hurt of living apart from their children, which all of the mothers experienced to at least some degree. Although a significant percentage are unhappy with their situation, a significant percentage are content with the way things have worked out and are confident that the custody arrangement is best for all concerned.

I had conducted a number of interviews between 1983 and 1985; however, when it was time to go ahead with the book, I asked Mary Pabst to collaborate. I believed that a female interviewer would make the mothers feel more comfortable and would be able to get different information from them. I also recognized that Mary's clinical skills, perspective, and extensive experience with female-related issues would add value to the project.

We hope this book will be useful to those interested in single-parent families and in the evolving roles of women as well as men.

Geoffrey L. Greif

Acknowledgments

T HE list of those to thank is always long. The grantors who helped get the study off the ground with their ongoing vote of confidence cannot be thanked enough. The staff at Parents Without Partners, particularly Ginny Nuta and Ann Parks, were extremely supportive. Lee Robeson's help with the statistical data and interpretation was invaluable, as always. A number of experts were interviewed for background information: Dr. Alice Dvoscan, with the Baltimore City Courts; Dr. David Arnaudo of the OCSE; Tom Ries, J.D., of Frank, Bernstein, Conaway, and Goldman; Stan Rodbell, J.D., L.C.S.W.; and Dale Blanchard and Angie Mease from Mothers Without Custody. We would also like to thank Dr. Judy Coché and Ann Boyer, L.C.S.W. for offering encouragement. Margaret Zusky at Lexington Books has provided continued interest in the topic and has made the writing of this book so much easier because of her enthusiasm.

Most important, we would like to thank the children, the fathers, and particularly the mothers whom we interviewed. We hope that this book can begin to compensate them for the hours they spent talking to us.

All names and identifying information from our surveys have been changed.

1

"How Could a Mother Do That?"

F ROM the beginning of our work on this book, we constantly heard:

"How could a mother do that? I'll never understand how a mother could give up her children." Despite the fact that more and more mothers are living away from their children following marital break-ups, people have difficulty accepting the situation. Of course, they say, it is fine for a father to be raising children following a divorce. Of course it is wonderful that fathers have become more involved with children and housework. And of course it is marvelous for a woman to get out of the house, to pursue a career, and to broaden her involvement in society. Even in statements of support, however, doubt about the mother's competence begins to creep in. Questions arise about her morality, her sanity, her nurturing abilities, her warmth. Was she unfaithful to her husband? Was she having emotional problems or abusing alcohol? Was she an uncaring, selfish person?

Most of us were raised in a time when a mother's place was in the home. Motherhood, apple pie, and America were inseparable. The role of mother is so important to us and is so linked with being a woman that we do not know how to react to a woman who is not raising her children. As a result, she is misunderstood.

The number of mothers without custody is increasing. Although no definitive information is available from the census bureau, we know by charting the rise of single custodial fathers that a comparable number of mothers also exists. In 1985, more than 700,000 fathers were raising children alone.[1] For every single father with custody after a divorce, there is a mother without custody. Yet the numbers are even higher, as many fathers with custody have remarried. If we use as a guide our research finding that half of the mothers' ex-husbands had remarried, we can estimate that there may be well over a million mothers living away from their children.

The purpose of this book is to further our understanding of this growing population of women. Just as myths have developed about single fathers with custody and about other single-parent groups, so have they developed about mothers without custody. Most damaging is that these myths have negative connotations. We hope to lay these myths to rest so that this growing segment of the parent population—and by extension their children and ex-husbands—will be more easily accepted. If we continue to judge harshly and to base our reactions on a lack of understanding, we do harm to the mothers and especially to their children. Children draw a sense of themselves from their parents. If a noncustodial mother feels under attack, it makes it more difficult for her to have a positive sense of self. The children may see that their mother feels embattled and misunderstood. They may hear unfair assumptions made about her. They may absorb the prevailing societal view about noncustodial mothers. The mother's value to the children may be adversely affected.

These mothers are fulfilling what is still a nontraditional role. They are living in a "no woman's land," where they are caught in double binds. On the one hand, they have benefited from increased opportunities for women in many areas of society. Women have more choices educationally and occupationally than at any time in recent history, and they are also better off financially. The income gap between women and men has been steadily decreasing.[2] In many ways, these changes make it easier for a mother to be noncustodial, because they are signs of a fundamental shift in the expectations for women's behavior. Yet although opportunities for women have grown outside of the home, the beliefs that people hold about how women should act inside the home have not necessarily kept pace. Many people believe that it is good that women have more choices than before, so long as the changes do not take away from their time with their children. Studies confirm that among divorced parents, mothers without custody are viewed the most negatively.[3] Although women have more choices educationally and occupationally, they have to be careful how they use their choices if they have children at home. That is the double bind. The new opportunities they have achieved have not extended to permission to live away from their children. Thus, a divorced mother is in a precarious position—encouraged to pursue life outside the home but discouraged from doing so without her children. Thus, women are penalized if they are mothers.

This book discusses noncustodial mothers—some of whom have adjusted quite well, some of whom are deeply troubled. We will describe how these mothers became noncustodial and how they are faring in this nontraditional role.

Who Is the Noncustodial Mother?

We define a noncustodial mother as a mother who is living away from her child or children a majority of the time. She may have given birth to the child or she may have legally adopted the child. She may be never-married, separated, divorced, or married. She may have custody of one child but have another child living elsewhere, a situation known as split custody. (Mothers with joint or shared custody, who have their children half the time, are not considered noncustodial.) For the purposes of our study, mothers were considered noncustodial if they described themselves that way and if they spent eight overnights a month or less with their children. In our survey, 90 percent of the mothers spent five overnights a month or less with their children. A mother may be noncustodial at one point and then regain custody. Some of the mothers we interviewed told us about frequently changing custody arrangements, though they had to be noncustodial at the time of the study to participate.

We believe that a mother's role shifts substantially once her child is spending a vast majority of time with another custodian. In most of the arrangements discussed in this book, the father is the custodian. When he assumes responsibility for the child on a full-time or nearly full-time basis, the parenting demands on him increase. All the chores associated with parenting—cooking, cleaning, doing laundry, arranging child care, helping with homework, disciplining, setting curfews, carpooling, and so on—fall to him. There is thus a complementary reduction in the mother's parenting chores. If the mother does not have split custody (see appendix for further discussion), she is going to assume what is basically a single person's lifestyle.

This is when the shift comes for the mother. Still a mother, but no longer spending her time parenting, she becomes a noncustodial mother. (Being noncustodial does not mean she is no longer a parent.) She may announce her status to the world, or she may try to hide it. Many mothers who remain involved with their children find that the quality of their time together improves when they begin living apart. Some help make decisions about schooling, religion, discipline, and other parenting concerns. Others are quite unhappy with their situations. One mother wrote, "No woman should ever give up her children no matter what the circumstances!"

The noncustodial mother may have willingly sought out her status. She may want the freedom of living away from her children, of having the children establish a closer bond with their father, or of pursuing personal or educational goals. She may feel that the children will be better cared for, either financially or emotionally, if they live with their father. She may believe, for many reasons, that she is doing the best for the children, for herself, and for the father if she becomes the visiting parent. Sometimes these beliefs are acted upon gradually, with forethought. In other cases, the mother may have deserted.

Some mothers have assumed the noncustodial status reluctantly or have vigorously fought against it. The children may have chosen to live with their father because he was the more nurturing parent or because he could better provide for them materially. The mother may have lost a court battle with the father, or a protective service agency may have removed the children from her custody. She may have felt mentally or physically incapable of raising them, reluctantly turning them over to the father. She may have relinquished them to avoid a court battle that she believed she could not win or that she believed would be detrimental to the children. She may have thought the children would be better off living with the father because of her own lack of financial resources. Mothers also become noncustodial because of physical or financial threats. A father who wants custody and recognizes the mother's often precarious earning capacity may threaten to withhold child support and alimony if she attempts to get the children.

In some instances, the noncustodial mother has remained on good terms with both the father and the children. In others, the family breakup is tinged with a great deal of animosity and mistrust and the terms are not so amicable. As we will discuss, whatever the reasons are for a mother to become noncustodial, they have a strong bearing on how the mother fares once she becomes noncustodial.

A Historical Perspective

Mothers without custody are not a new phenomenon, either historically or in literature. Phyllis Chesler (1986) recounts horrifying stories of the separation of female slaves from their children when slave families were divided and sold to different plantations. Charlie Chaplin spent a good part of his childhood, nearly a century ago, away from his mother, who was deemed mentally incompetent. So did Cary Grant. More recently, Yoko Ono waged a losing battle to gain custody of her daughter, Kyoko. Joanna Kramer, in the book and movie *Kramer vs. Kramer,* is perhaps the best known fictional noncustodial mother. (Meryl Streep seems to have cornered the market on movie roles of mothers living away from their children. In addition to portraying Joanna Kramer, she was also a noncustodial mother as Karen Silkwood and a tortured mother who had to choose which child to give up in *Sophie's Choice.*)

We do not have to look too far back in history to find a period when women did not have the vote and children were the property of the father. As noted by a number of sources,[4] as recently as the late 1800s, mothers were considered in need of protection and thus unsuitable for parenting alone. Without a viable income or career outside the family home or farm, it was difficult for a mother to support her children if there was a divorce.

With the coming of the twentieth century, this situation began to shift. Mothers began getting custody after marital breakups, for a number of reasons. First, as a result of the Industrial Revolution more fathers went outside the home for work and left the care of the children to the mothers. Thus, the importance of the mother to the family increased. Second, the progressive era in American history meant greater rights for children. They were no longer considered their father's chattel, which meant that the father's grip on them was loosened. Third, women began acquiring rights of their own, such as the vote, which opened the way for a stronger legal identity. Finally, mental health experts, led by Freud, became interested in the role of the mother in child development. Within this context, the relationship between mother and child was considered essential for the child's well-being. This laid the foundation for the "tender years" doctrine, which came to represent the prevailing belief that the mother was the most important parent when the child was young.

Perhaps also reinforcing the mother's position with her children in the early decades of the twentieth century was the marked increase in an often-mentioned social problem—desertion. Desertion became a major problem for social service agencies, which were called upon to care for the children and the custodial parent (usually the mother.) In a 1904 study of 591 families that sought social services following a desertion, Lillian Brandt (1972) found only 17 in which the mother had been the deserter. Why was there an increase in desertion at this time? William Baldwin (1972), also writing in 1904, blamed the rise on the ease with which a man who had learned a skill on one machine could transfer it to another (a post–Industrial Revolution phenomenon), on improved travel between cities, and on a greater knowledge of other cities through the newspapers. Desertion became known as the "poor man's divorce"—a way of avoiding court costs and being held accountable for family support. Mothers were not likely to desert, because they had few skills that were marketable outside the home. More recently, Alvin Schorr (1982) notes that mothers who work are more apt to desert than those who do not work; their ability to support themselves provides them the opportunity to leave.

The ensuing decades only helped to reenforce the position of the mother with the children. In the 1940s and 1950s, with World War II and the Korean conflict, children were further separated from their fathers and left with their mothers. During this period, the mental health profession continued to focus on the importance of the mother–child bond. In one review of the literature conducted between 1929 and 1956, the researchers found only 11 articles dealing with father–child interactions, as compared with 160 centering on mother–child interactions.[5]

It was not until the 1970s that the mother's position as primary caretaker was questioned. The women's liberation movement, the increased divorce rate, the improved economic situation of women, fathers' greater interest in parenting, and a new legal climate that reduces the traditional bias toward women are all related to mothers' increasingly living apart from their children. At the same time, there has been an increase in the use of joint custody as an option for divorcing parents, further reducing the number of mothers with sole custody.

Clearly, the topography of child custody has changed greatly in this century. Debate continues as to whether mothers or fathers now have a better chance of winning custody.[6] Child support payments to custodial fathers, usually unmentioned in the past, are becoming an issue. Recent federal legislation has put pressure on states to get more involved in the collection of child support payments.

What we are facing at the end of the twentieth century is the result of a slow but powerful steamroller effect. Women have seen their hold on their children slowly chipped away while they have gained opportunities in other areas. For some mothers, the changes are a breath of fresh air; they have provided an atmosphere in which a mother can more easily become noncustodial. For others, the changes have meant confusion and unhappiness. These mothers feel stripped of what is most important to them. Regardless of how well they may be adapting now, all the mothers encountered had felt some pain in living apart from their children.

A New Approach

Little prior research has been conducted on the experiences of non-custodial mothers. The studies that have been completed have rarely exceeded 100 subjects, and they were gathered from a variety of sources, including responses to media announcements, word-of-mouth recommendations, court-related referrals, mental health referrals, and self-help groups. Almost all of the studies have drawn samples from only one area of the country. Some knowledge of noncustodial mothers has also been gained secondarily from recent studies of fathers with custody, in which the fathers' accounts of their own experiences have shed light on the mothers.

The research that forms the basis for this book began in 1983 and was carried out primarily with the membership of two self-help groups: Parents Without Partners (PWP) and Mothers Without Custody (MW/OC.) Parents Without Partners is the largest self-help group for single parents in the United States, with a membership of approximately 200,000. It was founded in 1957 and has chapters in all fifty states and some foreign countries.[7] Its membership tends to be primarily white and middle-class, with representation from most minority groups. People generally join PWP to meet other single parents, for educational programs geared toward parents and children, and for family-centered activities. The membership is nearly two-thirds female. Mothers Without Custody is a self-help group designed to meet the emotional needs of noncustodial mothers and to help influence social policy and legislation pertaining to this population. It is a grass-roots organization that has existed for almost ten years, with a membership of approximately 1,000 in 1983.[8] Married women may belong to MW/OC, whereas active membership in PWP is restricted to singles.

Following a procedure used by Greif in 1982,[9] an eighty-item questionnaire was published in the June 1983 issue of *The Single Parent*, the membership magazine of PWP. Mothers who were living away from children aged 18 and under a majority of the time were invited to complete the questionnaire, fold it into a postage-guaranteed mailer, and mail it to PWP. Because PWP does not keep data on the custodial status of its membership, an estimate of the return rate is impossible.

The sample was enlarged when the questionnaires were distributed to presidents of various chapters of Mothers Without Custody at their annual convention. The presidents then handed out the questionnaires at their local chapter meetings. Because the authors were not present at the meetings where the questionnaires were distributed, an estimate of the return rate is unavailable. The sample was further enlarged when PWP and MW/OC members distributed the questionnaires through networking to other mothers who did not belong to either group.

Questionnaires that were received between June 1983 and January 1984 comprised the sample. The final sample totaled 517, making ours the largest study of its kind to date.[10] Approximately 75 percent of the sample came from PWP, as indicated by a response to a particular item on the questionnaire. The remaining 25 percent came either from MW/OC or from networking sources. Sixteen mothers left the item about membership unanswered and could not be classified in either group.

Between 1983 and 1987, we conducted telephone and personal interviews with more than a hundred mothers. Some of these interviews lasted many hours. A few were videotaped. Although most of those interviewed had completed questionnaires, a number of interviewees came from other sources. Some had heard about the research and contacted us. Others were mothers one of us had met while giving lectures on single parents.

A number of limitations on this type of research must be mentioned. First, the sample was drawn largely from self-help groups. We can only speculate on the differences between mothers who join such groups and mothers who do not. Do the mothers who join the groups have more needs than those who do not join, or do they have fewer needs because they have joined and are having certain needs met? No easy answer is available, but this issue must certainly be considered. Second, the sample was self-selected. The mothers chose to participate in the study. Therefore, we do not know the characteristics of those who belonged to the self-help groups but did not complete the survey. Third, the sample is largely white and middle-class. What these limitations mean is that certain segments of the noncustodial mother population are not represented. Thus, generalizations to the population at large must be made with caution.

Despite these limitations, the regional diversity in the sample (respondents came from forty-five states and Canada) and the large sample size enabled us to gain a better understanding of these women than had been previously gained. With a sample size this large, we were able to run certain statistical tests that would not have been as effective with a smaller sample. A sample size this large also permitted us to learn about a wealth of experiences from a hard-to-reach population. In addition, the two methods of data gathering—questionnaire responses and in-depth interviews—provided a balancing factor. The interviews allowed us to gain a more complex picture of the experience of the mothers. By comparing the information from the questionnaires with that from the interviews, we were able to approach many issues from two different angles. We came to rely on both sources in drawing our conclusions about the mothers.

Perspectives on Noncustodial Mothers

To help us understand our findings, we found it best to employ several theoretical perspectives. No single view of human behavior can capture and interpret the variety of backgrounds and experiences that we came across. By using multiple perspectives, we hope to gain a broader understanding of how the mothers achieved their nontraditional status and of their experience in society.

We have divided the book into two distinct time periods. The first period is the time leading up to the transfer of custody to the father. We can best understand how and why the mother achieved her noncustodial status by examining the intertwining of several factors: the mother's childhood, her experiences with her husband and her children, the role of women in society, whether the mother relinquished custody voluntarily, her personal characteristics, and the opportunities available to her. The second time period involves what has happened to the mother since she became noncustodial. Although the same factors affect the mother in both periods, the applicability of a theory to explain the mother's experiences in the two periods may differ slightly. For example, in the first time period, a mother's loss of custody in a court battle may be due wholly or in part to her lack of financial resources. Such a loss could be linked to issues surrounding a woman's role and her inability to earn an income equal to a man's. But in the second time period, a mother's style of coping with being noncustodial once she has lost custody may have more to do with the role models she had when she was growing up or with the support she receives from friends. Although these sources of strength could be linked to women's issues, they also could be explained by other theories. What we wish to present are a number of theories that we have found helpful and that we hope capture much of what is experienced by these mothers.

These mothers' experiences are the result of a complex interaction of factors that include, but are not limited to, the following:

1. The moment in history in which the mother lives
2. The mother's personal experiences, characteristics, and perceptions
3. The family history
4. The status of women in society
5. Support systems
6. The developmental stage of the family

The Moment in History

The notion of the moment in history in which a person lives was put forth by Erik Erikson, a psychohistorian and a leading theorist in human development. Erikson's conceptualization of a person's identity is built on three stepping-stones: "the personal coherence of the individual and role integration in his group; his guiding images and the ideologies of his time; his life history—and the historical moment" (Erikson, 1975, p. 20). Thus, a person's identity crisis is shaped and can be resolved, in part, by what is happening historically. Similarly, a collective crisis among members of a particular society can form a positive identity when appropriate outlets are available. However, such avenues are not always available for the individual or for the group. There may not be a meshing of history with a personal crisis. For example, a student who found an identity through vocal protest in the 1960s would have to adapt a different form of expression twenty years later, when social protest does not play the same part in the culture.

The point we wish to make here is that in understanding noncustodial mothers, we must consider the available sources of identity. It is obvious that these mothers would have had greater difficulties as recently as thirty years ago, when the United States had not experienced its most recent women's liberation movement. How this actually affects the mother is difficult to ascertain. The sticky and perhaps unresolvable question is the *extent* to which the historical moment at the end of the twentieth century is different from previous periods in history. How supportive is our culture, and how much support do mothers receive from family and friends? One resource for mothers that exists in the 1980s but did not exist before is the self-help group. These groups provide a context for a positive identity that was unavailable in previous periods.[11] Also, as noted earlier, women now have more opportunities to define themselves in non-traditional roles. The impact of these opportunities on a mother's self-image varies from woman to woman. What are we to conclude about the prevalence of self-help groups and the economic opportunities for women that did not exist before? As with many of the issues concerning identity, it may be best to consider their impact along a continuum. Some mothers will feel that the time for being noncustodial is optimal, while others will feel that the time has not yet arrived.

Personal Experiences, Characteristics, and Perceptions

The mother's personal experiences, characteristics, and perceptions may affect her more strongly than anything else. A person's quality of life while growing up, interactions with others, and sense of self, and the amount of reassurance or abuse she receives all shape her perceptions. An optimistic person who believes that things will work themselves out most likely has experienced a variety of successes or has witnessed others overcoming adversity. This person's self-esteem and belief in the ability to overcome difficulties is high. Changes in her life will be viewed more as opportunities for growth than as earthshaking crises. Certainly, a mother who emerged from childhood with a sense of competence and mastery will approach adult crises with an outlook different from that of someone who feels she has few interpersonal skills to draw upon.[12]

It is important to consider whether the noncustodial mother's path through life leading up to her custody arrangement has been different from that of a mother who retains custody. To what extent have the mother's childhood experiences shaped her adult actions? Does she lack self-esteem? Or does she view being noncustodial as an opportunity for growth for herself, her children, and her husband?

Robert White (1974) has written about the search for competence that underlies many of our attempts at coping and adaptation. People generally strive to find a niche—a place to belong. It is our view that people often look for opportunities to make themselves happier, to solve their problems, and to cope with crises. We therefore choose to view the mother's behavior as a search for growth as she copes with her nontraditional status.

Family History

When we speak of family history, we are including both the events that happened in previous generations and the current events that have an impact on family members. For example, the experiences of a noncustodial mother who was raised by a single father will be quite different from those of a mother who was raised by two parents. She may have a sense of repeating history through her own actions. She might feel handcuffed by this history and believe that her becoming noncustodial is predestined—that she is acting just like her own mother. Or she may feel freed by her previous experience. Feeling good about herself, she may have no concerns about her own children being raised by their father.

Murray Bowen, one of the founders of family therapy, has written a great deal about this point.[13] In his view, resolving one's relationship with one's family history is the first step toward becoming a healthy person. Without an intellectual understanding and separation from one's parents, for example, one may repeat the same patterns even if they are not healthy ones. For these reasons, knowing how the mother sees her family can be vital in understanding what she experiences as a noncustodial mother.

Current family events can also be relevant in shaping our perceptions of the mothers. A mother whose children have moved a great deal since she became noncustodial may feel differently about pursuing custody than a mother whose children have had a stable existence in the same home.

The Status of Women

When we refer to the status of women, we are referring to the opportunities available to women, the costs and benefits of exploring those options, and the understanding that people have about women's behavior. We use a feminist perspective to help us frame what these mothers experience. A great deal has been written in the past twenty years about feminism and about the impact of sexism on women. A number of theorists have looked at these issues in great depth.[14] It is relevant for us to examine here some of the recurring issues, as the role of women in our society has a direct effect on these mothers. We cannot pursue our discussion without considering the political and social pressures on these mothers from the culture.

Although there is no single generally accepted definition of a feminist perspective,[15] many common threads weave together the issues that such a perspective covers. Central to all discussions is the inequality that exists between men and women in our society. It has been abundantly and well documented that women do not have access to the same opportunities in society that are available to men. The reasons for these inequities have been tied to differences deriving from gender and differences deriving from sex. Kaufman (1985) believes that gender is linked to the socialization process that begins in early childhood. The belief is that attributes related to males and females are linked to conditioning; they are culture-bound, not inbred. On the other side of the fence are those who argue that the differences between men and women stemming from sex are biological. Kaufman states that, now, differences between males and females cannot be easily explained by either perspective. Although there are obvious sex-based differences between men and women, these differences do not have to play themselves out in the way the culture is organized.

Gilligan's (1982) research on men and women has also turned up sex-based differences in experiences of adults and children. Like Kaufman, Gilligan argues for the need to understand female development in its own right—*different* from male development, but not inferior.

The impact of gender-related differences on society has been great. Kravetz (1976) states: "Women and men both have been socialized to view the characteristics, activities, and work of males as superior to and more valuable than those of females" (p. 421). One of the detrimental results, according to Kravetz, is an underutilization of women's capabilities and talents, which reenforces a sense of powerlessness. Coupled with this process are male dominance and male privilege, which contribute not only to powerlessness in women but also to their victimization. The relevance of this analysis is that through socialization, not solely through biological sex, women are in a one-down position. It is not an inherent inferiority that currently victimizes women but rather a society that is structured by both women and men to offer men more opportunities than it offers women.

Hence, women do not place themselves in the role of victim but rather sometimes find themselves there through a complex series of interactions that involve the social structure, history, and the points of interaction between themselves and others. We say "sometimes" here to emphasize again the variability in experiences among people in general and among noncustodial mothers in particular. We must assess what has happened to a mother before we can apply any one perspective.

The victimization process wears a variety of faces. It appears in the ongoing threat to women of being raped. It appears in a marriage in which the wife is being physically or mentally abused. It appears when an abused wife feels that she has no choice but to stay in the marriage, because she perceives life without the income or protection of a husband as the harsher of two evils. It appears when women are held to a higher standard of appearance than men and when being attractive is linked more closely with success in the work and social world for women than for men. It appears in the workplace itself, where men dominate the administrative structures of most large corporations. Finally, the victimization process appears when women are held to a different parenting standard. Their relationship with their children is seen as more important than the father's. The result is that women are victims because there is a greater pressure for them to be full-time mothers. We wish to emphasize that in the family, men are victims, too. Their involvement with their children is often blocked by the same pressure that pushes women into the primary parenting role. The socialization process works against men, too, as it cuts them off from their own feelings and from many aspects of parenting.[16]

Legal, social, and therapeutic actions have begun to change this victimization process. These actions began on a widespread basis with the suffragette movement. Whether it is support for the ERA, a men's or women's consciousness-raising group, or therapy that specifically addresses the role of women in society[17] or the role of women in the family,[18] the imbalance in male-female roles is being reevaluated and addressed. Being a noncustodial mother does not necessarily mean that the woman has been victimized. Many noncustodial mothers chose the role and are quite comfortable with it. Thus, the victimization metaphor may be appropriate for some of those who are having a hard time but not for all of them.

The feminist perspective has greatly influenced our view of the women in this book, and it is a major, though not exclusive, perspective we have used in trying to understand them. The literature on feminist therapy, which has also had an influence, will be discussed in chapter 12, where we talk about clinical work with the noncustodial mother.

Support Systems

In looking at support systems, we used systems theory to examine the mothers' interactions with the members of their family as well as with institutions in society. We asked the mothers how supportive their children, parents, and friends have been, how supportive the workplace has been, and how supportive the legal system, the community, and their ex-husbands have been. Systems theory tells us that people do not live in isolation from others but affect and are affected by them.

The prevailing norms and values that the mothers encounter vary from mother to mother and from system to system. We know from theories of deviance, for example, that when someone goes against the expected, he or she may be viewed in a variety of negative ways. The mother who feels accepted by her parents or her children will have a different parenting experience from that of the mother who is made to feel guilty. These systems of potential support must be considered when we examine the mothers' experiences. The systems themselves are affected by the prevailing view of women and men. The mothers are embedded in a culture and in a variety of systems, which is why looking at issues systemically provides a valuable tool for understanding.[19]

One way of thinking about how others react to the mother and how the mother feels in turn is the concept of role ambiguity. This concept can be applied to situations in which the expectations associated with a role are unclear.[20] The lack of expectations makes the methods for fulfilling a certain role and the consequences of carrying out that role unclear.[21] When people feel uncertain about their role, they may experience depression, anxiety, low self-esteem, futility, and even poor job performance. The applicability of this theory for these mothers is obvious. As they move into a role for which there are few clear expectations, they may experience both a negative reaction from others and many of the feelings just described.

Developmental Stage

Finally, we also have been influenced by theories of life cycle development.[22] As part of normal development, all families pass through certain stages as they mature. Negotiating each new stage can be a time of crisis for a family. For instance, the departure of the youngest child for college or the work world marks a new stage for the family. The child's leaving home results in a redefinition of the family members that remain. A marriage that has been kept together by the presence of that child may suddenly fall apart. This perspective on families also tells us that when children reach adolescence, new demands are placed on parents to provide both continued parenting and the freedom to explore the world outside of the home. Conflicts between parents and children are normal at this stage. It is often during this particularly difficult stage that many mothers who have had custody turn the child over to the father, who is considered more strict and better able to handle the adolescent. We wish to emphasize the importance of this theory, as it should not be assumed that all of the problems between mothers and their children described in this book are the sole province of a noncustodial mother–child relationship. When mothers describe how difficult parenting has been for them, it must be remembered that parenting can be difficult regardless of the sex of the parent or the number of parents in the home.

We would like to add one final note regarding theoretical perspectives. We have been influenced by much of the research by Clarke-Stewart (1977), Lamb and Lamb (1978), Rutter (1972), and others, which has pointed out that successful adaptation of a child can be brought about by any consistent and nurturing adult. The mother is not the only one necessary for a child's psychological well-being.

The Mothers in Our Study

Of the 517 mothers without custody who completed our questionnaire, 97 percent were white and 96 percent were single. Their average age in 1983 was 38.9 years old (90 percent were between 27 and 49). The ex-husbands' average age was slightly older, 41.8 years. Most of the mothers (66 percent) were married between 1960 and 1970 and were separated or divorced in the mid to late 1970s, following ten to twelve years of marriage. Almost half of the mothers gave their religious affiliation as Protestant, one-quarter were Catholic, and 5 percent were Jewish; the rest gave other religions or said that they were unaffiliated.

On the average, the mothers had lived away from at least one child for 3.9 years; two-thirds of the sample had been noncustodial for four years or less. Twenty-six percent of the mothers had split custody, with at least one child 18 or under living with them. Another 7 percent had a child over 18 living with them. Sixty-six percent had had their custody situation legalized, and 61 percent had had custody when the marriage first ended. (For the purposes of discussion in this book, the term *custody* is used to refer to the living arrangement of the children, regardless of whether or not it has been legalized.) A total of 785 children were reported to be living elsewhere, the vast majority with the father. (To facilitate later discussions, we consider the father to be the primary caretaker.) Thirty mothers reported that their children were staying with either a grandparent or another relative. One mother reported that one of her children was institutionalized. Slightly more than half of the mothers reported that they had only one child 18 years old or younger living away from them. Another third had two children living away from them. One mother in eleven had three children living away from her, and one mother in thirty had four or five children living elsewhere. The children living away from the mother were more likely to be male than female (by a ratio of nearly three to two). The average age of the children was 13; twenty-nine were under 5 years of age. Fifteen mothers indicated that they had given birth to children from different marriages.

Although it may not be surprising that mothers are more likely to have boys living away from them than girls, there was also a greater percentage of boys (a ratio of six to five) living with the 26 percent of the mothers who were raising some of their children. The mothers with split custody were raising 181 children (an average of almost 1.4 child per mother with split custody). The average age of these children living with the mother was 12. Sixteen children in this group were under 5, a higher percentage than among the children being raised elsewhere (9 percent versus 4 percent).

Almost half of the mothers said that a stepmother was currently involved in rearing their children. As mentioned earlier, the mothers came from most states in the United States and from Canada. Some lived in small rural areas; others came from large urban centers. The five states that were most highly represented were California (eighty-three respondents), Ohio (forty), Texas (thirty-two), Michigan (thirty-two), and New York (thirty). When respondents were grouped by region, no significant differences were found in the answers given.

The average annual income, including alimony, of the noncustodial mothers was $16,298 in 1983. The incomes varied widely—from $3,000 to $60,000—indicating a potential for a great range in the lifestyles of the mothers who took part in the study. Some of the mothers were scraping by on their incomes; 10 percent reported incomes of $7,500 or less. This income level can be compared with that of noncustodial fathers, which, according to a census report for 1983, was $16,520. These mothers' income was more than $2,500 above that of the average working single mother in 1983, yet lower than the median income of U.S. families in 1983, which was over $23,500.[23] Moreover, the poverty level for 1983, not including in-kind benefits, such as food stamps and Medicaid, was just over $5,000 for one person.[24] Only 5 percent of the mothers in our study reported incomes of $5,000 or less.

In reviewing these statistics, we see that the mothers in our study were earning more than many single mothers, about the same as the average single father without custody, and, for the most part, well above the poverty level. As we will show later, however, these mothers were earning substantially less than a group of single custodial fathers who were studied in 1982.

The mothers' occupations varied from maid to lawyer and professor. By far the most frequently given occupation was secretary, cited by 15 percent of the mothers who gave an occupation. The next most common occupations mentioned were office manager, salesperson, nurse, teacher, teacher's aide, office machine operator, counselor, and engineer.

Educationally, the mothers had completed an average of two years of college; nearly a third had completed some graduate education. Another third had stopped their education after high school. The median number of school years completed nationally, 12.6 years, was lower than this sample.[25] The higher education level among the noncustodial mothers would be expected since their income is higher, and income and greater educational attainment are usually linked. Also, many of the mothers had a chance, since they became non-custodial, to pursue educational goals that were stalled when they gave birth to their children.

Overview of the Book

Our purpose in writing this book is to explore the lives of the mothers up to the point when they became noncustodial and to describe their experiences as noncustodial mothers. The major findings are based on the 1983 survey of 517 noncustodial mothers and on subsequent interviews we conducted between 1983 and 1987 with these and other mothers we encountered. We have also undertaken three other research projects in order to better place our findings in context. In 1986, we surveyed forty-seven single fathers without custody. By asking them to complete the same questionnaire completed by the noncustodial mothers, we were able to derive comparisons between the experiences of noncustodial mothers and noncustodial fathers. These comparisons are discussed in chapter 11.

In 1987 we also reviewed 400 divorce decrees documenting custody and child support awards in Baltimore County. The 400 decrees were selected from seven different years between 1968 and 1987. Some of them were examined in depth. This research turned up some interesting trends in who is getting custody and who is paying child support. That information appears in chapter 10.

In addition, a telephone survey was conducted in 1987, nearly four years after the questionnaire was first published, in an attempt to gain some follow-up information on the permanence of the custody and living arrangements of the mothers. Information from those interviews appears in chapter 15.

Finally, we have relied for further comparison data on the findings from Greif's 1982 study of fathers with custody, which used the same research methodology as this study, centering on the responses of members of Parents Without Partners to a questionnaire and in-depth telephone and personal interviews. In that study, 1,136 custodial fathers were surveyed about their parenting experiences. As part of that research, 150 mothers with custody were interviewed.

Those findings are woven into the book at different points to provide a context for the information gained from the mothers. The focus of the book, though, will remain on the noncustodial mothers, for it is their story that needs to be told.[26]

Chapter 2 focuses on the lives of three women whom we interviewed in depth in 1985 and 1986. They represented to us mothers who had followed different paths in becoming noncustodial and were adapting to their situation to various degrees.

Chapters 3, 4, and 5 cover aspects of the time period before the mothers became noncustodial. Chapter 3 deals with the mothers' childhoods, their relationships with their own parents, and other family characteristics; chapter 4 examines the courtships, marriages, and divorces of the mothers; and chapter five zeroes in on how the mother became noncustodial.

Chapters 6, 7, and 8 discuss the mothers' experiences as noncustodial mothers, focusing on their relationships with their children, their relationships with their ex-husbands, their social and work lives, and the comfort they feel in being noncustodial.

Chapter 9 looks at the issue of child support, and chapter 10 covers the mothers' experiences with the court system (our research into the court records). Chapter 11 presents comparisons drawn from our surveys of noncustodial fathers.

In chapter 12, we examine the clinical and therapeutic implications of our findings. This chapter is geared toward mental health practitioners who work with noncustodial mothers in need of service and single parents who run self-help groups.

Chapter 13 centers on interviews we had with children raised by custodial fathers in the 1950s, 1960s, and 1970s. We learn from some fascinating descriptions what it was like for them to be raised away from their mothers at a time when mothers were expected to be home with their children.

Chapter 14 is the story of one family that we feel provides a model for working out successful relationships when the mother is noncustodial. The chapter includes interviews with the noncustodial mother, the custodial father, and their son.

The final chapter presents the findings from our telephone calls to fifty mothers almost four years after the original survey began. In that chapter, we also attempt to draw some conclusions from our findings and look toward the future.

2

Three Noncustodial Mothers

I let them have him. He was four. It was probably a mistake because it did not work out the way it was supposed to.

—Carol

I could not raise the children half time on what I was making as a student on a grant. So I let him have them and the house. The kids really loved him a lot.

—Barbara

My oldest son and I always had trouble getting along. He's too much like me—quick to temper and our values are different. My ex is more tolerant.

—Wilma

WE have chosen to highlight the stories of Carol, Barbara, and Wilma in this chapter because we believe their experiences exemplify the range of events that may occur in the lives of noncustodial mothers. Of course, three stories cannot adequately explain every mother's situation, yet we saw many commonalities among these mothers and others we interviewed.

These three were also chosen because they are all at different points on a continuum. Carol lost custody partly because she was young and naive. She has not talked with her son in many years, and she hides her identity as a noncustodial mother. Barbara had struggled with feelings of incompetence but has maintained contact with her children and is trying to put some perspective on her situation.

Wilma, who has split custody, willingly gave up custody when her sons requested it. She believes that the custody arrangement is best for everyone. As we will see, one of these mothers has had a continuously difficult adjustment, one has recently overcome some self-doubts, and one feels very comfortable with her situation. Their stories reflect many of the recurring themes in this book. In examining the different stories, it becomes clear that one theory explaining how mothers become noncustodial is never sufficient, nor can one event in someone's life sufficiently explain the resulting events.

Carol's Story

Carol is a 35-year-old paralegal working in New York. She has not spoken to her son in thirteen years. It is not that she has not tried desperately to see him. It is he who has refused to see her or even to believe that she is his mother.

Carol is a tall woman with shoulder-length light brown hair. When she speaks, her eyes dart back and forth, usually resting on the listener. During the course of the interview, she occasionally becomes tearful and asks to have the tape recorder stopped. When she regains her composure, she says we can turn it on again. She gives the appearance of physical strength but also of weariness, as if she just about makes it through the day before going home for a hot bath. She is reserved and tends to reveal the most about herself when asked directly.

The oldest of two children, Carol was 13 when her parents' marriage ended in divorce. Unusual for those times, the children were split up: she stayed with her mother while her brother went to live with her father. Prior to her parents' breakup, there had been a good deal of fighting in the home. Carol thinks that it was her mother who finally ended the marriage. Her parents did not stay on speaking terms, and Carol has seen her father only once since then. She maintains infrequent contact with her brother.

When Carol was 17 and a high school junior, she met Bill, a senior at the same school. They began dating and were married a year later. Carol regrets the decision to get married so young and gives the following explanation:

> The real reason was back during the Vietnam war. He was going into the Marines and he was afraid I wouldn't wait. If you waited

to get drafted you went to Vietnam. So he enlisted, and when he got out of basic training was when he wanted to get married. I would have waited longer but he was afraid I wouldn't wait, but I would have.

Her mother opposed the marriage, but to no avail. A Catholic wedding was arranged.

Shortly after the wedding, Bill was assigned to an army base in a southern state, and Carol moved in with her mother. Bill was then reassigned to a six-month training program in Florida, where Carol joined him. It was during that stay in Florida that Carol became pregnant. Bill was subsequently assigned to Germany, and Carol returned to her mother's house. While Bill was overseas, Mark, their only son, was born. Six months later, Carol and Mark joined Bill in Germany. The couple had not seen each other for ten months. Carol thought Bill had changed during their absence:

I didn't like the way that he acted. It seemed all he did was whine about his getting out on a hardship [being a father]. He would say to me, "If you loved me you would get me out of the service."

Carol refused. She thought he should serve his country.

In spite of Bill's behavior, Carol liked the time spent in Germany. She worked as a secretary at the base, and Mark was enrolled in a day care center. Their life took on a semblance of a happily married couple. But Bill became increasingly jealous.

I remember one time we had our picture in the paper and people started calling the house and saying how beautiful I was. He threw a fit, saying I was not going out of the house anymore. Another time we were out with another couple to celebrate my twenty-first birthday and this guy came over to our table and asked me to dance. Bill caused a scene, saying, "How dare you ask my wife to dance." Then we were at another restaurant and Bill went up to get drinks and this man came over to ask me to dance and I knew his family was back in the states so I danced with him. Bill threw a fit that night and left. I stayed out with the other couple and when he came home that night he had drunk about a case of beer and he came after me with a knife saying he would fix my face so no one would look at me. He threw a lit cigarette and burned me.

That was probably the worse it had ever been. It wasn't that he was violent, it was just that he was so jealous.

Carol was feeling a lot of other pressures at that time. She and Bill shared a car, and she frequently had to sneak out of work to drive him to his station. Mark was thrown out of nursery school because he was hyperactive, and Carol had problems getting baby-sitters for him. As a result of these pressures and her mounting marital difficulties, Carol began suffering from what she described as psychosomatic stomach pains.

A year later, Bill was discharged from the army and the family moved back to the states and into Bill's parents' house. Carol was unhappy there.

It was terrible. Every time you left a room you were told to turn out the light. Bill's sister would go into my things all the time and just help herself to my jewelry and clothes. I would tell Bill she had no right to be there but he wouldn't back me up.

Three months later, they moved into their own apartment. This was the happiest period in the marriage for Carol. She enjoyed being a full-time mother. Bill began working as a real estate salesman, and the relationship was improving. But this period was short-lived, and problems returned when she learned that Bill was not being honest with his co-workers.

No one at his job knew he was married and that is where he got his girlfriend. We had an unlisted phone number and the operator put through an emergency call from this hysterical woman who turned out to be his girlfriend's aunt asking for her. At that point Bill grabbed the phone out of my hand and I knew something was going on. He gets on the phone and tells the aunt he'll be right over to see her. He had stood her up on a date. After that I told him to leave. I found out during that time I was pregnant. He said it was my problem. I gave it a lot of thought and abortions were hard to get so I went to some psychiatrist who presented me to the medical board and I got it done.

When Bill left, Carol had custody of Mark, who was then 3. She returned to work at two different jobs to earn enough money to support the two of them. Her mother and Bill's sister helped out with child care. For the next year, Bill rarely visited but usually contributed some child support. Then he began seeing Mark a good deal. He continued to date the same girlfriend, and even moved in with her, but he and Carol began seeing each other again. At one point, he asked Carol to call his girlfriend and ask her to move out so that he could move back with Carol. When Bill brought Mark back after a weekend visit, Carol would find love letters to her that Bill had hidden in Mark's clothes.

> That's when I called his girlfriend and said I think we have to straighten this out. So we met and we found out that he was lying to us both. He found out about the meeting and said he thought the three of us could move in together. It was crazy. After too much of this I formally filed for child support. I got a child support order even though he had been paying regularly. That aggravated him.

Bill wanted Carol to rescind the support order and threatened to kill himself if she did not. Carol told him to go ahead. Three months later, he married his girlfriend. Almost immediately, they began asking Carol to turn over custody of Mark to them.

> I had heard that she really loved Mark and took good care of him when he visited them. At this point I was going through a rough time because I was working constantly and Mark was crying all the time, saying, "Please mommy don't go to work." So I let them have him. He was 4. It was probably a mistake because it did not work out the way it was supposed to. I had legal custody. Of course, when they got him they moved to a new address and I never knew where he lived. But I knew where Bill worked and where Mark went to day care. So I went to the day care center and the counselors advised me that Mark was very mixed up and if he was going to live with his father then I should stay away from him for awhile. That was the next mistake because the time to see him was never right after that.

Carol kept calling Bill at work and asking to see Mark, but Bill, picking up on the theme introduced by the counselors, said that a visit from Carol would make Mark more confused. Carol did not dispute this at first. But after many months, she finally decided to take legal action to regain custody. Carol's income put her in a precarious position, though. Legal Aid told her that she earned too much money to qualify for their services, but she did not think she could afford a private lawyer. She felt stuck. Bill continued using stall tactics.

> Over the years I would keep calling to see Mark, and Bill kept saying, "Okay I'll talk to him and you can see him" or he would say he wasn't doing too well in school and this was not a good time and he would always talk me out of it.

Nothing changed for the next few years. Carol remained out of touch with Mark and then lost contact with Bill when his company went out of business. Despite the lack of contact, Carol began getting harassing phone calls from Bill's new wife.

> She would call and say, "You call yourself a mother. I'm the one who takes care of him when he's sick, you bitch." I was so upset I began calling up every real estate company looking for him. Well, I finally found him and told him about the phone call; he denied it, and I said, "Let me see Mark," who was 13 at this point. I had not see him for nine years. Bill said, "Let me ask him about seeing you. Please do not get a lawyer." Well, he called me back and told me Mark did not want to see me. I asked to speak to Mark and he said no.

At that point, with the financial help of her mother, Carol hired a lawyer. A custody battle followed. Mark said he wanted to stay with his father, and Carol lost the suit. The judge denied visitation. No reason was given. Carol also lost the appeal.

During that time, Carol's mother went to Mark's school to make a direct appeal to Mark on Carol's behalf. She told Mark that she was his grandmother. It was a mistake. Carol remembers:

> He got hysterical. He said, "You're not my grandmother. I don't have another grandmother." I was sitting in the car watching and was going to go up to him at that point but he ran away. [That was the first time Carol had seen him in years.] It was then decided by the courts that until he was 18 I could not make any contact

with him. He was just 18 two months ago and I'm waiting to hear from him. I keep sending cards. I don't know if he gets any of them, though.

Over the years, Carol has handled questions about whether she has children by saying that she does not. It is only when she has known someone for a long time that she explains her situation. She believes that most people will not understand. It is not that she has received a negative reaction from people when they hear she is non-custodial; rather, she feels that the story is too complicated and that people might react negatively to her if they knew that she did not have custody.

Carol thought when she gave up custody that she was making Mark happy, but now she is ambivalent. Although she thinks it has been hard on Mark not seeing her, she also says, "I think that even to this day I probably did the best thing for Mark by turning him over to them." Even with the arguments they have had, Carol's favorable impression of the parenting abilities of Mark's stepmother has made the lack of contact easier for her. Despite Carol's various attempts to get custody and her feeling that Mark is better off where he is, she feels guilty: "I was young then but I should have tried harder. [She gets teary-eyed.] I should have tried harder."

Carol has been dating the same man for the past ten years. She has found the romantic security she never had with Bill. He has no children, and she says she does not want to have any more children after what has happened to her.

In her concluding comments during the interview, Carol says:

It's not fair to the child to not have contact with both parents. It's also not fair to grandparents. I think if I had been older I would have been more insistent about seeing Mark. I would not have let them push me off. It was always assumed that it was best for the child to be with the mother but that is not always the case. Sometimes the father can provide better for them. A lot of my friends are divorced and with their kids and they never got child support from the fathers. Just because my case turned out like this doesn't mean other mothers should hang on to custody. If Bill had lived up to his word, everything would have worked out fine. And it doesn't mean things did not work out well for Mark.

Barbara's Story

Barbara, 46, is the mother of an 18-year-old daughter, Jean, and a 15-year-old son, Jerry. Ten years ago, the children went to live with their father. She begins our interview by saying, "It has a strange effect, being a mother and not being a mother." She is a woman of medium build, with blond hair and blue eyes that twinkle when she smiles. As she talks, she twists her hair, adding to its natural curl. The interview takes place at her place of work, a small mental health center in a Philadelphia suburb. There are pictures of her children in her office. Trained in asking other people about feelings, she is very articulate and comfortable in expressing her own.

Barbara was born and raised in San Francisco. Her parents ran a small hardware store, where they both worked long hours. They were orthodox Jews and raised Barbara in a traditional way. Barbara remembers them fighting with each other every day and also fighting with her. The conflicts were most intense between Barbara and her mother.

> I don't remember ever getting anything positive from her, any stroking. The emphasis was always on the negative. I remember having a real low self-esteem because of it. I even did the emotional parenting of my younger brother, who also got nothing from her.

Barbara graduated from high school without difficulty and began college, maintaining her residence at her parents' house. But when her brother got married, she sensed that the pressure on her would be too great, and she moved out.

> I did not want to be alone with my parents anymore. I was kind of a free-thinker, a beatnik, I guess. So I moved into an apartment and continued going to school. Then I really broke the mold. I became a cocktail waitress in the biggest folk club in the city. That was an incredible statement for me to make. I was considered a rebel by my parents. It was very positive, because working as a cocktail waitress I was making a statement to myself that I was attractive enough to do that kind of work. It was a big step for me to make that statement. It was also a very stimulating atmosphere.

In the folk club, she found acceptance for herself that she had never had before.

This period of going to school during the day and working at night was one of the best periods of her life up to that point. It was also the time when she met her future husband, Sam, a fellow student. Sam came from an Italian background and was not Jewish. Barbara describes him as a very big-hearted person who was good at taking care of people. "I had been involved with a few other guys who were less stable but that I loved more. I decided that this was the kind of person I should marry, though." They dated for a year before her parents found out he was not Jewish. Her father was so upset that he did not speak to her for the next year—until her wedding. "He came up to me and kissed me, but we really did not have much to say to each other."

Immediately after the wedding, Sam and Barbara moved to Pennsylvania because Sam received a job offer from the government.

> The first six months of the move were terrible. I had never been away from home. I was scared to drive. I was not very adventuresome. Sam was very supportive during this time. He was my best friend.

Barbara was working at the time as a teacher but not enjoying it: "I was nurturing to the kids but did not feel I was doing a good job."

About this time, Sam's mother died of a heart attack, and he was devastated. Barbara decided that she wanted to have a baby, partly to help Sam with the loss.

> It seemed like something I could give him to help him with his mother. Before that I had thought I never wanted to have children. I felt very inadequate and I looked around and everyone I saw looked very inadequate. I did not want to feel the guilt of being an inadequate parent. Sam was the opposite. He wanted children very much. His father had not been around when he was growing up, and he convinced me that he would be around. I did not think I could do it myself and I thought that he could. I suppose that's why I married him.

When Jean was born, Sam did help out a great deal, in spite of a heavy work schedule. Barbara began feeling depressed.

> When I was in my twenties I was just so unaware of myself and my feelings. I still felt very inadequate. Jean was adorable and

charming and had me wrapped around her finger. But I was not feeling good about myself and would try to make things as easy on myself as I could. I think I had been depressed even as a child but no one saw it, including me. The important thing that happened here was that after I had Jean I became much less sexual. The doctor said that was natural, but it never resolved itself and I think I was never that attracted to Sam sexually and never really felt love for him. That became a real hard area in our marriage. Sam responded by feeling very rejected and could not understand what was going on. I did not know what was going on either.

Even though they remained close emotionally, the sexual aspect of their marriage was gone. "I would still make love with him occasionally when I felt sorry for him and fake it. Or I would just make an excuse." A second child, Jerry, was born three years later.

Six months later, Barbara began therapy. The reason was, "I felt like I could not do a thing around the house. Besides, seeing a therapist was included in our health plan." The entrance into therapy marked a change in her life. She began to feel good about herself and to appreciate some of her own strengths. Sam entered therapy with her. Barbara also began doing volunteer work and became involved in peer counseling, which later led to her decision to become a counselor.

This was also a burgeoning time for the women's movement, which had a profound effect on Barbara. She joined a consciousness-raising group and found that she had a great deal in common with the other women. Her marriage, though, was not improving. Other things began to change. Although she was not sexually attracted to Sam, she did begin feeling attracted to other men.

This was during a period of open marriage and greater sexual expression. I encouraged Sam to find a lover. Then I realized I wanted a lover, too. I started opening up to my own body and became sexual. I became involved with one or two other men. I also started questioning the marriage, of course. It was not working and that was very frightening to me. He was a decent, loving man who was very committed to the children and doing everything for me. But I did not love him.

During a therapy session, she told Sam that she wanted a divorce.

I was committed to making that as open and painless as was possible. We got a lot closer, and there were many tears during the session. But we got closer and stayed together for the next few months until finally he left. Way back when, before Jean was born, I had decided that if anything happened, he should have the children. But over the years I decided that was not the way it had to be. That I could be a good parent. I kept the kids for eighteen months. I was a terrible parent. I did not know I was going to be so distraught over the divorce. I also got involved in a bad relationship two weeks later which did not work out. I did not give the kids very much. Sam was angry for everything he did for me that I could not pay him back for. He was angry that he was paying me support and a lover was coming into the house. He was furious, furious, furious.

So we went into counseling to try and work out some of these issues. Sam was complaining that he lost his family, and the therapist started to suggest that we do an experiment where Sam moved into the house for six months and I move out.

Barbara thought this was a good idea for many reasons. She knew how much he missed the children, she wanted a break from the children to finish her school work, she was not doing a good job as a parent, and she was trying to have a new relationship. "It was a break for me and I thought something good would come of it." Barbara began visitation every other weekend, when the children would come and stay with her and her new boyfriend, who later became her second husband. The experiment continued for another six months while Barbara took more courses. Sam then asked for custody. Barbara wanted joint custody but knew she could not afford it and stay in school.

I could not raise the children half-time on what I was making as a student on a grant. So I let him have them and the house. The kids really loved him a lot. They loved me, too. The year he had them he did a lot better job than I did. Of course, he had that year and a half after the separation to get his shit together. Economically and practically it seemed to make sense for them to stay with him, and emotionally, too, because they were doing real well.

To a later question concerning the role money played in her decision, Barbara responded that it was a contributing factor but a

minor one. In addition, she says that she always could have taken a
higher paying job and kept them.

The next period of her life was very difficult.

> It was awful. I never thought I had any prejudices or any thoughts
> of inadequacy about mothers who had given up custody but . . .
> I went back into therapy and the therapist told me, "You are going
> to have to face that you failed as a mother. A lot of people do not
> understand that we all fail to some degree as parents." I cried a lot
> and did agree I had failed. The only hard part was telling my
> parents. They reacted terribly, but they always did. But with this
> one, I was unsure of myself.

Barbara never paid child support. A complicated formula was
worked out in which she would start paying when her salary reached
a certain percentage of his. It never did.

The children who were 8 and 5 at the time, did not play an active
part in the decision to grant custody to Sam. Over the years, Barbara
has kept a fairly active visitation schedule, usually taking one or both
children during all holidays. Within the past year, new problems
have arisen. Two years ago Sam remarried and moved out of town.
Jean, a high school senior, did not want to leave her old high school,
so she boarded with a family in the school district. Barbara offered
to have her come and stay with her, which also would have meant
a change of school district. She refused. Problems developed between
Jean and Sam's new wife. Jerry moved with his father and also
developed problems with Sam's new wife. Sam kicked Jerry out of
the house, and Jerry elected to go to boarding school rather than
move in with Barbara. Sam and Barbara, because of disputes over
the recent treatment of the children, have not spoken for over a year.
Yet Barbara celebrates holidays with her parents and Sam's parents,
who have become quite fond of each other despite past problems.

Does Barbara feel guilty now about being a noncustodial mother?

> I felt guilty for so many years, I just got tired of it. But I still think
> of myself as a mother who had an empty nest at a very young age.
> My role as a mother has never been very clear to me from that
> time on. Sometimes it has been sad and sometimes it has been very
> joyful. When Jean called me recently and said she wanted to take

me out to dinner, I felt wonderful. Now we can become close. She's reaching out and that feels good to me.

Wilma's Story

Wilma is different from Barbara and Carol in that her custody situation has evolved into a split situation in which she has one of her three children living with her. Her 13-year-old daughter lives with her, while her 14- and 16-year-old sons live with their father. Now 44 years old, Wilma lives in New Mexico and works for a small manufacturing company as an administrative assistant. She is interviewed at a convention hotel. She is short, with long brown hair that has started to turn gray. She laughs a great deal during the interview. She exudes a great deal of energy, in contrast to Carol's weariness and Barbara's calm.

As Wilma tells her story, there is little evidence of bitterness or remorse. She does not deny that there has been pain, but she states, "I believe in self-determination and I have become a realist."

Wilma spent the first fourteen years of her life in a two-parent home with a brother three years her junior. She never considered the possibility that her parents could divorce. Then, suddenly, her father left. It was a complete shock. She does not know precisely why he left, but she is sure that it had something to do with his business failing. She was never told the reason for his disappearance and just accepted it as a fact. She does remember him fondly and says she was closer to him than to her mother. The reason is easily apparent: Her mother emotionally and physically abused her. Wilma says that her mother had no idea how to raise children and that her mother had been spoiled when she was a child. When Wilma and her brother made the normal demands on a parent that children make, she could not handle it. Wilma says that her mother was more interested in social climbing than in being with the children. If the children interfered, there was severe discipline. Wilma says that it was probably especially hard for her mother to social climb because Wilma and her brother "were nonconformists—black sheep. I wanted to be a tomboy."

By the time she reached high school, she felt quite inadequate, both socially and intellectually. She had few close friends until her senior year. Eventually, and largely because of the influence of a

journalism teacher, Wilma began to excel academically. With the
help of that teacher, she began writing and was elected editor of the
school newspaper. Although these positive experiences helped improve her self-image, she maintains, "I was always a little different.
I was the only girl living on our block and never played with dolls."
She did baby-sit occasionally and says of it, "I didn't enjoy it—it
was an inconvenience. It was mostly infants. I would have liked
older kids because they are more responsive." When asked if she
ever saw herself in the role of mother Wilma says, "Yes, I felt I had
a lot of love to give and could raise kids. In fact, this year we have
an exchange student from Germany living with my daughter and
me."

Two years after her father left, her mother remarried. Her relationship with her stepfather was satisfactory, but she was so "dam-
aged" by her mother's abuse that she left home when she was 17.
Her brother left three years later, when he was 17.

Continuing her pattern of being a nonconformist, Wilma moved
into a commune with about twenty other people. She remained for
three years. "It was the sixties and communal living arrangements
were fairly prevalent elsewhere, but not in my small town. It was
probably the closest thing to a family that I ever really had." After
the communal living, she moved in with an aunt and some other
single women. Two years later, she met her future husband and
moved in with him for a year before they married.

Wilma was attracted to Michael because they were opposites,
which, she claims, was the reason for the breakup of the marriage.

> He was laid back and calm—I was hyper. He was tall—I was
> short. He was athletic—I was not. We liked to do different things.
> He had come from a large happy family. I obviously had not. In
> fact, I fell in love with his family almost as much as him. One
> problem from the start was that he wanted me to stay home and
> I wanted to have a career.

Things began well in the marriage. She was successful as a writer
and got some of her stories published. She and Michael developed
a few mutual interests but still preferred to spend their time
differently.

Then Wilma got pregnant. Including two miscarriages, she was
pregnant five times in 4 years. She remembers being happy about

being pregnant but feeling that it was a mistake for her to stop working. Having three children so close in age was very difficult for her. When her youngest started school and she at last felt free to go to work, a major blowup occurred because Michael wanted her at home. "I really enjoyed being with the kids, but I needed to do something else with my life to maintain my sanity." Her battle won, she first worked for an insurance firm and then opened a bookstore.

During those years, her relationship with her husband was compatible but not exciting. The marriage began to slowly unravel. Wilma explains it:

> He made a fair income as an electrical engineer. There was enough money for the essentials—food, clothing, the kids, our home—but he wasn't practical. He wanted to spend money on golf, fishing, and going to the ballgames. There was little time for the two of us to develop a relationship. His time would be with his jock friends. Gradually I developed some outside-the-home activities and we grew apart. I think maybe he felt too much responsibility too quickly. We also never really talked about our problems. We just did not communicate well. The only thing we really shared was the kids. He was always very involved with them—a good father—and still is. He was always mild mannered—to a fault— and still is. I tried to provoke him to argue or at least have an opinion on something, but he did not have it in him.

Wilma woke up one day and knew, after fourteen years of marriage, that it was over. "On my birthday. It was a present to myself. I left." She had not discussed it with anyone in advance, including her children. She went into counseling for a short period of time and then joined Parents Without Partners for two years. "PWP was an emotional support after the breakup. I stopped going when I had the strength to go it alone."

Wilma had custody of all three children when the marriage first broke up. She moved them all to a small town thirty miles away because of a job offer. After a year, her sons wanted to move back to their old town and be with their father. Wilma does not resent their moving out. "My oldest son and I always had trouble getting along. He's too much like me—quick to temper and our values are different. My ex is more tolerant. My other son wanted to go so he could be with the men." Would Wilma have been upset if all three children had gone? "I wouldn't have liked it, but that's their choice. I feel comfortable with that."

Since the new custody arrangement, her ex-husband has faithfully paid child support. Wilma has also stayed close to his family. "The grandparents are important to my kids. Especially since they do not see my parents at all."

Wilma has adjusted very well to the role of noncustodial mother. Regarding her relationship with her ex-husband, she says,

> He has remarried a very nice woman. I have no hard feelings. He was very good to me. He has always helped out financially. He has become my best friend over the years. We get together once a month to talk about the kids and share what is happening in our respective lives. He has taught me how to trust and in turn I have taught him how to feel. I know he was devastated by our divorce. Although it was not a huge suprise, he was deeply affected. There was nothing to be bitter about or blame on the other person, so I think we respect each other now. We feel each other is a good parent and should not be interfered with in parenting. We were just unhappy together—now we are happy apart.

Wilma adds with a smile, "In fact, we get together each year to celebrate the anniversary of our divorce."

Wilma believes that the children are doing well.

> They took things hard at first, but once the new custody arrangement got worked out and the boys were back in their hometown, things improved. We all see each other a lot, and my daughter visits them often. I do wish I was closer to the boys, though. They are starting to think about careers, and that's always interesting.

In talking about her own adjustment, Wilma reports:

> Life is now exciting. I am impulsive. I will do whatever I want to do within limits. I don't want to feel restricted by a mate. I love to attend the symphony, opera, art fairs, camping, and canoeing. I will do things alone or with friends or my daughter. I date some, but I am not interested in getting married again. Of course, if Prince Charming walked through the door I might reconsider.[She laughs.]

Conclusions

These women represent three different paths to becoming noncustodial mothers as well as three different lifestyles as noncustodial mothers. Although their stories all include disruptive or unhappy childhoods, the types of experiences they had were vastly different. Their stories are meant to introduce the broad range of situations that mothers experience as noncustodial parents. These women describe friendly and acrimonious divorces, custody loss because of money as well as by mutual agreement, and relationships with their children that range from the warm to the angry. In considering these mothers' experiences, we could say that Carol's situation is the least voluntary and the most painful and that Wilma and Barbara have made the better adjustments.

Although these mothers, like those described elsewhere in the book, are vastly different from each other in many ways, they are similar in that they are all noncustodial mothers—a role that makes some people renegades and others role models. They are renegades in that many people see them as having broken the basic and traditional rule that a mother should be with her children. To others, they are role models because they are seen as having been freed from those same traditions.

3

The Mothers' Own Childhoods and Family Backgrounds

M ANY of the mothers we interviewed had experienced some rough times as children; many had unhappy childhoods, absent fathers, or unloving mothers. Others, however, described very content early lives, with one or two supportive parents in the home. Although childhood and adolescent experiences can play an important role in what happens to people in later life, we wish to emphasize that a mother's early life is not a certain, and regular, predictor of her becoming noncustodial. Early experiences may have provided a springboard for some mothers, but not for others.

We certainly do not wish to imply that "bad" early experiences result in a mother's becoming noncustodial—that is, that being noncustodial is aberrant or unnatural. This book is not intended to judge the normality or abnormality of being noncustodial or to look at the mothers in good or bad terms. Nevertheless, because we do see noncustodianship as a nontraditional role, we are interested in what early experiences, if any, may have paved the way for the mother to become noncustodial and to adapt to being noncustodial.

In some cases, the mother's early experiences can be linked, in her own opinion, with becoming noncustodial. In other cases, we *and* the mothers see no connection. We do feel that, for some mothers, early experiences have the *potential* for setting the stage for later ones. For example, a mother who was happily raised by a custodial father is probably more likely to consider that form of family life for her own children than a mother who was not raised in that manner. Yet we make this statement with a great deal of caution. The link between early experiences and later lifestyles is extremely fuzzy.

People often believe that one's experiences as a child can account for how one turns out as an adult. In examining the development of children, Jerome Kagan (1984) has reviewed a number of studies concerning the relationship between the personalities of infants and children and their later personalities as adolescents and adults. Although some personality characteristics, such as aggressiveness, remain constant from childhood into adolescence and adulthood, studies of normal children show that behavior does change over time. One conclusion reached by Kagan is that behavior can be carried over from one developmental stage to the next but that the behavior may need support from the environment for it to be continued. This fits in with our view that later events influence a mother's becoming noncustodial.

We are not talking specifically here about the carry-over of personality from childhood to adulthood; those patterns of behavior can be traced. Rather, we are looking at the home life and relationships of these mothers in a search for predictive clues. We wish to emphasize that we believe that early personality is not related to becoming noncustodial; however, mothers' experiences that are distinct from personality traits may be.

In her in-depth look at the early life experiences of 100 noncustodial mothers, Paskowicz (1982) found what she considered a strong connection between a mother's childhood experiences and her later life experiences. Nearly one in five of the mothers she interviewed were raised in homes away from their own mothers. Another significant percentage were raised in homes where the mothers were described as emotionally absent or where the mothers had died. Thus, nearly a third of her sample were raised by someone other than their mothers.

In striking contrast to Paskowicz's findings, we rarely encountered a mother who had been raised by a single father. Most commonly, the mothers in our study were raised by two parents or by their own mother and a stepfather.

Childhood Living Arrangements

In considering the relationship between childhood living arrangements and becoming noncustodial, it is important to note that children whose parents divorce are themselves more apt to divorce.[1] Thus, it might be assumed that a higher percentage of noncustodial mothers than other adults would come from single-parent families.[2]

About 20 percent of the mothers we interviewed were raised in a single-parent family, almost always by a mother who remarried at some point. One-third of the mothers came from two-parent families in which one of the parents living in the home (usually the father) was physically or emotionally absent because of either work schedules or alcoholism. The remaining mothers described close relationships with both parents. Some mothers lived with a number of siblings; others were only children. No pattern was found in birth order or in the number of children in the family. We surmise that these mothers' living arrangements as children did not vary significantly from those of others who later experienced marital breakups as adults.

Although a relatively low percentage of the mothers were raised in families in which there were divorces, this should not imply that the rest of the mothers came from happy homes. A high degree of family stress seemed to be present in some of the families. Sometimes this was evidenced in mental illness in one parent, alcohol problems, or a working father's long absences from the home. The parents may have had years of marital problems, even if they never divorced. The noncustodial mothers' relationships with their mothers or fathers were strained in some cases, idolized in others.

Many mothers' impression of their parents were different now from when they were still living with their parents. The mothers who had accepted themselves as noncustodial mothers tended to see their own parents in a more realistic light.

Relationships with Fathers

The noncustodial mothers' fathers, more than their mothers, were described in negative terms. Approximately half of the mothers said that their fathers were absent, emotionally distant, or tyrants around the house.

Nora, a 33-year-old schoolteacher, was raised in a two-parent home. She rarely saw her father because of his work schedule; he was home only on weekends. When he was with Nora and her sister, he was "always playing, always having fun." Their mother "was the strict disciplinarian who would do the screaming and keep the house running."

Nora's father was an alcoholic who was fun when he was sober but very difficult to be around when he was drunk, which was fairly often. Nora grew up with a mixed view of men and women. Men were seen as both fun and dangerous to be around. Women came to be epitomized by her mother, always screaming and always disciplining. The result is that when she became a parent, she did not want to be the disciplinarian. Instead, she wanted to leave everything to, in Nora's words, the "stronger gender."

Nora has been married twice and was physically abused in both marriages. Her husbands were described as dictatorial men who were loud and insulting. She initially had custody of the children from the first marriage after she was divorced but gave them up when she went to work and her ex-husband, who was unemployed, had more free time. The second marriage yielded no children.

Beverly, a 45-year-old housekeeper, also came from a two-parent family. Her parents are still married after fifty-two years. Her image of her father is of a man who was very distant. He traveled because of his business and was away an average of one week every month. Her parents never argued, and she described their marriage as loving, although affection was never shared openly. At home, her father was an unapproachable man who was always sitting in a chair and reading. She felt much closer to her mother.

Beverly married a man who became an equal partner in parenting. She described him as a more effective disciplinarian. When the marriage fell apart, both Beverly and her husband wanted custody, but she lost it in a court battle because he had a stronger financial position. During the custody trial, her parents were very supportive of her. She now has a much softer image of her father.

A third mother, Cora, 40 years old and "between jobs," has only vague images of her father. He and her mother were divorced when Cora was 6. Her mother married a man with whom Cora and her sister lived for a number of years until that marriage broke up. He never felt like a father to Cora. Her biological father rarely visited her following the breakup. He never seemed very interested in his children and went for years without seeing them. He visited Cora once after her first child was born but has since lost contact. Cora later lost custody in a court battle because her husband had remarried and could provide a two-parent home. Her father remains peripherally involved. Her mother is now on her fifth marriage. Cora grew up with a negative image of men. Her stepfather raped Cora's sister when Cora was 15 and her sister was 13. Cora never forgave either her stepfather or her mother for that.

Some of the mothers described their fathers in positive terms. The women who grew up feeling close to their fathers often felt that their mothers were distant. Elissa, a 32-year-old social worker, was raised in a two-parent family. She felt closer to her father, who was described as the more nurturing and compassionate of the two parents. Her mother was "void of emotion. She could not express her feelings and was rarely there. She did not do enough to help out." It was Elissa's father who helped with homework, taught the family the Bible, and was respected in the community. Despite these characteristics in her parents, she described their marriage as a happy one. Elissa felt good about herself growing up in the home.

Elissa's own marital history was less stable. She married for the first time at 15 and was divorced six months later. The next year, she married for the second time and had a son soon after. That marriage also ended in divorce. Her third marriage, her longest and her best, lasted nine years. This man was described by Elissa as a "a lot like my dad." She was looking for emotional support after two failed marriages, and her third husband fit the bill. That marriage ended because she and her husband grew apart. She lost custody when her son chose to live with his father. Elissa feels comfortable being noncustodial.

Margot, a 43-year-old secretary, also described a close relationship with her father and a feeling of distance from her mother. Her parents divorced when she was 12. Her father was in the Navy and the family had always moved around a great deal. Margot felt closer to her father than to her mother, even after the divorce, when her father's visits were sporadic. "I was always daddy's little girl." Margot believes that her mother did not want her in the first place, that the pregnancy was a mistake, and that she was resented. Margot did feel accepted by her mother's second husband. After her mother and stepfather had three children together, Margot became their primary caretaker.

When Margot divorced her second husband, she thought that her son would be better off with him. She was not earning much money at the time and worried about the effects of a custody battle on the child. Like Elissa, Margot has not had much difficulty assuming the role of noncustodial mother. She believes that her son is better off with his father, which makes being away from him easier than it is for those mothers who do not view the ex-husband's parenting abilities so positively.

Other accounts of the women we interviewed who were close to their fathers follow similar patterns. The mother was close to her own father, but not to her mother, who is described as rejecting or as having emotional problems. With these women's early reliance on their father, a two-tiered pattern may have been set in place: They may have more positive images of men, which makes it easier to relinquish custody to their ex-husbands; and they may have less positive images of their own abilites to nurture. If the opportunity to relinquish custody presents itself, they may be more willing to do so than some of the mothers who have different early experiences.

Relationships with Mothers

Approximately two-thirds of the women we interviewed described positive relationships with their own mothers, who were described as warm, caring, and good role models. These women seemed to have mature, nonidealized impressions of their own mothers. Shortcomings were recognized, especially if the relationship was maintained into adulthood, but those shortcomings did not affect the relationship.

Lucy is a 38-year-old waitress whose mother died recently. She describes both her parents as very supportive, but she felt especially close to her mother when she was growing up. Lucy's mother did not work until Lucy was 11. Lucy describes her as always being at home and involved in activities around the house, including teaching Lucy and her two other sisters how to cook. Lucy remembers that her mother took them to many after-school and cultural activities. But she gave the children more than just an active after-school life; she also helped them acquire a positive self-image, "Mom gave us kids the feeling that we were each individual and special. There was no competitive sense about it and we were all very close." Lucy's parents loved each other but fought a great deal, often over money, of which the family never seemed to have enough.

After Lucy had her first child, her mother became "overinvolved" with helping out, while her father took a backseat. When Lucy divorced and kept one of her three children, her mother continued to stay very involved. Lucy maintains her respect for her mother and appreciates her helpfulness but is also aware that there is a negative aspect to their relationship; she frequently feels that her mother is interfering in her life.

Mary, who is 43 and describes herself as self-employed, also had a good relationship with her mother. Mary came from a large family in which she was the oldest of eight children. She was very close with her mother, in part because she was always helping with the younger children and in part because her father, a pilot, was away a great deal. Although Mary described her father as not being "tuned into the family," she characterized her mother as "touchy, feely, warm, and devoted to the children." At the same time, Mary's mother was totally devoted to her husband, despite his frequent absences and his alcoholism.

Mary's mother centered her whole life on the children when they were young. As they became more independent, she started her own life outside the family. At 42, she learned how to drive and began racing cars. Mary's father died recently, and Mary's mother has begun traveling with a stock car show that puts on daredevil shows in various cities. She is the ticket taker.

Mary has always felt supported by her mother and believes that she can call on her for help wherever she is. "If my mother was working in Texas and I called her for something, I know she would drop what she was doing and come help me out."

Despite the warmth Mary felt from her mother, problems surfaced in the family. Her father's alcoholism led to a career-ending accident when Mary was 15. Afterward, he was home much more and began verbally abusing the children and being very demanding of Mary. When Mary left home, she entered an abusive marriage, in which she stayed for many years. She "escaped" from the marriage eighteen years later, taking her youngest child with her but leaving three others.

A few of the women we interviewed did not get along with their mothers. Some of these situations are reflected in the relationships between the women and their fathers, described earlier. In those, the mother's lack of affection or parenting was often balanced by the father's presence. In a smaller number of cases, the women described unsatisfactory relations with both parents.

Childhood Experiences and Self-Esteem

As Robert Beavers (1985) has written: "There are two main sources of self-esteem: (1) being heard, understood, empathized with (not necessarily agreed with) and (2) having success experiences as defined by the person" (p. 127). People who feel good about themselves— who have high self-esteem—are going to have greater potential for coping with life crises.

The mothers we interviewed described their childhoods in terms that ranged from glowing to unhappy, with the majority tending toward unhappy. Even when parents were seen as helpful and supportive, the mothers were likely to say that their childhoods were more unsatisfactory than satisfactory. A number of mothers, though not a majority, said that they did not have many friends or that they felt like outsiders among their peer group. About three-quarters said that their self-esteem as a child was low.

One mother who described her childhood as unhappy said that she always felt loved by her parents and that she was a good student in school. Her difficulty was that she was shy around people outside the family. This interfered with her ability to make friends.

Another example is provided by Pam, who was raised by her mother after her parents divorced. She described herself as a good student in school but a loner. "I felt I never fit in any place. I wanted to move out of the house but was not clear why. I did not feel real good about myself even though I was doing okay in a lot of areas." She daydreamed about being a mother when she grew up. This was easy for her to do, because she was raised in a traditional household and her mother always bought her dolls. This early social conditioning for motherhood does not have much impact on her now. She is involved in a split custody situation and finds that not having her oldest daughter living with her is easier to deal with than being divorced.

Pam is not alone in having been raised to play the part of mother. Most of the mothers we interviewed were given a clear message from their parents that womanhood and motherhood were inextricably linked. Thus, in many ways, these mothers' upbringings do not seem to vary from the norm. Most were raised with dolls; some babysat for pleasure, money, or both; and many dreamed of one day having a family of their own.

One exception was Michelle, who knew from earliest memory that motherhood was not for her. "I could never picture myself as a mother. It just did not interest me. I was the tomboy on the block and was into all of the boys' sports."

The mothers' early lives tended toward introversion. We had wondered if rebelliousness as a child or adolescent might lead to the adult assumption of the nontraditional role of living apart from the children, but this was not the trend we saw.

The fairly common picture was a mother who was successful academically but had low self-esteem. Many of these mothers were high achievers, wanting to please their parents or themselves. Being successful, though, did not seem to erase their doubts about themselves. Many felt constricted at home and looked forward to the day they could leave, but they were not openly rebellious about wanting to leave. We rarely heard a description of an adolescence in which the woman had felt extremely comfortable at home and reluctant to leave. As discussed in the next chapter, marriage provided an escape for many of the women.

Conclusions

We have concluded that the connection between childhood experiences and becoming noncustodial is a weak one. Unlike Paskowicz's (1982) finding that a significant percentage (20 percent) of noncustodial mothers had been raised by custodial fathers, only one of our interviewees had had this experience. Although some mothers' experiences—notably positive relationships with their fathers and negative ones with their mothers—may have made it easier for them to give up custody and to adjust to being noncustodial, this does not fully explain how they became noncustodial. As stated earlier, many mothers *with* custody could describe the same kinds of relationships with their mothers and fathers.

We also found a large number of mothers suffering from low self-esteem as children, although almost all of these mothers did well in school, many described happy home lives, and some felt accepted by their peers. Moreover, none of them described patterns of pathological conditions, extreme withdrawal from peer groups, or other types of abnormal behavior patterns as children. These mothers' childhoods do not sound markedly different from those of the general population. Further research with other groups of mothers is needed to determine the relevance of this pattern of self-esteem.

It is a vitally important point to note that we are not implying that being noncustodial should be equated with being rejecting, with having low self-esteem, or with having been raised in a tension filled household. For many mothers, being noncustodial could be equated with a strong affirmation of the role of mother or parent. Many are in such a custody situation because they consider it best for the children. Thus, they may have overcome their feelings of low self-esteem by the time they reached adulthood.[3]

Theoretically, the possible beginnings of a noncustodial lifestyle could be traced to the childhoods of a few of the mothers and might be related to their low self-esteem. For the majority of the mothers we interviewed, however, no event or series of events stands out as an experience that would help us predict the assumption of this nontraditional parenting arrangement.

4

Marriage and Divorce

F OR many people, marriage is the biggest risk they will ever take. The choice of partner is a statement about the way one feels about oneself that is more revealing than any words could convey. Because it is such a revealing statement, marriage often exposes aspects of people that they did not know existed or that they did not want revealed. Although marriage is such a big decision—one toward which many people gear much of their younger life—mistakes are made. People choose the wrong person, get married for the wrong reasons, or marry before they are ready. Sometimes potential problems are recognized during the courtship, yet the marital plans continue. Other times, problems surface soon after the marriage and are pushed aside or ignored. Often, they may not be recognized until the couple has been married for a few years and has started a family— or even until the children have left the house and are no longer there as a diversion. When the realization finally hits home that the marriage is not a happy one, the decision has to be made whether to divorce, to continue in an unsatisfying relationship, or to try to improve the situation. If the decision is made to divorce, the couple will join ranks with millions of others.

The married lives of the mothers we interviewed were often unhappy ones, as would be expected since they all ended in separation or divorce. The stories tell of dashed dreams, incompatibility, distrust, and abuse. In some of the marriages, the father was very involved in child care and housework; in others, his participation was negligible. Sometimes the marriage ended quickly; others dragged on and on for years.

It is well known that divorce is more common now than ever before. Between 1960 and 1983, the percentage of divorced people in the population almost tripled, while the percentage of married declined.[1] If we look back further in time, we can see how the divorce rate has grown. In 1910, for example, there were 948,000 marriages and 83,000 divorces—less than one divorce for every ten marriages. By the end of World War I (1920), the rate was slightly more than one divorce for every ten marriages. By the end of World War II (1945), it was slightly more than one divorce for every four marriages. Although this trend reversed itself for a few years, it resumed until it peaked in the early 1980s, when the rate was slightly more than one divorce for every two marriages in any given year.[2] This chapter focuses on the marriages and divorces of the mothers we interviewed. As will be shown, the relationships during the marriages varied as much as the causes of the divorces.

Over the years, a number of reasons have been cited for the increase in the divorce rate: the women's movement and the changing status of women; new economic opportunities for women; a loosening of sexual and social mores, including increased premarital pregnancy; greater physical mobility and the transferability of jobs from one location to another; a turning away from religious values and an increase in interfaith marriages; a distrust of government and social institutions; and a repetition of a pattern begun by parents who divorced.[3]

Kitson et al. (1985) reviewed nine research studies that asked people the reasons for their divorce. The studies spanned the twenty-eight-year period from 1956 to 1984. The reasons mentioned most frequently were nonsupport, sexual incompatibility, lack of communication, mental cruelty, personality problems, feeling unloved, and extramarital sex. The studies also examined the period of the marriage up to the divorce. Some studies found long spans of unhappiness or ambivalent feelings before the breakup. Others found that some marriages ended because of a single final event—a "last straw."

Researchers have also studied what happens to people after the separation/divorce. Common findings are pain and isolation, loneliness and feelings of loss, a sense of failure and, at times, relief accompanying a marital breakup. It is believed that most people go through specific stages as they adjust to their single status. Salts

(1979) reviewed leading theories of the adjustment process and found that most theorists tend to break down that process—which may begin well before the actual divorce—into four stages:

1. *The preseparation stage:* In this stage, the couple is together, but the marriage has turned sour and an emotional divorce has begun. There is denial, anger, erosion of love, and disillusionment.

2. *The separation stage:* The couple has split up and is experiencing feelings of depression, anger, guilt, bargaining, and relief.

3. *The stage between separation and the legal divorce:* The couple mourn the loss of the marriage, focus on themselves, and begin restructuring their emotional, legal, economic, parental, and social lives, while trying to work out a co-parental relationship.

4. *The adjustment stage:* This stage, which is the goal, is characterized, ideally, by acceptance of the breakup, a "second adolescence," recovering, reconnection, a restructuring of one's life, and achieving a divorce recognized by the community.

These stages concentrate on the divorcing individuals as spouses and, to some extent, as parents. Certainly, when children are involved, the demands on everyone are greater. The parents are concerned not only with their own needs but also with those of the children. If there is a disagreement concerning custody, the emotional and financial tensions increase greatly, and the stages of the adjustment process can be slowed or stopped. We introduce the different postdivorce stages of adjustment here because the mothers in our study were at various stages in the process. For some, the custodial arrangement may have slowed their adjustment. Moreover, the nature of the divorce may have affected what has occurred regarding the custody situation and the mother's adjustment to being noncustodial.

For the children, the divorce means an end to family life as they have known it. Regardless of where they live, the children will undergo a multitude of emotional, financial, and physical changes in their new lives. These changes may be positive if they result in a diminution of tension at home. But frequently, the children perceive the divorce negatively. They may be used as pawns in a custody game. They may be made to feel responsible for the divorce. The parents may need to nurse their own wounds and, in attempting to make sense of what has happened to them, may shut the children out. The children's emotional needs may not be met because the parents may be so wrapped up in themselves. The children may stay in their old home or move to a new one, to a new neighborhood, or even to a new part of the country. Material things may vanish as the house is divided. Financial resources that were once available may become greatly restricted, especially if the children live with the mother.[4] How the children are coping with the divorce certainly affects how the parents will cope, too. For example, if the parents see that the children are relieved, they will feel better about the decision. Conversely, if the children are suffering, the parents will also have a more difficult adjustment.[5]

The Mothers' Married Lives

To achieve a well-rounded picture of who these mothers are and what led to their being noncustodial, we must attempt to understand the lives of the mothers before their divorces as well as the reasons for the divorces. Paskowicz (1982) offers a number of descriptions: The typical woman in her study married at a younger age (19) than the national average, which at the time was between 20 and 21. The women tended to work in low-status jobs until the birth of the first child. The first and second children tended to be born close together, and most of the mothers had two children. Most interesting is Paskowicz's finding that only one-fifth of the children born to the mothers were conceived because of the mother's desire to have a child. Two-fifths were unplanned pregnancies; one-fifth were conceived because the mother wanted to please someone; and the final fifth "were simply allowed to happen." When the mothers were asked about their memories of living with the children, slightly more than half spoke of both positive and negative aspects of parenting; slightly less than half had positive things to say; and a handful said that they did not enjoy their children at all. Twenty percent were sorry that they had children. Almost a quarter of the mothers had a handicapped or problem child. Almost half of the mothers were unable to see that they had needs separate from those of their husbands and children. The mothers had a range of emotional problems during the marriages, and six had attempted suicide.

Paskowicz concluded that her sample of mothers came from high-pressure situations, with suffocating marriages and difficult child-rearing arrangements. The husbands of these mothers were described as more involved with the children than the average father. In fact, 70 percent of the fathers took part in the child rearing to a significant degree.

Almost half of the ninety-nine California mothers in the research by Berke et al. (1979) did not have happy relationships with their husbands before the children were born. Four-fifths of the mothers in that study described their relationships with their children during the marriage as loving, and two-thirds described themselves as actively involved. About a third thought that there was tension and strain between them and their children. At the same time, 72 percent described the fathers' relationships with the children in positive terms, considering them as "loving," and 40 percent went further and described them as "active and involved with open talking and sharing" (p. 58).

Marital Patterns

We were particularly interested in finding patterns in the marriages that might point toward the mothers' not having custody of the children or that might indicate how well the mothers would adjust to being noncustodial. In looking for those patterns, we were aware that we were dealing with a population of divorced people. Many of the mothers' characterizations of their marriages could have led us to predict the potential for a divorce, but we were attempting to find clues that could lead to a prediction of a nontraditional lifestyle for the mother and father and later adaptation by the mother.

We began by hypothesizing that there might be a cluster of characteristics present at the beginning and throughout the marriage that would lead to the mother's being noncustodial. We looked first at the age of the mother at the time of marriage and the period of time between the marriage and the birth of the first child. We considered whether the mother married out of love or as an escape and what the roles were in the marriage.

Two-thirds of the mothers in the study were married between 1960 and 1970. The average age of the mothers when they were first married was between 20 and 21, the same as the average age of women nationally in 1965.[6] Thus, since our sample of mothers was not significantly different in age from the average woman in the United States, age at marriage is not a factor.

The vast majority of mothers we interviewed did report that they were pregnant when they married or had become pregnant within the first three months of marriage. Although a few of these pregnancies, particularly those that occurred after the marriage, were planned, most were not. The majority of the mothers who had planned to conceive wanted the baby. A few felt forced into pregnancy by demands from their husbands, pressure from parents, or the feeling that it was the "right time" to get pregnant. Among the mothers whose pregnancies were unplanned were both those who wanted children and those who did not. One or two mothers had abortions early in the marriage or wanted to but were talked out of it by their husbands. Sally is an example of a mother who had not wanted children. Married for two years, her pregnancy was accidental. "I did not want to have any children because I had babysat so much as a teen-ager." When her marriage fell apart, she voluntarily gave custody to her husband so that she could pursue a career.

One possible impact on those mothers who gave birth early in the marriage, whether the birth was wanted or unwanted, was an added pressure to parent. This pressure sometimes manifested itself in the mother's feelings of resentment toward the child and of being tied down to parenthood and the home. This seemed to be especially true for the younger mothers. Christine, for example, was married at 19. Two planned children quickly followed. Now 38, her memories of those years with the children are not pleasant ones. "I felt tied down, had most of the responsibilities, and got no, I mean no, help from my husband."

Problems in the marriages mounted if one or both of the parents were too dependent on their own parents. If the mother had never been on her own, she might rely on her parents too much or feel that they were interfering in her life. This could add to her feelings of being tied down. Some mothers we interviewed said that their husbands had never made an appropriate separation from their parents. Christine said: "My husband always put his mother ahead of me. She wanted him to call her every day and he would talk to her instead of helping me or being with the kids. His parents treated him like a baby and they did not like me."

Approximately half of the mothers entered marriage as an escape from their home lives, which they often depicted as being too confining. Their husbands offered them a chance, as one mother put it, "to move out and start to enjoy life." Their reasons for selecting their husbands varied from "he was responsible and would provide a good home for me" to "he was cute and fun to be with." Some admitted that they were not in love with their husbands when they married but admired their qualities.

Overwhelmingly, the mothers described their marriages as "traditional" ones, in which their husbands were usually the primary breadwinners and they were the homemakers. Many of the mothers worked part-time outside the home. Most of the husbands were described as being peripherally involved with the children during much of the marriage. This is consistent with findings from the study of custodial fathers, who also described their marriages as having a traditional division of roles. Notable exceptions were a few mothers who worked when their husbands were unemployed and the child care and housekeeping roles were reversed.

The majority of the mothers described very close relationships with all or most of the children for whom they eventually relinquished custody. Many of the mothers centered their lives on their children and received a great deal of satisfaction from those relationships. Some, however, struggled to meet the demands that parenthood placed upon them. Their relationships with their children were stormy. They viewed their children as demanding, and the mothers felt unappreciated. The husband's behavior toward the children, as described by the mothers, also varied. Some were considered distant or verbally and physically abusive; others were described as warm and nurturing.

Two stories illustrate the types of married lifestyles of the mothers. Constance met her husband when she was 18. He was in the Air Force, and she was starting college. They dated for two years before they married. He was physically attractive to her and treated her with respect. Constance thought he would be a good provider, that he would work steadily and be reliable. She thought she loved him at the time but wonders now, fourteen years later, if she was perhaps looking for an escape from the demands of college and the pressures of dating. When they married, she felt very dependent as a person and was happy to latch on to a husband.

Constance's first pregnancy was unplanned and came six weeks after they were married. This was satisfactory to her, because she had wanted to have children. During the first five months of the pregnancy, her husband was stationed overseas. Marital difficulties developed between them because of the prolonged absences. She felt that they never appreciated each other. Three months after the birth of her first child, she became pregnant again. Whereas the first pregnancy was unplanned but wanted, this pregnancy was neither planned nor wanted. Constance considered an abortion, but because she was a Catholic she dismissed it. By the time her second child was born, her husband had left the service and was in college. Although she carried primary responsibility for the children, he helped out a great deal.

Her husband was overinvolved with his family, and her in-laws' interference, plus her desire to work outside the home, began to drive a wedge into the marriage. She felt that her husband wanted more of a "buddy" than a wife. Their sex life was totally unsatisfactory to her. "I was raised a Catholic and I think somehow conditioned to not like sex. I was a virgin when I married and did not know anything else." Problems in their relationship were exacerbated by her parents. Constance's mother was domineering. "She wanted to be a grandmother and helped out a lot with the children. But she wanted to control everything." Five years after the marriage began, Constance sought a divorce.

Winnie married at 19 and was quite aware at the time that she was escaping an unhappy home. Her husband was "charming, handsome, a real doll." She wanted to get pregnant and conceived three months after the wedding. "I felt if I was a mother I would be free of servitude and abuse. People respect mothers and take care of them. I have found that in motherhood. My in-laws did take care of me." When her only child, a daughter, was 5 years old, the child had a kidney removed. Winnie did not realize at the time the gravity of the situation but became very close to her daughter throughout the ordeal. Her husband was working and did not help much. He also began drinking heavily. "Despite having to take care of my daughter all alone, I loved being a mother."

Winnie fell in love with her second husband while she was still married to her first. They had an affair and then ran off together. She left her daughter with her first husband and his parents. She went back three months later and fought for her daughter in court, but she lost. Now remarried and the mother of two more children, she regrets how the first marriage ended. She has not seen her daughter in four years. "I think it would be painful for all of us if I visited. She now has a stepmother who I hear is a very nice lady."

Physical and emotional abuse were not uncommon patterns in the marriages of the mothers we interviewed. We estimate that the mothers suffered these abuses at the hands of their husbands in about a quarter of the marriages. Many mothers were ashamed to tell us they had been abused. One they had admitted it, however, they often said that the abuse was the impetus for the divorce.

Patterns of Divorce

Sandy, a 30-year-old secretary, wrote at great length about her marriage and divorce:

> I was a young mother who had to get married at 18 because I was pregnant with my daughter. I had become pregnant my first sexual encounter and was naive. My parents encouraged the hasty marriage. We were really in love—but I feel we were both too immature. There was drug experimentation (mostly my husband's) and all the 60's things—I was unhappy after I had the baby—I realized what an enormous responsibility it was and I resented not being free (to party, etc.). Also, the baby had colic; nothing satisfied her. I wanted the divorce, not fully realizing the consequences."

Like Sandy, a majority of the mothers in the study (55 percent) said that they had initiated the divorce. This finding is consistent with other research showing that women are more likely to end the marriage.[7]

The mothers were asked to describe their reasons for the divorce, and many gave more than one. The ten most frequently cited reasons, in order, are shown in table 4–1.

As shown, the reason given most frequently was marital incompatibility. Responses grouped in this category implied that the dis-

Table 4–1
REASONS THE MOTHERS GAVE FOR THEIR DIVORCES

(n = 482)

Reason	Number of Mothers	Percentage
Marital incompatibility	223	46.2
Husband was unfaithful	113	23.4
Husband had emotional problems	49	10.1
I was mentally abused	44	9.1
I was physically abused	43	8.9
Husband left me (no explanation)	28	5.8
I had affair/wanted to leave	24	4.9
I had emotional problems	16	3.7
Husband was emotionally immature	12	2.5

Note: Thirty-five mothers did not respond.

solution of the marriage was the result of problems between the spouses and that the responsibilities for these problems were shared. These responses are in marked contrast to those of the mothers who assigned some blame by saying that the marriage ended either because of their own problems or problems attributed to their husbands. In citing incompatibility, no single person is blamed. In the four categories cited next most frequently, the husband is blamed.

Specific answers that were grouped in the category of imcompatibility were "We grew apart," "We fell out of love," "We had sexual problems," and "We could not communicate." Sometimes these problems led to others. The story of Barbara, told in chapter 2, illustrates this. She was never sexually attracted to her husband, and as they grew apart in this area, she became attracted to other men, leading to an affair and the eventual breakup. As in the example of Barbara, there is often a trial separation and a reconciliation before the final divorce.

Toby, a teacher, wrote about the incompatibility in her marriage:

> At the time of the first separation, my daughter was 12, my son was 8. My husband and I agreed we could not continue living together; we constantly quarreled and the stress was becoming unbearable. He agreed to move out. During this time, the children remained with me. We had an informal agreement between ourselves, nothing legal. He supported us and visited on an unlimited basis. During this time, he was very despondent, often came to

the house to visit the children and cried to them and me. At the time of the original separation he refused my suggestion for marital counseling. Three months later he wanted to come back and agreed to counseling. We started going and with my okay, he moved back in. Within a month he was threatening me with loss of custody, had doubled the children's allowances, and was telling all of us he was not going to leave his house. Three months later we both agreed our differences were irreconcilable.

The second most frequently cited reason for the breakup was that the husband had been unfaithful. Here, the mothers' responses included "He fooled around," "I did not want to put up with his mistress," "Husband became involved with a younger woman," "He was seeing someone else during the marriage." The tone of these responses varied from matter-of-fact, to hurt, to angry. In twenty-four cases, the mothers said that they were the ones having the affair or that they wanted to leave the marriage in order to be with someone else. The mothers in this latter group gave such responses as "I fell in love with someone else" and "I left for someone else."

Ten percent of the mothers said that their husbands' emotional problems had caused the divorce. The range of problems given was grouped differently from the next two categories, physical and mental abuse. Answers placed in this category were "He was depressed," "He was an alcoholic/drug abuser," "He was emotionally unstable," and "He was crazy." At times, these reasons appeared with others, especially those having to do with physical and mental abuse.

The fourth and fifth most common reasons for divorce were mental abuse and physical abuse. The incidence of family violence in marriages in the United States has been estimated to be as high as 50 percent,[8] so this type of behavior is clearly an unfortunate but common feature of our society. What is also worth noting is that although the father may have been abusing the mother, he may not have been physically abusing the children. Hence, the courts could decide that he was a safe parent for the children to live with, forgetting that he was the perpetrator of some family violence. How these children will do in these situations over the long run is unknown. As one reviewer of the literature on family violence has noted, a child who witnesses violence between the parents is being abused, also.[9]

Only 3.7 percent of the mothers said that their own emotional problems were the primary reason for the divorce. As will be seen in the next chapter, this is a much smaller percentage than the mothers who gave emotional incapability as the reason for not having custody.

Using the responses from the study of single fathers, we can draw some comparisons. (Remember, these were not the mothers' ex-husbands but a different group of 1,136 custodial fathers.)[10] The fathers were also asked to state their impressions of the reasons for the divorce. The comparisons are as follows:

Incompatibility: noncustodial mothers, 46 percent; custodial fathers, 28 percent

Other spouse's infidelity: noncustodial mothers, 23 percent; custodial fathers, 24 percent

Other spouse's emotional problems: noncustodial mothers, 10 percent; custodial fathers, 15 percent

Physical and/or mental abuse: noncustodial mothers, 18 percent; custodial fathers, none

Spouse left: noncustodial mothers, 6 percent; custodial fathers, 23 percent

Taking these responses as factual, the comparisons are remarkable for what they include and for what they leave out:

1. Physical and mental abuse is not a problem for men, whereas it is for women. This confirms the obvious. Levinger (1966) reported a similar imbalance in his research comparing the reasons husbands and wives gave for the divorce. In his findings, wives were eleven times more likely than husbands to complain about physical and mental abuse.

2. The percentage of parents citing infidelity of the other spouse as the reason is remarkably similar. This may indicate that infidelity has little relationship to how a parent ultimately gains custody. Or it could mean that a custodial father could be unfaithful but his chances for custody would not be affected to the same extent that they would be for women.

3. The wives were four times more likely to be accused of being the one to leave the family. This, of course, makes sense given the nature of the custodial relationship.

4. Not shown in the comparisons, a small percentage of women blamed the husband's immaturity. None of the fathers thought that the wife's immaturity led to the divorce. We can conclude that men are more likely to be perceived as emotionally immature in these relationships.

The Impact of the Divorce

We wanted to explore the relationship between the reasons the mothers gave for their divorces and other important events in their lives. To do so, we used the five most frequently cited reasons for the divorce and explored the experiences of the mothers who gave those reasons.[11]

We hypothesized that the mothers who gave incompatibility as a reason for the divorce had been involved in marriages that ended on a better note than those who were either abused or had had an unfaithful husband. The incompatible marriages were ones in which both spouses were seen as having grown apart. Blame was not being placed on either spouse. It was further believed that they may have had a more compatible marriage, which led naturally to a more friendly termination.

We can contrast this with a marriage in which the wife was abused and might have left in a hurry because of the abuse. And we can contrast that with a wife who left after learning that her husband was having an affair. In these two situations, the marriage may have been unfulfilling for many years, and it may have ended with a great deal of recrimination on both sides. The mother may be feeling victimized. Her self-esteem may be lower during a marriage where victimization is occurring, and it would certainly remain low for at least some time after the breakup.

Our hypothesis was confirmed: There is a definite relationship between the reason the mother gives for the divorce and her later experiences. We also found a relationship between the reasons given for the divorce and those given for the custody decision. When we consider the impact of the divorce on the mother's later experiences, we must be aware that the reasons for custody play a part in the measurement of that impact, as does whether or not custody was given up voluntarily. This relationship between divorce and custody is discussed in the next chapter, but some points can be made here. Comparing the mothers whose marriages ended because of incompatibility with all the other mothers, we found that the first group of mothers possessed characteristics that have a much more positive connotation. For example, those mothers were more likely

1. To have found the decision to have custody reside elsewhere not stressful

2. To describe themselves as very involved with the children who are living away from them

3. To have the children sleep at their house when visiting

4. To be satisfied with their ongoing relationship with the children who are living away from them

5. To be satisfied with their children's progress in most areas

6. To be consulted by the children's caretaker about their upbringing

7. To have experienced little difficulty in not being with the children

8. To believe that the children are better off where they are

9. To be satisfied with their involvement with their children

10. To give their ex-husbands high ratings as parents[12]

We believe that the reasons these mothers are doing well are strongly linked to the mothers' view of the fathers. As stated earlier, when incompatibility is the reason for the divorce, both spouses are more likely to feel some responsibility, and there is less recrimination. This is correlated with a better feeling about the other spouse. These mothers would tend to have more positive views of their ex-husbands and to be less upset about their children being raised by them.

The fact that a mother has a high regard for the father with custody may be further tied to some preceding involvement. These fathers are described as having been more involved around the home than other fathers. From the interviews, we learned that the marriages of these mothers tended to be initially based on love, not the mother's desire to leave her parents' home. The marriages were also characterized by less fighting. One result is that the mother is more content with having the father raise the children.

Looking at the other three groups, we see that two of them, those whose husbands have problems and those whose husbands have abused them, consistently tend to have the hardest time adjusting and to be the least satisfied with their situation. The mothers whose marriages ended because of infidelity fall between those mothers having the least difficulty and those having the most.

Three Broad Patterns

From our interviews with the mothers, we see three broad patterns in the terminating marital relationships. In the first pattern, both parents were unprepared for marriage and parenting. The mother had chosen to marry because of a premarital pregnancy or to get out of her parents' home. Often, the mother was in her late teens at the time. She had never established an identity for herself that was distinct from that of either her parents or her husband. The births of the children were often a "mistake" or an event that, though planned, was not thought through. The ramifications and responsibilities of having children were not understood. Parenting presented a crisis for the mother either immediately or after a few years. The husband may also have been immature at the time of the marriage and often left the bulk of the child care and housework to the mother. The marriages were built on what Rhodes (1977) called *pseudoharmony*. No real intimacy or happiness was achieved and problems emerged, ranging from continued emotional distance to infidelity to verbal and physical abuse. The husband most likely became actively involved with the children as a reaction to the wife's withdrawal, rather than seeking out the active parent role on his own. The wife or husband ended the marriage because things reached an intolerable level within the marriage or because they found someone else who they thought was better able to meet their needs.

Ali is an example of this type of mother. She wrote: "I got married too young and for the wrong reasons. I did not love my husband. I was only 17 and pregnant when I married. I was still a child myself and having an identity crisis when I had two children." Five years later, she "needed to be free of husband and children responsibilities." Her husband did not want the divorce and kept the children because, according to Ali, he wanted to keep a link with her. That was twelve years ago. Now, Ali feels that she has grown up. She is a successful store manager earning over $50,000 a year.

In the second pattern, the husband was the one who changed markedly. It was his behavior that shook the marriage the most. Here, the wife and husband most likely loved each other at the beginning of the marriage but the husband, for a variety of reasons, changed. He may not have found the happiness he thought he would in the marriage or in work. He may have reached a developmental stage in his life at which his own inadequate parenting began to influence his adult behavior. For instance, some men may have had a very loving relationship with their wives but when the children arrived, they found it impossible to share their wife with the children. They may have witnessed their father abusing or withholding affection from their mother, and they may have adopted the same behavior in their own marriage. They may have learned from their parents that it was acceptable to have an affair. However, their own wives may not have tolerated it as their own mothers may have. The husbands may also have turned to alcohol or drugs as an excuse. In these marriages, the change in the husband was much more the cause for the breakup than anything the wife did.

A number of examples of this kind of marriage are available. Pamela was 21 when she married. She had known her husband for two years before they got married. During that time, he was in the armed forces and she was in college. She was attracted to him because they had a lot in common. When he was discharged from the service, they were married, and he began working as an electrician, a trade he had learned in the army. For the first ten years of marriage and three children, their relationship was solid. Then he started to abuse alcohol and to abuse her. Pamela thinks he became frustrated with their life and with not being able to go anywhere in his job. During the marriage he was a very involved father. He did much more housekeeping and child care than other fathers Pamela knew. After a few years of abuse, she left him. It is interesting that Pamela's own mother left her father when Pamela married. Pamela's mother took the remaining four children (Pamela's sisters and brothers) with her and raised them alone. Pamela hoped to get custody of her sons, but they chose to stay with their father in the family home.

Heather, another mother who experienced a marked change in her husband, wrote, "He decided early in the marriage that he did not like responsibility and did not want to be married to me for a lifetime. He was frequently unfaithful." Heather sensed that because of her own upbringing, she had made a bad choice in her husband, even though she was willing to make a go of the marriage. "As a child I was badly abused and battered by my father. I could see personality difficulties in the man I married but apparently overlooked them because my early experience was not good."

The third pattern we saw had to do with changes in the mother. She may have experienced emotional problems that hampered the marriage. She may have decided that she needed a complete change in her life and left the family altogether. She may have been seeking more equality than her husband was willing to give. These changes precipitated the end of the marriage.

Louise is a mother who fits this pattern. She was married after completing her third year of college. Her son was born two years later. Her husband had been a caring man during the early part of the marriage. When their son was born, he began showering all his affection on him. Louise describes him as loving children and being a natural father to all of the children on the block. She said that she could not stand the amount of attention given to her son rather than to her. "I retaliated—I found affection elsewhere. It was a bad move on my part. Live and learn."

Sandra said that her marriage ended because of her career ambitions. She was married at the age of 21, and her only child, a daughter, was born when she was 27. Her husband was somewhat involved in child care but did little housework. When she wanted to use her college education for work outside the home, problems began. Her daughter was 3 at the time and Sandra was trying to be a supermom: "I was totally exhausted and had a feeling of hopelessness about trying to keep a job, a home, and a child. I wanted out of the marriage." Had her husband been more flexible, the marriage probably would have endured.

Conclusions

In considering these marriages, we see some situations that potentially could have been early predictors of divorce and of some of the mothers' becoming noncustodial. The mothers who had escaped into marriage and who felt overwhelmed by the responsibilities of parenthood at the outset of the marriage were conceivably more likely to relinquish custody. This is especially true of the mothers who felt close to their fathers when they were growing up. Marrying young and not having been on one's own could result in a feeling of being tied down. Not getting help from a husband or feeling interference from parents or in-laws could add to this feeling. Although such experiences in a marriage can possibly point toward becoming noncustodial, we are aware that many divorced mothers *with* custody have had similar experiences. We believe, though, that these experiences might have set the stage for what happened later to some of the mothers.

Other marriages were not so predictable. Influences outside the marital relationship, such as the emergence of the women's movement, may have had an impact. Such sociopolitical considerations that might affect the marital relationship are difficult to track early on in a marriage and are more difficult to link to a mother's noncustodial status.

Thus, in considering the early childhoods, adolescences, courtships, and marriages of these mothers, we see possible links, but nothing that is substantially predictive of how most of the mothers became noncustodial. To best understand the process, we need to consider the experiences around the actual decision for custodianship of the children to go to the father.

5

How the Custody
Decisions Were Made

THE single most burning question people have about this population of mothers is: Why don't they have custody? What happened? Who was responsible? This aspect of the mother's life places her, in many people's minds, into a category of mother that is aberrant. Her noncustodial status becomes her identity, an identity to which many react negatively.

Trying to understand the reason or reasons the mother does not have custody is a complex process. There is rarely any single factor that can be held above all the rest and shown as the reason. Much more common are situations in which a variety of circumstances have come together. For instance, the mother's lack of guaranteed financial resources may be the final deciding factor for the mother, but her impression of the father's parenting ability may also play a major part in the decision. Determining custody is both an emotional and a cognitive decision that is frequently stressful for parents and children. Despite the careful thought that many parents put into this decision, custody may ultimately be decided rather irrationally. The mother's or father's anger may determine who ends up with the children more than considerations about the well-being of the children or the abilities of the individual parents. Threats may be made, stonewalling attempted, visitation denied, children's impressions poisoned—even child-snatching may happen.

There are two important points to remember: (1) custody decisions are often made within an atmosphere of tension and anger and (2) these situations frequently have a systemic nature. After a divorce, it is difficult to remove the cloud of animosity that exists between the spouses. When the children are added into the equation, the stakes are raised further. Regardless of how it turns out, it is often a painful transition for all members of the family. It is a change from the way the family has been. In cases where there has been abuse, the change often brings relief. But it is still a change that requires coming to grips with what has happened in the past and placing negative experiences in perspective. In addition, the decisions are not made in isolation by the mother or father but are the result of years of family interactions as well as current conditions in the family. To understand the custody decision, it is helpful to know about the family's situation.

For over three-quarters of the mothers in the survey, the final process of becoming noncustodial was described as very stressful. Less than 10 percent said that it held little or no stress for them. By the time of the survey most of the mothers had been without custody for a few years (3.9 years was the average); 40 percent had become noncustodial within the preceeding two years. Two-thirds had had their situations legally sanctioned.

Before presenting the reasons given by the mothers for why they are noncustodial, we should review the perspectives that were applied in understanding the mothers. These perspectives shaped how we consider the mother's situation. As we stated in the first chapter, more than one perspective was needed, as the assumption of any one perspective would preclude understanding many of the mothers. For example, if we viewed the mother's becoming noncustodial as a sign of failure because she has moved into what many consider an improper role, her situation would be the end result of a series of mistakes or weaknesses on her part. Conversely, we could consider her becoming noncustodial as a success, because she has moved into a new stage of her life and the father has gained more than the usual access to his child. In this view, a mother could be seen as having thrown off the "burden" of parenting that she had perhaps unfairly assumed. We prefer to consider the mother's status as neither a success nor a failure but, rather, as the outcome of several interlocking situational factors. In assuming this position, we are looking, to a large extent at "environmental" and social factors.

It is the reasons the mother gives for why she does not have custody that focus our analysis in one direction or another. An analysis of the mother who loses custody because of money requires that we consider different factors from those we would consider if the mother lost custody because of emotional instability that began in childhood. It is here that the systems view comes to the fore. With a systems view, we have to be cognizant of other factors that are influencing the custody situation—for example, the roles of the father and the children. At the same time, in explaining the mother's part in the system, we need to be aware that, in some of the cases, a feminist perspective is appropriate. The applicability of the various perspectives is thus modulated by the idiosyncrasies of each situation.

Review of the Literature

A few other researchers have looked at the reasons mothers become noncustodial. The emphases of these researchers tend to vary.

Todres (1978) reported the reasons given by thirty-eight "runaway wives" for their noncustodial status. The most commonly cited reason was the father's ability to fulfill the children's emotional and financial needs. The mother's inability to care for the children emotionally was also cited. Fischer and Cardea (1981; 1982) interviewed seventeen noncustodial mothers, the majority of whom lived in Texas. The reasons given most often were that it was in the best interests of the child, that the children were "bought off" by the father, and that the children were abducted.

Fischer (1983), in a follow-up article, described five common circumstances that lead to mothers living apart from their children: (1) the mother's choice to leave home to "find herself"; (2) the couple's choice, when there is a "commuter" marriage or a joint custody situation and the mother is away from the children part of the time; (3) the father's choice, when the father brings pressure to obtain the children; (4) the children's choice, when their preferences are considered; and (5) the court's choice, when a decision is imposed on the mother. At the conclusion of this chapter, we give further credence to these conceptualizations.

Herrerias (1984c), using a sample also largely drawn from Texas, studied 130 mothers who voluntarily gave up custody. The reasons given most frequently were emotional inability to handle the children, the father's threat of a legal battle, and the mother's involvement in a destructive relationship. To a lesser degree, financial difficulties, the mother's desire to attend college, and the nurturing qualities of the father were also held responsible.

Paskowicz (1982) described her own noncustodial situation as well as those of the mothers in her sample. Twenty-five mothers relinquished custody involuntarily either because of court intervention or because the children chose to live with the father. All of the seventy-five mothers who relinquished custody voluntarily cited money as one of the contributing factors. Also mentioned were the mother's emotional problems, a search for self-actualization, intimidation by the father, and the nurturing qualities of the fathers.

Meyers and Lakin (1983) drew from their own experiences as noncustodial mothers and from the experiences of women they had met in workshops, discussion groups, and their clinical practice. They cited the following reasons for mothers being noncustodial: financial strain, a desire for stability for the children, career demands, a desire to establish an identity, the father's wishes, and burnout.

The Mothers' Reasons

Our information was drawn both from questionnaire responses and from interviews with mothers. The mothers were asked on the questionnaires to describe, in their own words, the reasons their children were living elsewhere. They were also asked to indicate the reasons for split custody if some of their children were with them. Many mothers gave more than one reason. The responses provided by eight or more mothers in order of frequency, are presented in table 5–1.

There was a great deal of overlap among answers. For example, a mother who said her children chose to live with their father because the father was better off financially is giving a response that fits into both the first and the second reasons on the table. If a mother said the child was "bought off" we presume, though we cannot be sure, that she meant bought off with money, not love. When a mother said she abandoned the children, we cannot be sure whether there were other reasons that should have been included with the abandonment. She could have been abused or mentally incompetent.

Table 5–1
REASONS THE MOTHERS GAVE FOR WHY THEY DO NOT HAVE CUSTODY
(n = 502)

Reason	Number of Mothers	Percentage
Money	153	30
Children chose the father as parent	106	21
I could not handle the children; discipline problems	60	12
So children would not have to move	55	11
I was unstable; had problems	54	11
I lost them in a court battle	47	9
Father had good relationship; was best parent	43	9
My career made single parenting hard	35	7
Father remarried; two parents better than one	25	5
Children needed a male image	19	4
Schools/neighborhoods better where father was	18	4
Father "bought them off"	17	4
To avoid a court battle	13	3
Father persuaded them to live with him	12	2
Father abducted the children	11	2
I abandoned them	10	2
I was "burnt out"	9	2
I was physically ill	8	2
I left and could not get custody upon return	8	2
I left to find myself	8	2

Note: Fifteen mothers did not respond.

To learn the prevalence of similar reasons, we grouped those that appeared to address the same issues. The major groupings and their percentages are presented in table 5–2.

Money

The reason given most often has to do with money. Common responses included in this category were "I could not afford to raise them," "He could provide for them better financially than I could," "He threatened me with not paying alimony and/or child support if I took custody," "I could not afford a good lawyer," and "He wanted to avoid paying child support." Of these reasons, the first two appeared the most frequently. Sometimes, the mother had custody at the time of the breakup but turned the children over to the father because of a lack of money or because the father was not keeping up with the required child support payments.

Table 5–2
MAJOR GROUPINGS OF MOTHERS' REASONS FOR BEING NONCUSTODIAL
(n = 500)

Reason	Percentage of Mothers
Money	33.8
Mother's inability to parent	32.2
Children chose the father	23.5
Best interests of the child	23.1
Courts decided	11.9
To pursue a career	7.0

Note: Seventeen mothers did not respond.

With this response, nearly one-third of the mothers were saying that money was the reason for or a contributing factor in custody going somewhere else. A second question that asked specifically about money was also included on the survey. Respondents were asked to state their level of agreement or disagreement with the statement: "I do not have the children because my ex-spouse has more money than I do." Forty-six percent of the mothers agreed with this statement, 41 percent disagreed, and 13 percent were mixed. If we consider the group that agreed that money was a factor (although, arguably, the "mixed" group could also be included), we see that, when the question is posed this way, money affected almost half of the mothers, (and potentially as high as 59 percent). What we see, then, is that, depending on how we posed the question, between 30 percent and 46 percent (if not higher) believed that money was a factor in their not having custody.

Mother's Inability to Parent

Sixty mothers gave answers indicating that they did not have custody because they could no longer handle the children or were unable to discipline them. A few examples of answers in this category were: "My daughter is physically larger than I am; she began to try to control me," "I am not a mother in the sense of being able to handle the day to day of bringing them up," "My son was getting into trouble because he needed more supervision than I was able to give," and "His father can provide stronger discipline than me."

We also placed in this category reasons that were related to the mother's emotional instability, such as "I was unstable," "I had tried to kill myself after the breakup," "I was too emotionally sick to take them with me," "I couldn't raise them," "I abandoned them," and "I was burnt out."

In this category (32.2 percent total), we placed mothers who no longer felt competent to parent either all of their children or one specific child. The mothers' intent in these responses varied between blaming the children, blaming themselves, and blaming the situation.

Children Chose the Father

The reason given next most frequently was that the children chose the father. Responses in this category indicate that the children had a preference and/or were given the choice of whom they wanted to live with and chose the father. Here the intent was to reflect that the choice was made by the child, not by the parents or the courts. If the mother said that the child picked the father because of money, both this response and the previous response concerning money were coded.

In the majority of cases, the mother indicated that the father was picked either because he offered a change from the mother or because he had a good relationship with the child. An example of the former situation was provided by a mother who said, "My only child declared she was going to live with her father in the heat of an argument while I was trying to discipline her. Whenever she had been disciplined in the past her father had said, 'You can always live with me.'" An example of the latter situation was given by the mother who wrote, simply, "Father wanted son and son wanted father," and the mother who wrote, "My son chose to live with his father. I had had custody since he was four. I felt his being with his father would be good."

In some other instances, the implication was that the father persuaded the children to live with him. Here, the issue of a free choice was not so apparent; instead, the emphasis was on the father somehow "pulling the wool over the children's eyes."

Best Interests of the Child

Almost a quarter of the mothers said that they did not have custody because it was in the child's best interests. The mothers in this category indicated that they valued such things as the children staying in the familiar surroundings of the home, school, neighborhood, and friends for the children's adjustment. These mothers also considered the father's competence as a parent important. Answers in this category included: "The father loved the children," "So the children would not have to move," "The father was more nurturing," and "The neighborhood and schools were better where he lived." Altruistic reasons usually were reflected in the answers in this category.

Courts Decided

Twelve percent of the mothers replied that they lost custody after a court battle. We included in this category mothers who did not fight for custody because they thought they could not win. Court-related reasons were occasionally linked with others, most notably the implication that the mother was mentally incompetent. In this category, typical responses were: "My husband sued for custody and won," "The judge awarded custody to my husband because he took into consideration my emotional state at the time of the divorce," and "He sued me for custody and won. He produced lies to use in court against me and nothing my minister or many witnesses could and did say as to my excellence as a mother was worth anything."

My Career Made It Difficult

Thirty-five mothers indicated either that they wanted to pursue a career or that their current career was established and raising children alone would interfere. Sometimes they stated that the father's career allowed him more freedom or flexibility, which made him more able to do the child rearing.

Other Reasons

During the four years of interviews since the original survey, other reasons were mentioned that are worth noting. For example, wife abuse was given as a reason more than once (as discussed in chapter 4). In such situations, the mother had often been physically abused over a period of years, although the children usually had not been abused. To escape the abuse, the mother left the home and the children. The question asked about these situations is why the mother would leave the children if the father is abusive. The answer is not simple but usually revolved around four points: (1) the father may not have been abusing the children; (2) the mother believed that if she left the situation at home would become less inflammatory; (3) the mother feared that the father would become violent if she left with the whole family; and (4) the mother may have believed that she did not have anything to offer the children if they came with her.

One mother wrote:

> My husband took the Vietnam war out on me by beating and raping me. At the time of the breakup, I was emotionally unstable and afraid of my ex. I was forced to work a job involving travel and could not find another. I could not quit because I could not support the kids and could not have them living with me under the circumstances, either.

Sometimes the threat of violence from someone related to the mother can hurt her chances for custody. In one situation described by a mother who did not participate in the survey, two sons were taken away by the court because of neglect and were placed in foster care. The mother and father then divorced, and six months later the father remarried. His new wife was seen as a stabilizing influence, and they regained custody. In the meantime, the mother had become involved with a man who was both abusive and alcoholic. Because of him, the mother was refused custody but was permitted court-monitored visitation. The dilemma for the mother was that whenever her boyfriend learned that she was visiting the children, he became violent. She consequently went to the visitation meeting only when she could sneak out. A number of times she missed the meeting. Her children became increasingly disenchanted with the idea of seeing her, as she often failed to show up.

In another situation, the mother did not have custody because her husband, to use her term, "blackmailed" her. He was a respected member of the community and shocked her by threatening to abduct the children if she did not give him custody. She agreed.

Abduction of the child, though not mentioned by any of the mothers, was cited by a few of the fathers in the study of custodial fathers.[2] According to the Missing Children's Network, the majority of abductions are committed by noncustodial parents. Thus, we know that this reason for being noncustodial is present in the general population.

Lesbianism was also not mentioned as a reason, but through interviews, we learned of a number of mothers who had lost custody because they were gay. A few also decided not to pursue a battle because they believed a gay woman could not win. In Pisano's (1986) study, at least one of the eight mothers contacted through Baltimore County court records had lost custody because she was gay.

A few mothers said that they turned over custody to the father because of guilt. These women had ended the marriage and felt sorry for the father. They did not want to take everything away from him, so when he asked about custody, they agreed so that they would not hurt him further.

Though not reflected in our sample, social service agencies can also be involved in mothers' becoming noncustodial. A parent who is neglectful or abusive may lose custody to a foster home, a relative, or the other parent if the parents are not married.[3] Incarceration of a woman who has committed a crime as cited by Sametz (1980), can also be a reason.

Finally, there is the "supermom syndrome". Many mothers believed that they had to do everything for everybody. They ended up realizing they could not work, clean the home, be a good parent, and be a good wife. The result was that that they were burnt out. Giving up custody was one way to deal with the situation.

Three of the reasons require further discussion. Money, the reason given most often for why the mother does not have custody, is a markedly different issue for women than it is for men. It is our impression (see chapter 11) that most men do not say that they are noncustodial because of financial reasons or that a weaker financial position is the reason that their children live with the mother instead of with them. Fathers face important but different issues about money when they become noncustodial. For example, if custody goes to the mother, they may be unhappy about the child support and alimony award set by the court. They may be upset by the way they perceive the mother is spending the money on herself or on her children. They may be denied visitation by the mother because of nonpayment of support. Despite these complaints, the fathers are usually operating from a position of greater financial strength. At the same time, there can be a leavening effect, as many fathers believe the court system generally favors the mother.

The mothers in our research perceived themselves in a more vulnerable position. More often than not, mothers with custody have to rely on the good graces of the courts and the father for their initial financial well-being. If the father is conscientious in his payments and if the court has set an adequate level of support, all can go well. This is often not the case, however. Full support payments are made to custodial mothers in only about half of the cases (see chapter 9). If the father is unhappy about paying support, he can drag his feet in sending the money or continually pay less than expected. Such a situation keeps the mother off guard. It is well established that income is one of the key variables in how the single-parent family adapts. When there is less money, there are more difficulties. In one study, child support and alimony accounted for 20 to 40 percent of the single-parent family's income in the first year after the breakup[4]. Thus, financial support is vitally important to the well-being of many families.

For single mothers, therefore, there is often the fear that money will not be forthcoming either through the court process or from the father. This makes some of them wary of seeking custody. Some do not feel that they can hire lawyers as competent as their husbands' lawyers or that they can even afford a lawyer in the first place (see Carol in chapter 2). (This issue can also work against the father. If he earns income in a certain range, he may feel he cannot afford a lawyer while he watches his wife, with no income, get one through legal aid.) According to Polikoff (1982), some mothers fight for custody but lose because they do not earn as much as the father. Finally, there are mothers who survey the terrain and decide that what they have to offer their children is inferior to what the father with a higher income has to offer. They cannot afford the material things the children desire. If the father has retained the family home, the mother may have only a small apartment to offer. Thus, the mother's financial position can discourage her from seeking or getting custody.

The point we wish to make is that at the time of the breakup, although both parents are vulnerable in different ways, the mother is usually in a "one-down" position that is different from and can be potentially more damaging than that of the noncustodial father. The mother is vulnerable because of her sex. She is in the position of receiving while the father is in the position of giving the financial support that the family needs. For this reason, when a mother gives up custody because of money, it reflects the differential economic status of women in our society. If divorcing spouses earn close to the same income, they will have other issues to face if there is a battle. In such situations, the financial balance is even, and the scales may be tipped against the father solely on the basis of sex. This is clearly unfair to the father, and there is ample proof of such injustice. But when one spouse is earning less than the other, the less affluent spouse is potentially at a disadvantage from the outset unless the more affluent spouse takes steps to rectify the imbalance. The less affluent spouse is thus dependent on both the courts and the more affluent spouse. That is a vulnerable position to be in.

When we interviewed the mothers whose children chose the father as the primary parent, we did not find any common themes. The stories behind why each child picked the father varied a great deal. In some cases, the father may have had a nicer lifestyle to offer the children, often including a new stepmother. Or, the children may have wanted to move into a different neighborhood where they could make a fresh start or escape an area they disliked. Sometimes they chose the father so that they could stay in their old home if that was where the father was living. Other times the mother had a boyfriend, a husband, or stepchildren whom the children did not like, which precipitated the choice to live with the father. In some instances, the children were living with the mother for a while and were interested in seeing what life would be like with their father. Personality clashes also developed occasionally between the mother and the children. The father thus offered a respite for everyone.

In cases where there were personality clashes, the children may have found the mother too restrictive. The father, wanting custody, might have been egging them on. Following the argument with Mom that was the "last straw," they jumped ship for Dad, who was waving a flag of greater freedom in front of their eyes. Some children sought out their father even though they were well aware that life with him could provide a change, but no picnic.

Some mothers welcome the noncustodial situation. They may feel liberated from the responsibilities of day-to-day parenting. For mothers who have spent a good deal of their adult lives in child rearing, the chance to explore new options is a gift. It allows them to pursue their own interests, which can include careers or new friends. They may also feel it is good for the children to get to know their fathers.

Sometimes, though, the child's choice of the father is seen as rejection. The mother feels devastated and wonders what is wrong with her that she was not the children's choice. One mother stood up at a workshop and told the audience, "When my daughter said she wanted to live with my husband it was the worse thing that ever happened to me. I felt I had failed as a mother and I couldn't tell anyone about it for weeks."

Often, children go back and forth between parents. Sometimes one of the children may go along with the wishes of a sibling and go where that sibling goes. Sometimes, children's decisions are made based on impressions of a situation that change over time. When children are making the choices, because they are young, they often change their minds and go back to the other parent.

Toby, a mother mentioned in chapter 4, wrote a particularly detailed description of her situation over a three-year period during which she lost custody and then regained it:

> We agreed that we had to get a divorce and let the children choose who they wanted to live with and that that person could stay in the home. My daughter, who was the oldest, chose her father and my son wanted to stay with his sister.
>
> My ex-husband subsequently lost his job. Although he is legally responsible for their support, I now have legal custody of my daughter, who chose to live with me after completing her last year of high school. My son remains with his father.
>
> My daughter has now stated the reason she stayed with her father initially was that her father needed her more and needed to stay in the house. She has told me and our relatives that he knew "Mom would be all right." I am overjoyed to have her back with me. I am sorry they stayed with their father initially because I now see how much better they would have been with me. However, at the

time, my ex threatened that he'd never leave the house, and I felt
any more arguing and stress or legal battles for custody would have
caused more harm to our children.

The mothers who do not have custody because they could not
handle the children sometimes express a feeling of exasperation.
They often were raising children who, when they reached their teens,
became too difficult for them to handle. They might have been able
to handle their children's problems when the children were younger,
but when they reached adolescence, a new set of issues may have
arisen that made the situation unbearable. In some cases, the mothers
reported that their children had very severe problems with drugs or
with the law. A few mothers said that their children were institutionalized. In other cases, the problems were much less severe. The
father may exacerbate a tough situation by supporting the child in
disputes with the mother. The family members then become triangulated, with the father often incorrectly perceived as the child's
savior.

With what we know about families, we believe that much of what
these mothers experienced with their children may also be found in
two-parent families. The problems of raising teens are not unique
to one-parent families or to families in which a mother becomes
noncustodial. As part of the life cycle of the family, having a child
in the teens presents the family members with new demands for
behavior. For parents, new questions emerge when they have to
worry about a child who drives or one who is showing an interest
in sexual activity or illegal substances. When there is one parent,
though, there are fewer parenting variables to bring to bear in a
positive sense to help raise the child. This would be true whether
the single parent is a male or a female.

A number of mothers described themselves as emotionally unstable, as abandoning the children, and as being burnt out as parents.
Parenthood has never been restricted to people who are mentally
healthy. People can carry with them from childhood insufficient
means of dealing with normal stress, or they can develop an inability
to cope as they are faced with certain demands and pressures. Some
mothers had been hospitalized for psychiatric illness and were unable
to handle custody—or did not want it—when they were discharged.
Some mothers ran off impetuously with a lover and were unable to

regain custody or never tried to do so. There were also some who threw up their hands at their marriage and parenting, feeling that they had married too young. They felt chained to their home and their children and overburdened by the responsibilities. One or two mothers wrote that they lost custody because their husbands had them committed to an institution against their will.

The feelings the mothers had about themselves as parents at the time of the breakup were explored through another item on the questionnaire. They were asked their level of agreement with the statement: "My husband was a more competent parent than I was when he first got the children." Although 67 percent disagreed, 20 percent agreed and 13 percent were mixed. This response confirms that a significant percentage of mothers felt incompetent to parent— or less competent than their husbands.[5]

The Mothers' Perceptions of Why the Fathers Wanted Custody

Germane to the mother's reasons for being noncustodial is her perception of why the father wanted custody. Her perception of his motives has an influence on her own desire to be noncustodial. What do the mothers think about the fathers' motivation in seeking custody? Are they being good parents, or are they seeking revenge? The mothers were asked on the questionnaire: "Why do you think your husband wanted to raise the children?" This question was designed to gain further information concerning how the mother came to be noncustodial. It is different from the question that asks how the mother actually *became* noncustodial, because it seeks the mother's impression of the motivating forces behind the father's behavior.

The mothers' answers were grouped into six categories:

1. The father loved the children/The situation was a better one for the children: There were 161 responses (34 percent of those who answered) that indicated either (a) that the father loved the children; (b) that he had a good relationship with the children; (c) that it was best for the children; (d) that the children wanted to be with him; (e) that the schools were better where the father lived; or (f) so that the children would not have to change schools. The implication of

this response is that the father wanted the children because he cared for them and/or wanted the best for them.

2. Money was the reason: Eighty-five mothers (18 percent) indicated either (a) that the father wanted the children to avoid paying child support (approximately two-thirds of the respondents) or (b) that the father could afford to raise them and the mother could not (approximately one-third). The implications here are divergent. Some mothers believed that the father wanted the children purely for their own financial gain, while others believed it was for the benefit of all.

3. The father wanted custody because the mother was seen as being unfit: Eighty-five responses (18 percent), indicated that the father perceived some incompetence as a parent on the mother's part. The father wanted custody because (a) the mother was unstable: (b) the mother had abandoned the children; or (c) she was having difficulty with child rearing. The implication here is that the father needed to get involved in single parenting because the mother had abdicated the role.

4. The father wanted revenge: Seventy-seven mothers (16 percent) said that the father wanted custody of the children for revenge, implying that he wanted (a) to get back at the mother; (b) to show the mother she was a bad parent; (c) to get control of the children; and (d) to get control of the mother. The implication is that the father was angry at the mother and was not interested in the children per se but was using them to get back at her. The anger at the mother most often stems from her ending the marriage, from her being an unfit parent, or from her being unfaithful.

5. The father wanted custody for the sake of appearances: Thirty mothers said that they thought the father wanted the children either to make himself look good or to prove that he could be a good parent.

6. The father wanted custody because he did not want to be alone: Twenty mothers (4 percent) gave an answer indicating that the father was lonely, had lost his sense of family, and wanted the children so that he would not have to be alone.

Three categories clearly indicated that the mother felt that the father wanted the children for his own needs, not because it was best for the children. The mothers who cited "revenge," "appearances," and "to avoid being alone" as the motivating factors fall into this category. Also, we could place in this category the mothers who indicated that avoiding child support payments was the motivating factor—approximately another sixty mothers. This means that over a third of all the mothers gave a response indicating that they believe the fathers did not want the children for the sake of the children but rather for some other reason.

This could be a reflection of the continued animosity between the parents or of the difficulties that some of the mothers have in feeling content with the custodial arrangement. It is hard for a mother to feel good about the parenting situation if she believes that the father wanted the children for his own gain.

Betty fits into this group. A 49-year-old waitress who has now remarried, she wrote that after her husband lost the custody battle, he kidnapped all four of their children. The reason?—to avoid paying child support and alimony. Eventually, three of the children left him and came back to live with her. Two of the children are now living on their own, one remains with her, and the fourth is with him. She thinks her husband is a poor father and wishes that she could have regained custody of all of her children sooner than she did.

At the other end of the spectrum from the mothers who think the fathers are after personal gain are the mothers who feel that the father wanted the children because he was the parent best equipped to take are of them financially and emotionally. For example, Mindy, a 38-year-old nurse, wrote, "He's a good parent and the kids are happy. They are his whole life. He centers his social life around them (Little League, school, etc.)."

The answers provided by the mothers concerning custody show the depth of the problems many mothers face when the custody decision is made. Besides the wide range of reasons for why the mother loses custody, we have to consider the mother's perception of the father's part. This perception can help or hurt the mother in adjusting to her role of noncustodial mother. This adjustment is obviously easier for mothers who believe that their chidren are being well taken care of.

In analyzing the relationship of the main reasons given for custody to the later experiences of the mothers, we found that the custody situation can have a strong impact on the later experiences of the mother in relation to her children and, as will be discussd in other chapters, on how the mothers feel about themselves. We found, consistently, that the mothers who lost custody in court tend to have the hardest adjustment and the mothers who are noncustodial because it is in the best interests of the child tend to have the easiest. The mothers who gave the other reasons fall somewhere in between these two groups.[6]

The reason for divorce was also related to the reason for custody. Two trends were seen: (1) the mothers who gave up custody because it was best for the children were the most likely to be the mothers who said that the marriage ended because of incompatibility; and (2) the mothers who lost custody in court were those most likely to have said that they were mentally or physically abused in the marriage.[7] Again, two extremes are shown. Incompatibility as the reason for divorce implies a smoother end to the relationship, with no one being blamed. These situations tend to be coupled with those in which mother believes that the children can best be taken care of by the father. There is little recrimination in the relationship. For the mother who loses custody in court, there is bound to be a history of acrimony that resulted in the parents not being able to work these situations out on their own. Abuse is one sign of this acrimony.

We also found that the mothers who lost custody in court (1) are the least satisfied with their relationship with the children; (2) are the least apt to believe that the children are better off living with the father than with them; (3) are experiencing the greatest difficulty with the children living away from them; and (4) are consulted the least about the children by the father.[8] At the same time, these are also the mothers who spend the greatest number of overnights with the children, indicating a high level of visitation. What we are seeing is a group of mothers who have lost custody against their will and are very unhappy with their situation, which is clearly one that they have not chosen. They remain involved with the children, most likely because it has been mandated by the courts and because they feel they need to stay involved for the welfare of the children.

These women often feel terribly abused and victimized by both the father and the court system. The story of Carol in chapter 2 is one example of what can happen. She failed to go to court on a number of occasions because she wanted to avoid a court battle. Finally, she went, and she lost because it was believed that her having contact with her son would make things worse for him. In addition, her son told the judge that he did not want to see her. She remains bitter about her situation and feels that she did not get a fair deal. In her situation, though, there is no visitation.

We can contrast the mothers who lost custody in court with those who are doing quite well and who believe they are doing what is in the best interests of their children. These mothers do feel very involved with their children and are also quite satisfied with their lives in relation to their children. One reason for this could be that it was not forced on them. Believing that the children are better off somewhere else, they can then move on with their lives. Wilma, also described in chapter 2, is an example. This is not to imply that these mothers feel that their parenting responsibilities are over. Rather, they have placed them in a perspective whereby they are parenting best by not being the full-time parent. Mothers may also feel this if they gave up custody because of money or because of an inability to parent. In fact, there was considerable similarity in the levels of satisfaction and comfort among mothers who gave up custody because of an inability to parent and those who relinquished it because it was seen as being in the best interests of the child.

Margaret, one such mother, began working in a large city twenty miles from her home. When her marriage broke up, she retained custody initially but then found it too difficult to commute and be the parent with sole responsibility. Her husband was a good father and wanted custody of the children. Both parents wanted the children to stay in their small hometown rather than move to the larger, more impersonal city where Margaret was working. The decision was that Margaret could best pursue her career and the children would be better off if they lived with their father.

Voluntary versus Involuntary Custody Decisions

Another vitally important aspect of how mothers come to be non-custodial concerns whether custody was turned over voluntarily. The mother who gives up custody voluntarily usually has had a different experience during the custody decision process and afterwards than the mother who has given up custody involuntarily.

The mothers were asked to state their level of agreement with the statement: "I voluntarily do not have custody." Fifty-five percent agreed, 33 percent disagreed, and 12 percent were mixed. These responses provide us with a different way of looking at what has happened to the mother. A clear third to almost half of the mothers believe that they were involved in a situation that they did not choose. Slightly more than half willingly gave up custody, although many of those, when questioned closely during interviews, said that they did so reluctantly.

How do we judge or, more important, how does a mother judge for herself whether a situation is voluntary? Although it is clearly the mother's perception that is significant, it is necessary to discuss the kinds of situations that arise that may or may not be considered voluntary. The voluntary nature of the situation needs to be pursued because it proved to be a very reliable predictor of the mother's later adjustment (see chapter 8).

Consider, for example, a mother who gives up custody because of a lack of financial resources. She may or may not say that she has relinquished custody voluntarily. If she had more money, she might have retained custody. Does this mean that she voluntarily gave up custody? With a court battle, there is often a loser. A mother who loses in court would be in the involuntary group. Mothers who feel they wish to do something else with their lives and are acting in the best interests of the children are more clearly in the voluntary group. If economic or physical coercion was involved, these women involuntarily gave up custody. Yet suppose that a mother's new job requires that she work late hours and she decides, unhappily, that she cannot have the children and the job. If she had been on the job as long as her husband had been working at his, she might have had more work options; she might have been able to be home earlier and thus able to keep the children. Was her loss of custody voluntary or involuntary? (Fathers sometimes lose custody for this very reason— their work hours prevent them from being able to spend enough time with the children.)

A range of circumstances exists that can cause a mother to consider her situation voluntary or involuntary. Thinking of custody as being given up reluctantly rather than as an either/or situation may assist us in understanding the decision. When we looked at the relationship between the reasons the mothers gave up custody and whether they say they gave up custody voluntarily, we found some interesting correlations.[9] For example, the mothers who gave money as a reason are split on whether they gave up custody voluntarily. Again, great differences are seen between mothers who gave up custody because of the court system (7 percent were voluntary) and those who did so because of the children's best interests (83 percent were voluntary). We found close intercorrelation between whether loss of custody was voluntary, the reasons given for the custody decision, and other variables related to the mother's adjustment. Thus, we could expect, as was found, that the mothers who gave up custody voluntarily have had a smoother course both before and since the custody decision.

The impact of the voluntary nature of custody and the reasons why mothers are noncustodial is only one piece of the pie. As mentioned earlier, the father and the children have a part in the situation, too. The mother does not make her decision in a vacuum, nor are her decisions made for her in a vacuum. Having looked at the mother's side of the story in depth we can now look at other forces interacting in the system that result in custody residing away from the mother.

The Father's Role

The desire of the father to have custody, as mentioned by Fischer (1983), and his characteristics are pertinent to the custody decision. The father, like the mother, weighs a number of considerations concerning custody. He wonders who custody will best serve. Is he equipped to be a sole parent? Is his ex-wife? The decisions are not made lightly and often depend on the father's perception of the mother's ability to raise the children.

The findings from the survey of fathers with custody are relevant in this discussion[10]—first, because there was some agreement between the fathers with custody and the mothers without it when they were asked how custody came to reside with the father; and second, because the fathers' stories give further insight into what transpires.

Fathers may seek custody through both legal and illegal means. If a father feels that he is the better parent, that the children will be better off living with him for either emotional or financial reasons, or that he wants to maintain his family, he may seek custody through the court system. Many a father moves into the position of wanting to be a full-time parent because the mother has abdicated what the father considers her primary role. The father watches as she withdraws or invests her attentions elsewhere. As the children's needs continue, he moves in to pick up the slack. Some fathers do this involuntarily, in that they would rather not parent full-time, while others do it voluntarily, happy to become more involved.

If the father feels that he has little chance of winning custody or does not want to pay for a battle, he may seek custody through other means. What other means might he use? He may threaten the mother, either financially or physically. He may drag his feet about paying child support if the mother has custody when the marriage first ends. He may refuse to move from the house when the marriage ends. A father might feel that he has worked and paid for "his" house and will not leave it just because of a divorce. If the father refuses to leave, a woman who is at the end of her rope may feel compelled to leave without the children. This hurts her chances of regaining custody in the future, because she may be depicted as having abandoned the children. A father may try to gain custody by persuading the children with love, anger, hurt, or bribes. Finally, as mentioned earlier, he may kidnap them.

A father who wants the children thus has a variety of weapons at his disposal. The amount of force he brings to bear may or may not have a strong impact on the mother's decision, but it almost always has at least some impact. His desire is a force the mother has to contend with and a force that may affect the ultimate outcome of the custody decision. Conversely, if the father does not want custody at all, this may compel the mother never to consider relinquishing custody.

Mendes (1976) wrote of fathers who sought custody, a group she called "seekers," and fathers who reluctantly agreed to it, a group she called "assenters." These classifications, though correct in a one-dimensional sense, do not capture the depth that is behind many situations. We can add a third group of fathers to this understanding, a group of "capable fathers." The capable father is able to be a good sole parent and is recognized as such by the mother. By his competence, this father makes it easier for the mother to give up custody, because he offers a viable alternative. Although he might be either an assenter or a seeker, he may also have qualities that make him competent—such as interpersonal and financial qualities. The more the father is perceived as competent by the mother, the more likely it is that he will end up with custody. The opposite is also true. If the father is perceived as incompetent, the mother is more likely to want to retain custody or to be dissatisfied if the father does get custody. The point we wish to make is that the father's desire and actions, as well as his abilities, have a powerful impact on the custody outcome.

The Children's Role

Children are ostensibly at the heart of every custody decision. Yet experience shows that in some cases, the divorcing parents are not interested in the well-being of the children as much as in working out some of their own personal problems through the custody process. In those cases, the children are used as pawns in an escalating game of emotional chess. Fortunately, parents often do have their children's interests at heart. Three general patterns were found to apply to the children's role in the custody decision: (1) the children's needs are not considered; (2) the children's needs are considered but the children do not voice a strong preference or are not given a choice; and (3) the children express a desire to live with the father.

Why aren't the children's needs considered? Some parents may seek custody merely because it is expected of them, although they really would prefer not to have it. Others seek custody as a means of getting back at the other parent. In some situations, the parents may be wrapped up in their own needs. In these families, everyone suffers eventually.

In the second and more ideal situation, the children's needs are taken into account. At times, decisions are made by the courts and/ or by the parents on behalf of the children. The parents may meet and decide that one parent is better equipped for taking care of the children than the other parent. If the children are quite young, their preferences may be considered for them. The question of whom the children prefer is not given much weight because there may be no viable choice other than the father. Often the children's needs are considered on the basis of their age or sex. For example, judges or parents may decide that boys should be with their fathers.

The relationship the children have with one or both of the parents also plays a part. Consider the situation of a mother who has been raising a child alone for a few years. The child reaches adolescence and begins experiencing the normal emotional and physical developmental changes of the teen years. The mother and child have the normal clashes over curfews. In a two-parent family, there is one extra adult for these clashes to bounce off, an extra adult who can sometimes mediate these disputes or lend a hand to the parental side of the scale. In a one-parent family, there is less room for reverberation. The clashes shake the foundation of the relationship to a greater degree. The parents may decide that the father should take the child for a while, since men are often seen as stricter and more able to control a rebellious youth. Perhaps without being offered a choice, the child goes to live with the father.

In the third pattern, the children express a strong perference for living with the father. These situations may provide either a healthy change or an unhealthy one. In a healthy change, the child may want to live with the father because it is felt that the father is the more nurturing parent, has more time to spend with the child, or lives in an area that offers better schools or a better neighborhood setting. Some children, especially those who have lived with their mother for a few years, want to live with their father because they feel that they have never gotten a chance to know him. The children also may have gotten themselves into a rut with personality clashes at home, in school, or in the neighborhood. The best solutions to some of these problems can be a move to a new home, the chance to start again someplace else. For the child of divorce, having two families provides the potential for this kind of solution.

In the less healthy situations, children want to go with the father to avoid working things out with the mother, because the father has bribed the children, or because the father is more lenient. These situations can have a number of scenarios:

1. The child goes with the father to avoid working things out with the mother. In this pattern, the child and the mother fight continually and the child asks to go live with the father. The father has stayed out of the conflict but is willing to assume custody. The mother–child conflicts remain unresolved.

2. The child has been bribed by the father. In this situation, the child has been showered with gifts by the father, a pattern found also by Ambert (1982), and goes to live with him because of the material things he has promised. Sometimes, a war has gone on between the parents as to who can more effectively bribe the child. At other times, it is only the father who is doing the bribing, because

the mother either cannot afford to take part in the game or chooses not to.

3. The child chooses the father because he is more lenient. Here the father either is openly promising the child (usually an adolescent) more freedom or, merely by his presence, gives the child the hope of more freedom. Rather than working out some of the normal developmental issues about freedom that arise between children and parents (in this case, the mother), the child runs to the father. The pattern may be repeated when the father, after allowing more freedom for a few months, feels the need to pull in the rope. The child then runs back to the mother.

The child may express a desire to live with the father at the time of the breakup or after living with the mother for a period of time. In some cases, after one child expresses an interest and changes residences, a sibling, usually a younger one, will want to go, too. It is difficult to know whether the the second child's desire to live with the father is based on the qualities of the father and the mother or on the desire to stay with the sibling who has moved. Parents often like to have children stay together.

In addition, the expression of the desire to live with the father may or may not be solicited. The children may be given a voice or they may demand to be heard by either their verbal or their nonverbal behavior. Obviously, a child who is turned down after making a request can make life difficult for the parents. Difficult behavior can escalate to the point that the child goes to live with the other parent even though it was something neither parent wanted.

Like the father and the mother, when they are given a choice—and even when they are not—the children weigh many factors in deciding who they want to live with. Their part in custody decisions cannot be ignored.

Putting the Pieces Together

We have been looking at a number of factors that are present when the decision surrounding custody is made. Many of these factors interact with each other and affect the way in which the father gets custody and what happens to the mother. The reasons for the divorce, the voluntary or involuntary nature of the custody decision, the individual characteristics of the mother and her status as a woman, the characteristics of the father, and the personalities and wishes of the children can all combine or work on their own to result in the custody situation. These pieces tend to fall together in certain patterns that show a path leading to the mother being noncustodial.

It is our impression that what sets some of these mothers apart from some mothers with custody is the presence of many of these variables leading up to the custody decision, as well as the presence of many of the reasons given for the custody situation. As we stated earlier, it is rare that one thing can explain such a complex phenomenon. The more that these different reasons are occurring with the other variables, the more likely it is that a mother will be noncustodial. If you begin with a situation in which a mother has been feeling unable to raise her children, is having trouble financially, and wants what is best for her children and add to that a father who wants custody, children who want to go with the father, and a fairly compatible marital breakup, you clearly may get a noncustodial mother. The different variables add up until the balance of the scale is tipped toward the father's getting custody.

If we wished to look further, we could add some of the trends found in the relationships between these mothers and their own parents or in other aspects of the mothers' premarital lives. Looking at those trends may help put some of the pieces in place for some of the mothers, but, like any other single variable, these trends cannot explain everything that happens; at times, the early experiences have no impact. The point is that it is these variables that *begin* to explain the differences between these custody situations and the more traditional situations of custodial mothers and noncustodial fathers.

The Mothers' Stories

We conclude this chapter and this first period of study of the mothers' lives with the mothers' stories. In moving from the general to the specific, we can see how how many of these custody situations evolved.

Sandy, who was introduced in chapter 4, described her life after she got her divorce:

> I was awarded minimal child support and received welfare. I had only a high school education. I had difficulty finding jobs. My

inexperiences with men caused me problems. My own parents were divorcing after twenty-five years of marriage. Neither of them were able to be concerned about me and the baby or to offer help.

Things went from bad to worse. An involvement with a boyfriend became physically abusive. One day I sold my car, got a ticket to New York, called the nursery school and said my mother was picking my daughter up. I flew to New York, dropped in on a couple I knew, and was generally unhappy and terrified. I saw a counselor and flew back home. My mother had received a call from the nursery school to pick up the baby and called my ex-husband to take care of her. When I got back he had her. I was so depressed and run-down and my boyfriend was still playing games with my head. I tried a suicide attempt with pills. I believe I was so ill I sometimes did not know my daughter was gone. Other times I would miss her. My husband kept her, which was okay with me at the time. A few years later I agreed to forgo legal custody. My husband remarried a woman who has her own child. It seemed the best thing for my daughter both financially and stability-wise.

Sandra, also introduced in chapter 4, was described as the super-mom who left the marriage because of exhaustion from trying to balance motherhood and a career. She had custody of a 2-year-old when the marriage first ended. She wrote:

I had custody of our daughter for one year after our dissolution. During that year our daughter's behavior changed dramatically. She became very difficult to handle, plus she would wake up at night screaming and crying for her father. She cried for him at least twice every day. During that same year, I had a serious skiing accident, my uncle died, and I was raped. I was an emotional wreck and I finally relented to my husband's constant requests for custody. I tried to justify my decision by telling myself that one miserable person is better than two."

Constance, also described in chapter 4, is now a schoolteacher. She has split custody of her children. The older child wanted to live with his father and stepmother, and the younger child chose to stay with Constance.

Marta, 35, gave up custody in the best interests of her children, because of money, and to make the separation easier for her husband. She told this story:

Greg and I had made a joint decision to end the marriage. I no longer loved him; he knew I had been very unhappy for a long time. Although he did not really want the divorce, he knew it was for the best—I would have soon grown to hate him and that would not have done anyone any good. Greg had always taken care of the children and been good to them. Over the years I taught him how to relate better to them. When the decision needed to be made where the children would live, I felt I would cope better than he without the daily support they could provide. I had basically said, "I reject you, husband." I could not rationalize taking the only other people who had been dear to him. At the time, I made the best decision for my ex-husband and the children. He may not have survived without them. He also made two to three times as much money, which meant he could offer the kids a better standard of living. And their home and schools did not have to change.

Belle, who is 40, had a different ending to her marriage. Her husband fell in love with someone else and wanted a divorce because he said he could not handle the responsibility of a family. Belle tried to keep the marriage together but after a while could not tolerate his indifference. During the next three years, Belle stayed in the home with the three children. Belle had difficulty finding satisfactory work and felt most of their friends chose her ex-husband over her. Things got worse:

> Our house was about to be repossessed so I moved out of state with the children to be closer to my sister. It was a mistake! My job was okay but the children were unhappy as it was all foreign to them. Child support payments stopped altogether. He never objected to my leaving the state with the kids. I had to sell some furniture and move back to the hometown where I was raised to live with my mother. She supported us until I could get on my feet. Then she became ill and I began taking care of her. Maybe I was too tied to her because I had never cut the apron strings. The children were unhappy in the school system there. They began to visit their father, who still lived in their hometown, which was thirty miles from where we lived. My hometown offered nothing— theirs had a pool, skating rink, and a movie theater. That summer was hell. My mother got worse and the kids wanted me to move back to their home. I said no because I did not think I could handle it emotionally or financially.

It came time to enroll them in school again and my husband and I amicably discussed my moving back to town or having them move back to town with him. He did not think I could let them go. I told him my main concern was for the children's happiness. They were not happy where they were and wanted to be back with their friends. He said his only concern was for the children also. Throughout this the children assured me they loved me, would rather live with me than him, but wanted to be in their old school. In September they moved out of my mother's home. I stayed and took care of her. Six months later, he remarried. Her two children moved in with them. My children begged me to move back to town so that they could live with me. I was still taking care of my mother and couldn't find a place for us all.

I have a terrible guilt about the whole thing. If I had not left, this would not have happened. I miss them yet sometimes I don't want them to see me so depressed. They still assure me they love me and only chose their town, not their father over me.

Cathy, 45, sought a divorce from her husband after fifteen unhappy years of marriage. Initially, both children stayed with Cathy, but after two months her daughter wanted to live with her father because she "did not want him to be alone." There was a great deal of sibling rivalry between the daughter and an older brother, and Cathy believes her daughter was the "apple of her father's eye," while the son was often at loggerheads with him. It was arranged between the parents that the children would alternate months with each parent. A year later, after Cathy's husband had remarried, the son no longer wanted to visit his father because he was getting into fights with his new stepmother and stepsister. In the meantime, Cathy and her daughter were fighting constantly. A split custody situation was legalized whereby the son lived full-time with Cathy and the daughter lived full-time with her father.

An example of how timing can affect the custody outcome is provided by Babs. Babs, 30, and her husband were separated after a thirteen-year marriage. Their son, who was 12, had just begun to establish a relationship with his father—one that the son wanted to continue to cultivate with his father, who had never had time to spend with him because of his busy work schedule. Babs was willing to turn custody over to her husband for a variety of reasons. She "needed her space." It was important to her to figure out who she was, and she felt capable of fending off degrading comments about being noncustodial. She had suffered from ten years of ileitis and had a partially completed college education and a long history of unsatisfactory work experiences. She saw this as a chance to get a good foot into a career. Although her relationship with her son was very strong, she felt she "needed time not being someone's wife or mother." Babs was also aware that her husband's income of $30,000 was nearly five times what she was earning. After her son went to live with his father, her own life was comfortable for her: "I had always trusted men and knew my husband would do a good job."

Annie, 30, felt that she was a victim of the court system, inadequate representation by her attorney, and numerous manipulations by her husband. Divorced after seven years of marriage, Annie raised her three children by herself in a one-bedroom apartment. After a lot of wrangling, she finally was able to bring her husband to court, where she was suing him for increased child support. Her husband, who was financially well off, lied in court about his financial situation. Annie believed that her attorney, whom her husband was paying, was working for him sub rosa. He kept postponing further hearings and jeopardizing her case in other ways, particularly by not questioning her husband's false testimony. The outcome was a minimal and quite insufficient increase in child support. Annie felt emotionally and financially helpless to continue to plead her case, so she made the decision to turn over custody of her children. "I decided it would probably be better for them to live in their father's big house and be able to go to a good school. I just couldn't manage financially and was forced into it."

In contrast, Stella, 39, reported a much more equitable and comfortable arrangement for herself and her children: "Once I discovered that the main reason I had been refusing to let them go was because I did not want people to think poorly of me, then the decision was already made for me." She said that her sons needed a strong male image and firmer discipline as they entered adolescence than she was able to give them. She had had custody for a few years and believed that her children should get to know their father. Stella reported:

> My ex is really a fine person and they all deserved the chance to love and respect him. The children are happier, more content people and I am a happier, more whole person. I can commit myself

to some of the things I always had wanted to do but never had the time for.

Marlene, 32, lost custody of her son in court. Her husband of twelve years ran off with his secretary. Marlene believed that the only reason he wanted their son was to reduce the guilt he felt about abandoning the family. "My son wanted to stay with his father. I guess $400 bikes and less responsibility can be awfully attractive." Marlene retained custody of an adopted daughter from a previous marriage.

6

The Mothers' Relationships
with Their Children

I T is in their relationships with their children that the mothers feel they have the most to justify to their friends, co-workers, family, children, and themselves. Accepting what has happened and is happening with their children is the hardest area for the mothers to reconcile. Some noncustodial mothers strongly believe that their children are better off living away from them. They are content with the living arrangements and feel that those arrangements are the best for all concerned. Many more of the mothers are unhappy. Living away from their children has been much harder then they had anticipated and is the most difficult area of their adjustment.

This chapter discusses the continuing relationships between the mothers and the children living away from them including a description of visitation patterns and the mothers' experiences with visitation as well as the findings concerning the mothers' continuing involvement with the children—how well they get along with the children, how well they believe the children are progressing, and the experiences they have living away from the children. The mothers' own stories and two interviews with children living away from their mother are included. The mothers' advice for other parents will conclude the chapter.

Review of the Literature

Our knowledge of the noncustodial parent has been gained primarily from studies of noncustodial fathers. These studies point out that for men, being separated from their children can be quite painful. The fathers have been found to suffer from depression and loneliness. Without daily contact with their children, men complain of feeling out of touch with their children, of rootlessness, and of lacking structure. They cite day-to-day problems in terms of visitation, child support payments, and regularity of contact with the children.[1]

Mothers without custody experience many of the same feelings. Two key factors make many of these mothers' feelings particularly stressful: (1) they have been conditioned to believe that their identity as a person is wrapped up in being a mother, and (2) they have often been more involved in child rearing than the fathers have been. Hence, they are likely to experience a radical change when they cease to have daily contact with their children, especially if they have been the primary caretaker. When the father has been the primary caretaker during the marriage, the change for her will not be so radical.

Noncustodial mothers in other studies expressed a variety of concerns related to living apart from their children. These concerns fall into two areas: missing the children and worrying about their continuing relationships with the children. Paskowicz (1982) reported that some felt very relieved by having relinquished daily contact. Others continued to question the decision even years later. She stated that 63 percent of the mothers felt that they were loved and accepted by their children. Berke et al. (1979) found that the quality of the mothers' relationships with their children actually improved for about half of the mothers after they became noncustodial. The majority felt that they had made the right decision.

Todres (1978) reported that missing the children was a major concern for 60 percent of the mothers interviewed. One mother, besides missing her children, worried that, when they were older, they would hate her for leaving them.

Fischer and Cardea (1981; 1982) identified a few mothers who felt "betrayed" by their children for choosing to live elsewhere. This certainly would put a damper on the ongoing relationship between the mother and those children. Noncustodial mothers were not very pleased with their relationships with their children—only 35 percent characterized it as close and comfortable, 20 percent were ambivalent, and the remaining 45 percent were split between describing the relationship as hostile or as too infrequent. A number of noncustodial mothers experienced a decline in the relationship over time. Some mothers never saw their children, and the custodial father was usually blamed for this. Generally, three types of relationships were found: warm and loving, hostile and angry, and ambivalent.

What the children are feeling in their relationship with the non-custodial mother is more difficult to pinpoint. Little research has been done in this area, though some studies do approach this issue by looking at the adjustment of children living with their fathers.

Luepnitz (1982) is one of the few to have done a comparison study of children of divorce. She looked at sixteen custodial fathers, sixteen custodial mothers, eighteen parents with joint custody, and these parents' ninety-one children. One of her findings relates to how well children adjust to being raised by a custodial father. She found among her sample that the adjustment scores of the children did not differ on the basis of the sex of the single parent who was raising them. She added the cautionary note that all of the children being raised by their fathers had spent at least the first two years of their lives being raised by women. She also found that children being raised by single parents were dissatisfied with their level of visitation with the noncustodial parent. They wanted more of it.

Ambert (1982; 1984) compared seven single father–headed families with eleven headed by single mothers at two different times post-divorce. She found that the families in which the children were being raised by a single father were functioning more smoothly than the single mother–headed ones.

But what of the child's feelings about the mother? Although no study has looked in depth at the child's feelings about the noncustodial mother, selected research does provide some impressions. Greif and Wasserman[2] interviewed twenty-one children living with their custodial father. The children were found to be protective of their relationship with their mother, describing it in guarded terms. These children might hold an idealized version of the relationship or might have a fear of losing it if they expressed negative feelings.

Visitation patterns of noncustodial mothers have rarely been examined. Furstenburg et al. (1983) are one exception. They looked at visitation between children and noncustodial parents of both sexes. They interviewed a large nationally representative sample of children ranging between the ages of 12 and 16 in 1,047 different households. Among their sample of children separated from a biological parent, only a third saw their noncustodial fathers once a month or more. Over 90 percent were living with their mother. In contrast, 69 percent of the twenty-five children living with their fathers were seeing their noncustodial mothers that often. Thus, the noncustodial mothers were visiting more than the noncustodial fathers. These researchers added that the amount of visitation was affected by a number of factors. For example, visitation went down with lower incomes and educational levels, remarriage of either parent, and with greater amounts of physical distance.

Putting the research aside, it is important to remember that children in a divorce situation usually experience a great deal of pain. Separation from one parent, and often from relatives and grandparents, can take an enormous toll. The confusion, loss, and anger that can develop are quite normal, though difficult, reactions to what is usually the most upsetting event in the child's life. Many of the mothers, in turn, consider this a major loss. For both parent and child, working to reestablish the relationship can be quite difficult.

Findings of Our Study

The information gained from the noncustodial mothers in our study includes the amount of the mother's contact with the children, her feelings about that contact, the part that the children continue to play in her life, and her relationship with the children.

When the mothers were asked to indicate the level of involvement they had with their children, they responded as follows:

Very involved, 22.6 percent

Somewhat involved, 33 percent

Slightly involved, 29.3 percent

Not at all involved, 15.1 percent

Here, we were asking for an impression of the mothers' involvement with the children, including phone calls, letters exchanged, and physical visitation. The question tapped into the mothers' impressions of their emotional involvement with the children, which are qualitative rather than quantitative impressions. For example, a mother may feel very involved with her children even though she lives in a different city and does not visit them frequently. As indicated, more than half of the mothers considered themselves to be very or somewhat involved with their children. Fifteen percent felt they are not at all involved. Whether this is a situation of their choosing will be discussed shortly.

We also asked the mothers about the frequency of their contacts with their children—a quantitative factor. The responses were as follows (because they could check all answers that apply, the totals equal more than 100 percent):

Once a week or more, 29.7 percent

Every other week, 21.7 percent

Once a month, 11.6 percent

Summers, 17.7 percent

Holidays, 20.8 percent

Never, 9.4 percent

Other ("sporadically," "varies with each child," "once or twice a year," "hardly ever," "four times a year," "frequently"), 31.1 percent

The mothers' responses showed that approximately half of them were seeing their children at least once every other week (a combination of the first two categories) and 63 percent were visiting at least once a month, a figure very close to the 69 percent reported by Furstenburg et al. (1983).

When the mothers were also asked how many overnights they spent with their children, the average was 2.1 per month. When the children were spending the night with the mother, the most common visitation pattern was a visit once a month, one night every other weekend, or two nights every other weekend. The vast majority of the mothers (90 percent) spent five nights or less per month with their children.

The responses of the mothers were remarkably similar to the patterns described by the custodial fathers who took part in the earlier study (Greif, 1985a). In that study, 46 percent of the fathers said that the noncustodial mothers visited at least every other week, and 9.3 percent said that the mothers never visited. The fathers reported the average number of overnights the children spent with their non-custodial mother as 1.9.

In this study, marital status was not related to visitation, nor were income, education, or the number of years of being noncustodial. Physical proximity most likely was related, although the question was not asked of the mothers. Fathers with custody reported that visitation from the noncustodial mother does decrease with distance.

The Mothers Who Were Very Involved

An attempt was made to learn more about the noncustodial mothers who reported that they were very involved with their children, usually in situations in which the continuing co-parental relationship was working to the optimum. The exceptions were when visitation was court-ordered following a custody dispute. A number of items on the questionnaire were examined to determine their correlation with the amount of involvement described by the mother. In considering these characteristics, it must be remembered that many of them are neither the cause nor the effect of involvement but rather are occurring simultaneously with the involvement. For example, mothers who are very involved with their children are also very satisfied with their relationships with those children. It cannot be claimed, however, that one factor is due to the other; rather, these characteristics of the relationships are commonly occurring together.

We found the following:

1. The mothers who were very involved tended to give "shared" reasons for the divorce. As discussed in chapters 4 and 5, when the marriage ends with both parents taking the responsibility for the breakup, there is usually less acrimony in the continuing relationship. This is further substantiated by other correlations to be discussed here. Similarly, these mothers were most apt to say that their marriages ended by mutual decision, rather than being initiated by the mother or the father.[3]

2. The mothers who were very involved tended to say that custody went to the father because it was in the best interests of the children.[4]

As with the reason given for the divorce, better feelings flow from certain relationships that tend to result in a better continuing co-parenting relationship. Following from this, the mothers who were very involved with their children also tended to say that they gave up custody voluntarily. (The relationship between the reasons given for custody and the voluntary nature of the custody decision were discussed in chapter 5.)

3. The mothers who were very involved tended to be child-free; that is, they did not have split custody.[5] The explanation for this is complex, but what can be said briefly is that split custody often does not occur when there is more resolution in the postdivorce family—that is, when the reasons for divorce are shared or there was a court decision. (See appendix for further information.)

4. The mothers who were very involved tended not to have a stepmother involved in raising the children.[6] Some mothers have given the father's remarriage as a reason for not having custody, claiming that their children (or the courts) preferred a two-parent family. In such situations, the children may tend to turn away from frequent contact with their mother. The mother, in turn, may feel replaced and may not maintain as high a level of contact. If the father has not remarried, the mother may feel more needed and be more needed.

5. The mothers who were very involved were the most satisfied with their level of involvement with their children.[7] A few mothers who were not very involved also preferred it that way. Clearly, staying in touch with one's children is not for everyone, but for the majority of the mothers it was preferable.

6. The mothers who were very involved were also the most satisfied with their relationships with their children[8] and with how the children were progressing.[9] The pattern here is that everyone gets along well so they see a lot of each other.

7. The mothers who were very involved gave themselves a higher rating as a parent[10] and also rated their ex-husbands higher as a parent.[11] As would be expected in most cases, the mothers who have frequent contact with their children felt that they were doing a better job as a parent than those who see their children less often. Possible exceptions would be those mothers who felt that they were doing a good job by turning custody over to their ex-husbandsand not having

contact with the children, though this would be a minority. It is easier and more likely for one to feel comfortable in the role of parent if there is visitation.

8. The mothers who were very involved felt less guilt than the mothers who maintained a little involvement, but the mothers who were the least involved felt the least guilt.[12] This finding may be an indication that for some of the seventy-six mothers who said that they were not at all involved with their children, having cut off almost all contact has been a freeing experience for them, one for which there are few regrets. This is most likely the group of mothers who never felt very good about themselves as mothers and who believe that the children are better off living away from them.

In a number of other ways, the mothers who were very involved with their children were *not* different from the rest of the mothers. They were similar in terms of their age, their income, and the number of years they had been noncustodial.

What is of interest is the fact that the mothers' degree of involvement, as a group, did not significantly diminish or increase over time. (Because we did not follow these mothers individually over time, we do not know how time affected each of them.) One explanation is that a level of involvement was reached relatively soon after the custody arrangement and that the level did not alter appreciably over time. This is of interest given the general belief that noncustodial parents (especially fathers) lose contact with their children over time (see, also, chapter 11). For these mothers, this pattern was not found.

The mother's religion and education were also unrelated to involvement, as were the age, number, and sex of the children living away from her. The finding that mothers were not more likely to be involved with daughters than with sons was surprising to us. Other factors, such as the nature of the parents' relationship, may be more influential than sex in the continuing involvement.

Feelings About Arrangements

Turning, now, from the noncustodial mothers who are very involved with their children and returning to the total sample of noncustodial mothers, we can look at the feelings the mothers hold about their involvement. Although more than half of the mothers described themselves as very or somewhat involved and visit their children at least once every other week, a much higher percentage (70 percent) were unsatisfied with their situations and wanted more involvement.

Closely linked to the desire for more contact was the ease with which visitation was arranged. Fifty percent responded that arranging visitation was "very difficult" or "difficult," 19 percent said that it was "slightly difficult," and 31 percent said that it was "not difficult." Some mothers in this last group may not have attempted to arrange visitation.

On another question, an even higher percentage (75 percent) indicated that not being with their children was very difficult or difficult for them. Only 8 percent responded that it was not at all difficult.

Two other questions probed the mothers' feelings about the custody arrangement. The mothers were asked their level of agreement with the statement: "Usually I prefer not having the children with me." Only 17 percent agreed with the statement, 27 percent were mixed, and 56 percent disagreed. They were also asked their level of agreement with the statement: "Not having the children has been harder for me than I anticipated." Nearly half (49 percent) agreed, 20 percent were mixed, and 31 percent disagreed.

What this group of responses shows is that the majority of the mothers were unhappy with many aspects of visitation and custody. Most wanted more contact and found visitation troublesome to arrange. Being apart from their children was difficult—harder than they had expected—and most would have preferred a different arrangement.

The Mothers and Their Children

How well do noncustodial mothers get along with the children living away from them? Are they happy with how their children are developing? Do they feel good about themselves as parents? These questions are central to the life of the noncustodial mother. To many, the answers reflect how successfully they are leading their lives and how well the custody arrangement has worked out. As will be shown, it is not always working out well. What emerges is a complex picture of relationships that shift back and forth and are marked by mixed feelings.

The mothers were asked to rate how satisfied they were with their relationships with the children living elsewhere. Although this question did not account for the individual differences in the relationships a mother may have with each of her children—that is, she may get along very well with one and terribly with another—it does allow for a global snapshot. Approximately one-quarter (26 percent) were satisfied with the relationships, 24 percent were mixed, and 40 percent were dissatisfied.

Despite the difficulties in their relationships with the children expressed by many of the mothers, visitation was helpful. A large percentage (82 percent) described "seeing the children" as very helpful or helpful to their adjustment as a noncustodial parent. Responses to a similar question showed that "spending time with the children" was difficult for 44 percent of the mothers. What these two sets of responses show is that a large percentage of mothers (82 percent) derive some benefit from the visitation, whereas a smaller percentage (44 percent) report difficulty with it. We interpret this to mean that the mothers view visitation as a positive activity for them, but the actual interactions that occur during visitation are frequently difficult for them to handle.

Further ambivalence in the mothers' feelings was found when we considered the responses to a question asking for the level of agreement with the statement: "The children are better off where they are" (living away from the mother). The mothers were split into nearly equal groups—32 percent agreed with the statement, 33 percent were mixed and 35 percent disagreed. The mothers were also asked to speculate about what would be the children's preferred living arrangement. Their level of agreement with the statement: "The children would prefer living with me," showed by far the highest level of responses in the "mixed" category of any question on the survey—27 percent agreed, 47 percent were mixed, and 26 percent disagreed.

What emerged from two other questions further illustrates the complexity of the mothers' feelings about their relationships with their children. The mothers were asked how satisfied they were with how their children were progressing in most areas of their lives. Again, individual differences in the children's progress could not be ferreted out, but a global picture was gained. Only 20 percent were dissatisfied, 35 percent were mixed, and 45 percent were satisfied.

The fact that over half were dissatisfied or had mixed feelings regarding how their children were progressing does not speak positively of the mothers' impressions of their children's growth and development, especially when compared with the responses of the non-custodial fathers (see chapter 11).

The second question asked the mothers to rate themselves as parents. Only 10 percent rated themselves as poor or fair, 20 percent described themselves as adequate, 53 percent as good, and 17 percent as excellent. It is interesting that 70 percent of the mothers gave themselves a rating of good or excellent, yet only 45 percent thought the children were progressing well.

It is important, given the often ambivalent feelings of the mothers about their situation, to look at the characteristics of the mothers who describe themselves as poor or fair parents. We have been slowly building a case for linking involuntary loss of custody to later problems with adjustment. Some other characteristics also emerged. Specifically, the mothers who gave themselves low ratings were the ones who were less involved with their children[13] and preferred not having their children with them.[14] These are also the mothers who were more apt to agree that "finding out who I am" has been difficult. What we are seeing is that they feel unsure of themselves in the role of parent and are also unsure of themselves as people. Distancing themselves from their children is one of the behaviors that may be connected to these feelings.

The Mothers' Ambivalence

Even though some of the mothers were perfectly content with their relationships with their children and gave themselves excellent parenting ratings, what emerged from the questionnaire responses was the more common picture of the ambivalence that we have already mentioned. It is not easy for parents (female or male) to be separated on a daily basis from their children. Whether the situation is of their choosing or not, we see evidence of strain in the relationships. It can be generated by the mother, by the children, by the father, and by all the parties. The *feeling* of spending time with the children, of being involved with them, can be quite reassuring to the mother, because it means that she is successfully holding up her end of parenting. But the *reality* of actually spending that time with them can be stressful.

Noncustodial fathers have long complained about trying to cram a great deal of parenting into a few short hours of visitation. "Doing things" with the children becomes the order of the day, rather than just "being with" the children. Many things can make it hard for the noncustodial mother. She typically cannot entertain the children in the children's home, and they may feel out of sorts in the mother's home. Her own living situation may not be adequate, because of space restrictions, to accommodate one or more children for the night or even for a few hours on a rainy day. Depending upon the children's understanding of why they are living with their father, they may overtly or covertly express feelings of rejection because they are living away from the mother. This can make the mother's situation even more uncomfortable for her and can increase her feelings of ambivalence. In addition, most of the mothers believe that their children would prefer living away from them, or are unsure about it. This is a reflection of their feelings about their relationships with their children. Many must accept the fact that their children are happier living with the father. Their role then becomes that of the parent of secondary importance. This is not to say that noncustodial parents are not vitally important to children but rather to point out that, in most cases, the parent with whom the children are spending the bulk of their time is the one they are likely to rely on the most. For many of the mothers, playing second fiddle is a difficult position to be in.

Conceptualizing the Relationships

Just as we conceptualized the custody decision as affected by the mother, father, the children, and the role of women in society, we wish to point out some of the multiple factors that affect the relationship between the mother and her children. Besides the personal characteristics of the mother and the children, we consider it necessary to include, as others have suggested:

1. The role played by the father
2. The role played by the history of the relationship

3. The role played by the developmental stage of the family members

4. The role played by the interactions between the mother and the children

The Father's Role

As indicated in chapter 5, the father is not a passive observer of the noncustodial mother–child relationship. In the best circumstances, he encourages frequent contact between his children and their mother. He is able to separate his relationship with his ex-wife from the needs of his children to have a relationship with their mother. As will be shown in chapter 14—in the interviews with Susan, Joe, and Mark— parents can draw that kind of boundary around their problems as spouses and not let it affect their continuing role as parents. In the worst circumstances, the father obstructs the mother's attempts to see the children. He may be interfering in the mother–child relationship in a variety of ways, including financial, legal, and physical threats.

The History of the Relationship

In examining the ongoing relationship between the mother and the child, we must consider what has transpired earlier between the members of the family. For example, how the children came to live with the father is vitally important. If the children chose the father, this may be a major roadblock to the mother's comfort in spending time with the children. If the mother has relinquished custody because she wants to pursue a different life, she may find the children rejecting her. Conversely, if these decisions were made without acrimony or recrimination, they may pave the way for smooth relations. The shifting of custody from one parent to the other can also have an impact. If the child is going back and forth between parents every few months or even every few years, there may be a different relationship between mother and child than if the mother has never had sole custody. The mother is most likely not dealing with the same sense of loss and may have an easier time with the parent–child relationship. The comings and goings of the child may signify different things each time there is a switch. When there is a custody arrangement that seems permanent, the opportunity exists for the mother and child to deal with a more stable situation, though often for the mother a less desirable one.

History also affects the relationship between mother and child if we consider the upbringing of the mother and father. Is this mother's noncustodial arrangement playing out a pattern started a generation earlier? Is there something of historical significance for which the mother is trying to compensate? For example, a mother who was raised in a two-parent family may have a much harder time dealing with the absence of her child than a mother who was raised in a one-parent family. This is particularly true if the mother in the latter situation was able to establish a very comfortable relationship with her noncustodial parent. One mother told us, "I always wanted a close relationship with my daughter because I did not have one with my mother." She had an especially difficult time dealing with being noncustodial.

Recent history can be equally important. If the mother believes that the father is a competent parent, she may worry less about what she must provide the children and hence may be able to establish a more relaxed relationship with them.

As noted, there is often ambivalence. The mother may feel that she has done the right thing by agreeing to have her children live elsewhere, yet she may have doubts. As she observes her children's problems, she may wonder whether things would have been different if they had lived with her. She may hear an unkind comment about noncustodial mothers from a stranger or see *Kramer vs. Kramer* and wonder whether she would give up custody again. The ambivalence that many mothers feel casts a shadow on their relationships with their children, which can lead to uncertainty or stress in the relationships. It also may cause the mother to fight harder to see the children or, conversely, to give up more easily. The normal angry feelings expressed by a child may take on greater significance for the mother because she is unsure of her own feelings.

Developmental Stages

When we speak of a developmental stage, we are referring to a new, naturally occurring phase that comes with growth. People sometimes have difficulties when they are not prepared to change with the demands of a new phase. As children grow older, whether they are in a one- or two-parent home, what they need from the relationship with their parents changes. The relationship between a 5-year-old and his parents is different from that of a 15-year-old and his parents. The 15-year-old will be more involved in peer relations, going to parties, after-school activities, and homework at night. Visitation with the noncustodial parent sometimes becomes an infringement on those activities. The time spent during visitation with the 15-year-old may entail supervision of homework or providing dinner and a quiet place to study for an exam. Visitation with a 5-year-old may mean stocking up on crayons and building blocks while keeping an eye on which cartoons are playing at the local theater. When parents are interested in providing the appropriate structures for 15- or 5-year-olds, things can go more smoothly.

Adults also go through different stages. Sometimes the needs of the mother and the child will not jibe. The mother who has deferred a career to raise her children and suddenly finds herself with extra time on her hands may need to pursue a job. If it interferes with visitation, there may be conflict. The father may remarry and introduce into the child's life a stepmother who is not working the long hours that the mother has to. Thus, one more potential for conflict is introduced into the relationship between the noncustodial mother and her child.

These normal changes in the lives of the children and the parent can enhance or hinder the relationship. When the mother and children have less time together because of increasing involvements in other aspects of their lives but are able to enjoy the time they do spend together, the relationship can be enhanced. But when the normal changes that occur in people's lives throw impediments into the relationship, problems can arise. It is like a marriage. When the couple's interests mature in similar directions, the marriage can continue to be a strong one, though quite different from when it began. When the couple grows apart and their individual growth results in a lack of interest in each other, they may consider dissolving the marriage. Ideally, as children grow into adolescence, what their parents expect of them and what they want from their parents and for themselves mesh to a large degree. In the relationship between the noncustodial mother and her children, when everyone continues to grow and still mesh, the relationship will be strong.

Interactions

The interactions between a mother and her children are shaped by the individual characteristics of the mother and the children and the three preceding concepts. The relationship is not preordained but can be changed by many factors. It can also have a life or direction of its own. Kind words from the mother to the child can elicit a kind response. If the child calls the mother to brag about a high grade on an exam or to cry over a lost pet, the mother can feel like an important part of the child's life. Sometimes, positive interactions can overcome a negative history. A child and a mother can get their relationship back on a good path by making an effort to do so. But a child or mother who does not return the other's phone calls or does not show up for visitation can reverse earlier positive steps.

What happens between mother and child is the result of a combination of factors that must be considered when we try to understand their relationship. It is not merely that a problematic relationship is the fault of the mother or the child. Many other pieces contribute to their interactions in both positive and negative ways.[15]

The Mothers' Stories

To illustrate the types of relationships that have developed between noncustodial mothers and their children and the mothers' impressions of their children, we will relate a number of the mothers' stories. The mothers had opportunities on the questionnaire and in the interviews to discuss any aspects of their lives as noncustodial parents. They mentioned their relationships with their children most frequently. Many mothers reported improved or continued warm relations since they became noncustodial. Others focused on problems. Some seemed to use the children's improved status as a way of reassuring themselves that the children were better off living away from them. Perhaps what comes through clearly from these stories is the pain that many of the mothers feel in being apart from their children.

A 40-year-old registered nurse with split custody wrote:

> Because of their ages (both teens), I felt residency had to be their decision and visitation is worked out between my children and me. I am not permitted to visit my son at my ex's house without his

consent (which he refuses to give) but legally, if the children are sick I have (and exert) the right to visit after notifying him. In day-to-day raising, my ex will have no contact with me and refuses any reasonable sharing of ideas. It is a very difficult situation that has deteriorated as the years have passed.

A 36-year-old divorced mother who works as a secretary and lives apart from her two daughters wrote:

We divorced because I was sick and tired of taking care of his sick parents and being stamped on. I did not want anymore so I left. There are no words to describe the feeling and emotion I went through when he took our 7- and 12-year-old from me. Worse than taking an arm off of your body. My 12-year-old did not want to see or come to me in eight years. She finally came to see me, bringing her fiancé with her. Quite a trauma. I could not believe she was really coming. The reason was to tell me of her wedding plans. In the meantime, her father was on wife number four. My daughter wanted to put that wife ahead of me. She really did not want me at the wedding. I did not go. In the announcement of the engagement she left my name out, which really hurt.

All during the eight years I tried everything in my power with love, waiting for her to come to me. Both girls blamed me for everything that is going on with their father and the fact that he has married three more times. I never remarried. Through all the pain and suffering I still love my ex-husband and always will. If I had to do it over again, there would not be a divorce. I have this to say—anyone thinking of divorce, think about it a dozen times or more before you rush into it, especially if there are children involved. My mistake was taking care of his sick parents. I should have refused. Instead I was taken for granted. As a result I lost everything and was left alone to pick up the pieces.

Bertha, a woman mentioned elsewhere in this book, wrote extensively about her relationship with her children:

The most painful thing about a divorce is that the children feel their loyalty must be divided and they must take sides. Since I walked out, they say I deserted them. I was the heavy in the scenario and their father could do no wrong. My oldest daughter was not talking to me and that hurt deeply. Later I discovered it really annoyed her whenever any of her girlfriends would relay to her my message of greetings. But I wanted her to know I loved her and was basically the same person I always was.

It was frustration with my daughter that caused me to leave. She kicked open the door when I was working and ordered me to wash the dishes. I was so frightened by the violence of that kick that I started to cry. When I walked into the kitchen to get support from my husband, he refused to enter into the fight, but continued to smoke his cigarette and drink his coffee while she yelled at me and accused me of trying to retreat to my room. I looked at their total lack of love for me and decided I should not suffer anymore. I grabbed the keys and left. This made my daughter guilty that she caused the divorce, but I have told her in letters since then that she was just the final straw. I was going to leave when I got more money. One of my other sons only came to see me because the court said he had to. He was torn between my desire to see him and his desire to be in his own home and neighborhood.

Finally he did begin coming for visitation. At first I had a tendency to be an entertainment agency, taking him to movies, ball games, and to places his dad never took him to show him that we could have fun together. Now, we may have quiet times with Monopoly or take special trips to Chicago together for the day. We began making things together and it became a hobby for us both. I hid from him the anger I felt when he would take all the things that he made that I paid for back to his father's house so it would be decorated.

There were times in those first few months apart from the children that were bad. I had a tendency to be bitter. I regret to say I acted quite uncharitably when my oldest son asked me why I attacked their father so much when he did not say anything bad at me. I pulled over to the curb, ordered him, sprained ankle, stocking foot and all, out of my car one block from a shopping center and left him stranded. I was furious at him for defending his dad to me who I felt had played on my nerves for years. We had not had sex in a long time and whenever I tried to initiate it he would ridicule me.

By a year later, time had healed many wounds. I had become less shrewish. All the children came for a beautiful Easter dinner. That occasion healed us all a lot. They discovered I was still their mother and that I did love them. Six months later a lot of tension, suspicion, and possessiveness finally disappeared between all of us, including their father. He has given me back many things from our old house that he does not need any more. As the cordial atmosphere and better understanding developed between us, my former spouse invited me in to see all the changes he had done to our old house.

This year has been so marvelous to me emotionally that I have built up my life, overcome my loneliness, and made new friends. My children come over and call often. We may go on a trip together. Of course, nothing is ever perfect! I still think about a lot of things my ex used to do to me and how much differently my life could have been with him. There is a lot of bitterness in me yet, but I have learned not to express it to the children but rather in letters like these. I have learned also that you get more flies with honey than with vinegar.

A 37-year-old woman who has remarried and works as a counselor wrote: "Very painful being without my daughter. However, I got very involved in my career and with my new husband and friends. Also, I keep in close contact with her even though she is 1,000 miles away."

A divorced secretary who had given up custody of her son because of her emotional instability wrote:

I am still remorseful (five years later) it turned out this way and sometimes am resentful my parents could not have helped me more through my difficult times. I missed out on raising him on a daily basis. I now have a 1-year-old son and am enjoying every minute I missed with my first son. The baby's father and I broke up before he was born and I have not seen him since. I still see my oldest son but never frequently. Truthfully, it was too painful to be reminded of my "neglect." Now I am making more of an effort so he can be with his little brother. I really care about him and his welfare but have a conflict sometimes in that I know I won't be as close to him as if he lived with me every day.

A 49-year-old separated sales representative living away from a 14-year-old daughter wrote:

I look on it as if my daughter had left home a little earlier than usual. I found it hurt me too much to try and stay involved with her, so I withdrew. Now, I am available if she needs me but I no longer consider her a part of my family. I do not feel close to her.

I feel betrayed and will not give her the opportunity to do it again.
I feel fortunate to have the daughter who stayed with me.

A 34-year-old divorced mother with split custody talked in an
interview about her reasons for the custody arrangement and her
relationship with each of her children:

> My son who is with his father needed to develop a relationship
> with him. Also, I felt his father would be (and has been) more
> sensitive and supportive of his actions. Our daughter stayed with
> me because she was being treated very badly by her father (just as
> I was—like shit). She now has the best of two worlds—one with
> me and one like a "princess" with her father. Hopefully, he is
> finding a middle ground with her and not treating her like a little
> girl. My son and I have a good emotional relationship where we
> communicate a great deal. This relationship allows us to be alone
> yet still aware of each other's needs. We periodically have lunch
> or dinner together just to talk. Long visits are difficult for him
> as he enters the full swing of the teen years. We talk about this
> too!

A 39-year-old secretary who is separated and living apart from a
14-year-old son told us: "It hasn't been easy, but I think things are
better. We do talk a lot and we do get along well now. It is just
different for all of us."

A 44-year-old divorced woman working as a bank teller and
living apart from two sons gave the following statement in an interview:

> He was violent during the marriage and I left him and was hoping
> to take the kids with me. They stayed with him, though. I see
> both of them once a week now. They were quite upset by the
> breakup. My oldest son is resentful of me now and distant. I will
> never totally get over leaving my youngest son.

Two Interviews with Children

To provide a different perspective on the interactions that develop
between noncustodial mothers and their children, we conducted two
interviews with children being raised by their fathers. As with the

interviews with adults who had been raised away from their mothers (see chapter 13), we wish to emphasize that these children are not necessarily representative of other relationships that develop between noncustodial mothers and their children.

Tammy's Story

"It was a case of two kids getting married young with not enough in common." This was Len speaking, describing why he and Tammy's mother broke up after eight years of marriage. Tammy was 4 at the time. Tammy, now 12—and pretty, with soft blond hair and blue eyes—said that she was not sure why she came to live with her father, but Len filled in the gaps. According to Len, Tammy initially lived with her mother during the period of separation. He visited on the weekends and had the kind of involvement that, he said, most divorced fathers have with their children. "We went out a lot but over time stopped trying to squeeze everything in. We became comfortable just being together." One day, out of the blue, Tammy's mother called Len and asked him to pick up Tammy. He did not ask any questions, but he knew that she had recently gotten a job that entailed a great deal of travel. They were still legally separated. When it came time for the divorce to be finalized, she did not contest his request for custody of Tammy. "It was a combination of financial constraints and she just wasn't interested in being a mother."

After the separation, there was a long time when mother and daughter did not see each other. Len said that he used to send cards to Tammy on holidays and sign her mother's name. Twice since their divorce Tammy's mother had tried for custody and lost. Even though she had remarried and Len was still single, the court decided in Len's favor. Len thought the reason she wanted custody of Tammy was so that she would not look like a "bad mother."

Visitation between mother and daughter is regular—every other weekend. They have worked out a routine in which they go out for dinner Friday night, shop and do errands on Saturday, and see a movie on Sunday. Tammy said that she is quite pleased with the relationship and that she gets along "okay" with her stepfather.

Tammy talked easily about her life with her father. She described a life that seems perfectly normal and happy. Breakfasts and dinners are made by Len, who Tammy described as a good cook. Tammy helps with the housework and has total responsibility for the family's two dogs. She is involved in many after-school activities and has a boyfriend who drops over her house from time to time. She is not allowed to date alone, though, so she and her friends go out together in a group. "I always have to let Dad know where I am. And I agree that is important." Len helps Tammy with her homework, particularly her math. "That's my Dad's strong suit. He's a real estate agent, so it makes sense."

The only time that Tammy's happy-go-lucky demeanor changed during the interview was when she talked about her mother. Her mood became subdued, and she answered questions a little more hesitantly. It is not as if she was protecting her mother as much as that she was protecting the relationship she and her mother have. The impression was that the relationship is still being formed and would have trouble withstanding too many ups and downs. Tammy has apparently formed an especially close relationship with her father as a way of coping with a distant relationship with her mother.

Timothy and Katie

Interviewing young children involves a different process. It first entails establishing a relationship with them, which may take a few hours. Then, through play and picture drawing, an attempt is made to learn about their impressions of their mother and the part that she plays in their life.

Timothy, 10, and Katie, 6, began living with their father, Alvin, two years ago. Alvin said, "Most of the marriage had been good, but a year before the breakup she began to go out to the bars with some of her women friends. She eventually became interested in dating other men." It was mutually agreed that Alvin would get custody. "I wouldn't have wanted it any other way, because I am the better parent. If it had been necessary, I would have fought for them in court." Unlimited visitation was arranged, but usually it has occurred infrequently on Sundays for two to five hours. "She has withdrawn interest in the kids. She doesn't even keep toys or clothes for the kids at her apartment."

Timothy's relationship with his mother was strained at first but has recently improved; Katie is described as being too young to understand what is going on, "She tends to block out whatever appears unpleasant to her." Alvin is asking for child support but does not expect to get it. He considers the children well adjusted.

Both children were warm and outgoing in the interview. They were neatly dressed, reflecting the neatness of the home. They were asked to draw a picture of their family. Timothy said that he could not draw people and instead drew an accurate picture of the solar system. Katie had her own way of responding to the assignment. She cheerfully drew several pictures of large hearts—all in pink. She worked quickly, as if there was not a minute to lose. By contrast, Timothy worked slowly and methodically. Katie was asked to draw a picture of her home and made a pink house with windows and trees. She did not place any people in the drawing. While drawing, they were asked a variety of questions about their lives.

Timothy said that he is a big help around the house to his father. He makes extra money by doing chores. He was the spokesman throughout the interview and described his and Katie's daily routine. Timothy usually makes breakfast for himself and Katie and then cleans up before the school bus arrives to take them to school. Timothy's fascination with the solar system comes naturally—his father is an airline pilot.

Timothy wants to be an astronaut when he grows up. On weekends he plays soccer with his friends. Katie just giggled when questioned about how she spends her weekends. Neither child volunteered information regarding their mother.

They said that visitation occurs on occasional Sundays. The usual pattern is that she takes them out to eat and buys them a toy. They then proceeded on a tour of their house. Displayed on a bookshelf in Timothy's room is a collection of educational Peanuts books that had been started by his mother. His reference to her was offhand. It was as if her involvement with him had little importance in his life. The only significant parental figure seems to be Alvin, with whom the children quite obviously have a warm and loving relationship.

After some intial difficulties, all three children seem to have adapted to their situation. For Tammy, it has meant growing closer to her father while struggling to establish a relationship with her mother. For Timothy and Katie, it has meant a greater focus on their relationship with their father. Their mother is there for them but is not the primary parent.

The Mothers' Advice to Other Mothers

Many of the mothers wrote short pieces offering advice about how other noncustodial mothers should handle their relationships with their children. Most of the suggestions revolve around the mother's staying available and keeping the lines of communication open. The prevailing tone of the advice, as shown in the following exerpts, is that the children's needs come ahead of the mother's.

Try to place the needs of your children first. They are not necessarily better off with their mother, especially if this involves financial deprivation.

Just remember: the kids are the most important. Their emotional well-being should come first, above anything else. After all, they are just innocent bystanders.

Keeping in contact is very important. Letters are good. Cooperation between parents is very important.

Always tell the children the truth about why they don't live with you, because they always find out somehow. Also, by being truthful, your relationship with them stays close. Mine has.

Don't try to child snatch! It hurts the kids—you will be better off to keep in touch and miss them. They will not forget you. They will try to keep in touch later if you can be found.

I believe children should be where they want—I don't like using children as tools to hurt others. Life is too short and they are very important to me.

I would advise any noncustodial mother to get involved with her children, especially where a stepmother is involved. Also, make the effort to be friends with the father for the sake of the children.

Try to keep the peace. Leave doors open. Tell them you love them as much as you can. Send cards. Call. Make your time together special. Do her nails. Polish his shoes.

Keep open lines of communication; let them know you still love them; don't get involved or take sides with whatever the custodial parent or stepparent is doing unless it is directly detrimental to the children's health.

7

Noncustodial Mothers and Their Ex-Husbands

He has done everything he can to make life miserable. He plays games with the kids that get me upset. He changes visitation times. He poisons them against me. We cannot get together and talk about anything without it ending in a shouting match.

T HE ex-husband is a constant thorn in the side for some non-custodial mothers. Conflicted feelings are more the norm than the exception, although a number of mothers are quite content with their relationship with their ex-husbands. The way the mother feels about the father is often related to the way the marriage ended and to her own role as a noncustodial mother. Some mothers, particularly those who were opposed to the breakup, admitted that they were still in love with their ex-husbands. Others hated their husbands at the time of the breakup and still consider them to be a threat to their happiness. For many, the ex-husband's success as a father is a double-edged sword. If he is parenting well, the mother is less concerned about the progress of her children. Yet if he is parenting well it also means that she is a little less needed by the children. And if she is fighting for custody, it means that a more difficult battle lies before her.

This chapter considers the relationships that evolved between the noncustodial mothers and their ex-husbands. The ex-husband is a gatekeeper to a host of different areas that affect the mother's life. He can facilitate access to those areas or he can keep the gate closed and block her efforts in a variety of ways. For example, in most marriages, the husband is the primary breadwinner and often stands on more financially secure ground than the wife. After the breakup, he is in a position to assist her financially if he so chooses. He can ease her visitation with the children, or he can make regular contact yet another hurdle for the mother. He can affect her emotionally— playing on her guilt feelings if she is experiencing any, or helping to minimize them. The mother who is on an emotional rollercoaster because of unresolved feelings from the marriage may be especially vulnerable to the father's manipulations. The mother does have some control over what happens in the relationship, however. She can make life easier or more difficult for the husband by her actions.

Residual feelings from a failed marriage are common no matter who has custody. Often, there is anger and rage at the other spouse, especially if abuse or infidelity occurred during the marriage. The greater the violation of trust, the greater the anger, hurt, and conflict. If the marriage has been a positive experience, it can be even harder to put the memories aside. Frequently, a marriage ends without a clean break. Trial separations turn into reconciliations, only to evolve into new separations. One spouse may leave, feel that a mistake has been made, and want to reconcile. One spouse may beg the other spouse to come back.

It is not uncommon for separated spouses to maintain a sexual relationship. Many remain friends for years. The family interviewed in chapter 14 is an example of a divorced couple whose friendship grew over the years. Another example is a father who was interviewed for the single fathers study. He noted that he and his wife never lost respect for each other: "We just found we couldn't live together though we still care about each other. She is very involved with the children. I guess I picked the right woman to divorce."[1] The feelings of love and hate that linger after the breakup make it difficult to establish a parenting relationship that must span two residences instead of one. Yet this is what the divorced couple must do when children are involved.

Feelings about Money

Besides having an impact on the custody situation (as discussed in chapter 5), money also affects the ongoing relationship between the mother and the father. About half of the mothers in our study believe that they do not have their children now because their husbands have more money then they do. Half also feel that they are not financially secure. In some cases, the ex-husband is assisting the mother by paying alimony or by relieving her of an obligation to pay child support. In other cases, money is yet another weapon used in a continuing and angry battle that is fought overtly and covertly by both parents.

How does money come into play in these relationships? From our interviews with the mothers, we gained the impression that in an overt battle, the children are bribed to favor one parent. Goodies are promised in exchange for staying with one of the parents. In the more subtle financial wars, money is never mentioned. Rather, certain benefits that were not there previously appear in the home of the father or the mother. In some cases, these benefits are not meant as a bribe but are there because the parent wants to enjoy them. But in other cases, a Ping-Pong table, a new car, or a VCR is used to make the home a more "fun" place for the child. When both parents are financially solvent, these battles can take on the tenor of an escalating arms race between two warring countries.

More fuel is tossed on the fire if the father has remarried and the stepmother is working. In this situation, the single mother feels outnumbered and outfinanced. Especially angry are those mothers who feel that they cannot compete against two incomes. In many of these situations, the mere presence of a stepmother adds to the mother's hurt and anger. She feels that she is not only competing against two incomes; she is also competing against two people for the affections of the children. (To many of the children, the two-parent family of the father's looks better than the one-parent family of the mother's.) However the financial war is waged, the mothers will often end up on the losing side, because most earn less than their ex-husbands. Suzannah, Ardenna, and Judy exemplify how money comes to play a part in the continuing relationship between father and mother.

Suzannah, a southerner, is 39. She works as a clerk and has two teenage children living with her ex-husband and his new wife. Her income is approximately $14,000. She lost custody in court and is very concerned about her ex-husband's influence on the children.

My children were against drugs at one time. Since they began living with their father, he has told them of the wonderful benefits of smoking pot and he has furnished it for them. So has the step-mother, who is only five years older than they.

Money is a problem in the relationship, too: "He and his wife make three times my income but are filing for child support—it is a revenge tactic to make me pay for embarrassing him by asking for a divorce."

Ardenna, a 30-year-old secretary living in the East, had a different problem with money:

He can buy the children anything they want. He earns $40,000 compared to my $17,000. What chance do I have to compete with that? He has the house, too. At least my daughter sees what he is doing and tells me she can get things from dad but she gets love from me.

Some mothers are upset when they see the father buying things for himself but giving little to the children. Judy, a 42-year-old in real estate sales, said:

My ex has a business, lives in a $200,000 house, and owns three very expensive cars. He also has property elsewhere. Even though he has all this, he is still cheap, and the children are still deprived of a lot of things that a man in his position could easily afford.

Feelings about the Ex-Husband as a Father

The nature of the parents' interactions concerning the children usually has the greatest impact on the mother's relationship with the father. It is here that many of the mothers feel the most vulnerable and the most powerless. The mother can attempt to resolve her own feelings about her ex-husband in a variety of ways, but when the children are involved, the stakes are greatly increased. The mother is in an emotional bind if she feels that the children are not benefiting from living with their father. Even if he is not blocking visitation, the mother can feel tortured about what she perceives to be a bad situation for the children. This translates into more animosity toward the father and sometimes increased self-hatred for having allowed the custody arrangement to develop.

Central to many of the relationships that work out well is the ability of the parents to separate their feelings for each other as ex-spouses from their feelings toward each other as the children's parents. Although a great deal of anger and hurt may remain between the spouses, many are able to deal with each other objectively as parents. An objective view helps the mother deal with the father without letting her emotions interfere with the parenting role.

The mothers' views of the fathers as parents tended to be favorable. When the mothers were asked to rate their ex-spouses as parents, more than 60 percent gave their ex-husbands at least a rating of adequate, and only 20 percent rated them as poor parents. This indicates that the mothers had some regard for the parenting of the custodial fathers. By comparison, in the single custodial fathers' study, the fathers viewed the noncustodial mothers' parenting abilities much less favorably: 26 percent described them as adequate or better and 50 percent said they were poor parents.[2] Given the usually positive societal view of fathers with custody and the usually negative view of mothers without custody, these responses are not surprising.

It must be noted that the father's view of the mother also affects the relationship. The fact that many of the fathers considered the mothers inadequate parents does not bode well for the development of an evenly balanced relationship. There is a disequilibrium when the mothers regard the fathers more favorably than the reverse.

An attempt was made to predict which mothers would view their ex-husbands as good parents and which characteristics would differentiate them from mothers who have less positive views of the fathers. We found that mothers who gave a high parenting rating were more likely to have given up custody voluntarily, to say that the reasons for divorce were shared, and to say that they gave up custody because it was best for the children. These mothers were also more likely to have younger children living away from them, to be slightly younger themselves, and to be unaffiliated with any religion. Conversely, mothers who gave worse ratings to the fathers as parents were the ones who gave up custody involuntarily, divorced because of the fathers' problems, do not have custody because they lost it in court, and are more apt to be Jewish.

Some of these variables, especially those concerning the reasons for divorce and custody, tended to cluster in those relationships in which the mother and father were getting along well. They are indications of harmonious relations between parents.[3]

The mothers who gave their ex-spouses high ratings as parents also described themselves as: (1) experiencing less stress concerning the decision to have the children live elsewhere; (2) being more involved with the children; (3) spending more overnights with the children; and (4) being consulted about the children more frequently by the father.[4] The mothers' other relationships also were characterized by a high degree of satisfaction: (1) they were more satisfied with their relationships with their ex-husbands; (2) they were more satisfied with their relationships with the children living elsewhere; (3) they believed that the children were better off living with the father; and (4) they were more satisfied with the children's progress.[5]

These relationships show the link between many of the factors we have discussed previously. When the mother respects the ex-husband's parenting abilities, other things are also falling into place for her. She is usually seeing the children more frequently and is more satisfied with their progress.[6] These relationships tend to develop from less troublesome beginnings—that is, divorces and custody situations arranged by mutual agreement. These situations can also evolve, regardless of how the marriage ended and how custody was decided, when both parents have decided to try to work together for the benefit of the children. The pain and hurt still remain from the marital situation, but it does not bleed into the ex-spouses' roles as parents.

Gina is an example of a mother whose custody relationship evolved comfortably even though there were some angry feelings remaining from the marriage. A reporter for a major city newspaper, Gina turned over custody of her 4-year-old daughter to her husband because she felt that her own "needs could not accommodate the constant demands children make on a mother." The marriage had ended because Gina needed more time to be by herself. She stated that her husband wanted their daughter because "he felt it was his duty as a father—also he had an element of fear of being alone." Gina believed that her husband was the more competent parent at that time and, wanting time to herself, she had only slight trepidations about turning over custody.

She felt that she and her ex-husband were "good business partners" concerning the welfare of their daughter:

> Personally speaking, we are not close. The problems that we had in the marriage continued after that for a while. We can never resolve those feelings. We just got involved in other things. But we are able to resolve things as far as our child is concerned.

Kate, an unemployed 38-year-old, also had a realistic view of her ex-husband:

> He is a good male role model, caring, a real buddy. He encourages sports for the boys. However, he acts like he hasn't reached puberty yet. The family is important to him. I don't feel he has ever cut the apron strings, although since he has remarried he has grown up a lot. He spends a lot more time with the children now.

The mothers also commented about the fathers' relationships with the children. Kate went on to say:

> I felt it would be in my sons' best interests to live with their father, as he had remarried. However, when things are rocky over there, my oldest son gets real angry at him. But he still lives there and I am not going to ask him to make a choice between us, even when things are bad.

Being Consulted about the Children

Part of the mother's relationship with her ex-husband is shaped by her access to the children, which is often facilitated when the father consults her about raising the children. A father may call the mother for help with picking out a prom dress, deciding on an appropriate curfew, approaching a school problem, or picking out a summer camp for the children. Such consultation, which can be a sign of trust and goodwill between the parents, can go a long way toward making the mother feel more a part of the children's lives. What we found, though, was that the mothers are not consulted to a great degree. Over half (54 percent) said that they were never consulted, 35 percent said that they were consulted occasionally, and only 11 percent said that they were consulted frequently. Because frequent consultation with the father and a high rating of the father as a parent are related, many of the characteristics of the mothers who were consulted frequently are the same as those of the mothers who gave their ex-husbands excellent ratings. For example, when the noncustodial mother is consulted frequently by the ex-husband, she also is more involved with the children and is more satisfied with her relationship with them, making loneliness less of a problem for her.

It is not surprising that consultation is more frequent if the father has not remarried. The single father may have a greater need for the mother's assistance than he would if there were a stepmother in the home. The presence of a stepmother also may make it more difficult for the father to seek out the mother's help, as the stepmother might interpret it as a lack of trust in her own parenting abilities. The stepmother might wonder why the mother needs to be called if it is the stepmother who is taking care of the child's daily concerns. The noncustodial mother is also consulted less if there is a split custody arrangement.

Although things are generally better when consultation is frequent, the mothers are not often called. A father may not initiate consultation for a range of reasons:

1. He may want to prove to people that he can raise the children without the mother's help.
2. He may fear that her continued involvement will improve her position in court if a battle is imminent.
3. He may have a negative view of her parenting abilities.
4. He may be angry at her for reasons stemming from the divorce or custody arrangement.
5. He may be using the children as pawns to gain child support payments.
6. The children may not want to see the mother.
7. He may feel that the children will want to go back with their mother if they see her.
8. He may not want to strain a new marriage.

It is clear that the impact of consultation on the relationship between the parents is similar to that of visitation. Frequent visitation and consultation can usually help the relationship, whereas infrequency can hurt it. When the mother is seeking visitation and it is blocked, the relationship between the parents becomes more strained. Mothers who do not have contact with their children may fear the worst. The father's continued attempts to block contact and to avoid consultation may push the mother to sue in court, to consider abducting the children, or to withdraw. It is not uncommon for mothers to take this last course. Faced with what they perceive to be insurmountable odds (for example, the father's physical possession of the children, his greater financial resources, and a fear of psychologically hurting the children by a court battle), the mother may eventually refrain from attempting to see the children. This can be the final blow to what has already been a bad relationship.

One mother wrote: "We were given joint custody but my ex wants me out of the picture so I hardly see my children. I hate this. I go back to court soon to fight again."

Sometimes, it does not matter to the father what the court decides. If the child does not want to see the mother, that can be enough of an impetus for some fathers to prevent visitation. Another mother wrote:

> I agreed to let Mark live with my ex and his wife on weekends so Mark could go to a better school. Now they won't let Mark come back to me. I must admit Mark said he likes it better there because there are boys to play with. But they refuse to let him come and see me. The judge who gave me custody says I will have to see an attorney again to get him back. My attorney won't do anything until I pay him $500, which I can't afford. My other son still lives with me. He does not like the woman his father married.

The Good Relationships

Let us emphasize that some mothers reported having very positive relationships with and feelings about their ex-husbands. Bertha described an ever-improving relationship between herself and her ex, though one that is tinged with bittersweet memories:

> When my former spouse began redecorating the home, he discovered many accent items that he did not need. As the cordial atmosphere and better understanding developed between us, he invited

me in to see all the changes he had done to the house. Being a female, the Lord blessed me with curiosity. That curiosity often led to frustration as I wondered what went on in that house. I joked about things it would be nice for me to have back again. A few months later, he appeared on my doorstep with them. For all the romantics who think a reconciliation is forthcoming, I hate to disappoint you. The reasons for the separation are still there, but it is a lot easier on the nerves if you can live apart from your former spouse harmoniously.

Polly, a 43-year-old teacher living in the East, has not been able to resolve her feelings as easily: "Through all the pain and suffering, I still love my ex-husband and always will. We get along very well. If I had to do it over again, there would not be a divorce."

Christine, 36, wrote: "My former husband and I still care about each other, though it is not the same kind of love as we used to have. Although there is occasional conflict, as with a close friend, our son's well-being is uppermost."

Rose, who is 32 and works as a cook in the Midwest, wrote: "I find it best to try to maintain a friendly relationship with my ex-spouse. It's easier on the kids when we get along."

Geri, a 39-year-old traffic analyst from Texas who has been divorced twice and has custody of a child from the first marriage but not of the child from the second marriage, also described a good relationship:

> My son's father and I are friendly and jointly make decisions regarding him. I am a full-time mom who both ex-husbands say is a good parent. My second ex-husband takes our boy out to McDonald's all the time for meals, even breakfast. My ex works full-time, including Saturdays. My son spends the time he is not visiting me in day-care centers. He likes living with his father, though. They share a bed and he gets lots of toys. He gets spoiled, too.

Despite these descriptions, in the majority of relationships between mothers and fathers, we saw a range of emotions: ambivalence, strain, distrust, and sometimes hatred and fear. These feelings may have originated in the marriage, in the divorce, or in the custody arrangement. In some cases, such as Gina's, they can be worked out.

In others, the strains between the mother and the father haunt them both for years to come.

The Variety of Relationships

From our interviews with the mothers and the information gained from custodial fathers, we can identify several different types of relationships that evolve between noncustodial mothers and custodial fathers. Whether or not they are in contact with each other, the mother and the father straddle the two worlds of ex-spouses and parents. Their relationship as a once-married couple needs to be resolved, as does the nature of their continuing parental contact. Just as they fulfilled the roles of spouses and parents while married, they continue in the roles of parents and ex-spouses when they are divorced.

In an ideal situation, the relationship as ex-spouses is marked by acceptance of one another and the ability to work together without being influenced by emotional ghosts lingering from the marriage. In some cases, the ex-spouses may call each other for advice about finances or dating. Here, the couple has grown to the point where they can accept the loss of the marriage without holding onto any anger that actively interferes with their contact.

It is more common, however, for the hostility that contributed to the breakup to remain between the ex-spouses or to turn into ambivalence. The couple is not able to interact without dredging up past memories of indiscretions, distrust, or victimization. Thus, when one spouse requests special consideration on a matter, the request is not handled at face value. Instead, hurtful memories come up, the chance for revenge is grabbed, and the request is denied. In these circumstances, the relationship between the ex-spouses has not been resolved in a healthy way. These unresolved feelings affect their ability to work together effectively as parents.

Sometimes, these hostile relationships are marked by distancing. One spouse may still be in love with the other but, finding that love unreciprocated, may withdraw from contact with the other as a form of self-protection.

The second piece in the evolving relationship between the mother and the father involves their roles as parents. Regardless of whether or not the noncustodial parent stays in close contact, a parenting relationship still exists. In the ideal situation, the parents are able to cooperate for the benefit of the children and for their own benefit. Here, the parents are able to clearly separate their role as parents from their spousal role. They recognize the importance for the children of making this clear demarcation. Friction in the spousal relationship does not affect the parenting relationship significantly. Bill and his ex-wife are an example of how this separation can be achieved. They had a very stormy marital and postmarital relationship, which included court battles and Bill's claims that he was physically attacked by her. Over time, though, Bill came to recognize the advantages for his daughter Peggy of seeing her mother on a regular basis. Although he admits that he does not trust his ex-wife, he also acknowledges that it is in Peggy's best interests to see her mother.

Of course, many parents are not able to maintain a cooperative relationship. Either they cannot separate spousal issues from parental ones or they do not feel that contact between their children and the other spouse is beneficial to the children. In these situations, hostility may remain from the marriage. This hostility may also be fueled by one parent visiting inconsistently, by visitation being blocked, by disagreements over how the children should be raised, or by any number of other events. Triangulation of the children between the parents is also common here. The children may be used as pawns or they may initiate disagreements by trying to play one parent off against the other. Sometimes, court battles or the potential for court battles may exacerbate an already difficult situation. Cooperation between the parents is thus seen as a disadvantage to the parent who wants to gain more control over the children or over the other parent.

A new spouse may also be involved in fueling the fire of hostility. Sometimes, the stepparent is sent to do battle. The remarried parent may not want to deal with his or her former spouse and may feel too angry to make the contact. The stepparent becomes triangulated into the unresolved parental and spousal relationship. When discussions arise regarding parenting questions, no one ever knows who is speaking for whom.

Sometimes, a cycle is set up that involves both the parenting and the spousal roles. For example, in situations where the stepmother does the talking for the father because the father and the mother cannot get along the following cycle may occur. The stepmother may request a change in visitation. The noncustodial mother denies it and may make a counter-request that is perceived as being tinged with anger. The stepmother, perhaps unsure of her support, withdraws. The father then steps in and adds fuel to the fire. The noncustodial mother responds with further escalation. At that point, the father or the mother may withdraw, and the stepmother is left in the middle.

The relationships between the mothers and the fathers can be broken down into three general types: (1) hostile in both the parental and the spousal roles, (2) accepting in the parental roles and hostile in the spousal roles, or (3) accepting and cooperative in the parental roles and the spousal roles. In general, it is more likely that the couple will be hostile in the spousal roles than in the parental roles, although we have seen the reverse. Therefore, our classifications of the roles are somewhat artificial, as the spousal relationship affects the parental relationship more often than the reverse. Yet this dichotomy is necessary to account for those relationships in which a clear division does exist between the parental and the spousal roles.

The three types of relationships between divorced couples with children can be conceptualized as follows:

Hostile–Hostile: In this type of relationship the parents have not resolved the feelings left over from the divorce—feelings of confusion, hurt, distrust, and anger. Hostility is also present in their continuing roles as parents. Each parent disagrees with the way the other parent is raising or wants to raise the children, and the disagreements are vehement. Some mothers complained about the lack of discipline their children were receiving since they had been living with their fathers. One claimed that the father had introduced the children to drugs. Another argued frequently with her ex-husband about the children's curfew. Other common complaints from the mothers were about the fathers' not making the children do homework, being too lenient, and being too strict. There were also more fundamental complaints from the mothers that indicated a deep concern and a lack of cooperation. Some worried about religious upbringing, choice of schools, and the relationships between the children and their stepmothers. Visitation and custody arrangements also led to hostile interactions between the ex-spouses in their roles as parents. Attempts to resolve these issues were often unsuccessful.

Custodial fathers also voiced complaints about the mothers. One father accused his ex-wife of being a "Disneyland Parent." He said that she picks the children up on Friday, spoils them, and returns them on Sunday. It then takes him two or three days to get them back to a normal routine.

One final note about this type of relationship: The levels of hostility in each role can feed on one another; that is, problems in one area can heighten problems in the other area. Because the separation between the two roles is frequently minimal, the potential for escalation of hostility in both roles is great.

Hostile–Accepting: In this type of relationship, the level of hostility in the spousal role may be lower than in the first type, but it still exists. The ex-spouses have been able to separate their spousal issues from parenting issues, however, and have established a form of truce. They may occasionally consult each other about the children while still avoiding contact with each other around issues unrelated to the children. Occasionally, problems appear in the parenting area, but after a cooling-off period, an accepting relationship is reestablished. The parents recognize one another's importance in the children's upbringing.

One example of how this works came from Rachel:

> He is good with the kids, though he was not good with me. We can usually talk about the kids and we agree on most things about them. We just can't talk about anything else without fighting.

The stepmother may play a helpful role in these relationships. One noncustodial mother, Leona, told us:

> I cannot talk to my ex at all about the kids. Communication goes through their stepmother, who is a wonderful person, very understanding, and truly cares for the children. I feel very fortunate they have her.

A few parents do claim to get along better as ex-spouses than ex-parents. We have found, though, when exploring the relationship further, that underlying problems as ex-spouses do still exist.

Accepting/Cooperative–Cooperative: A few couples have worked out a relationship that is marked by acceptance and cooperation. Here, the feelings from the divorce have been resolved for the most part and one or both parents may have moved on to new relationships. As ex-spouses, feelings of acceptance or of active cooperation have developed. The parents are able to work together for the benefit of the children and may consult each other about issues in their personal lives. As mentioned, the family interviewed in chapter 14 is an example of how this type of relationship evolves.

We found these three types of relationships to be the most common types in custodial father–noncustodial mother families. Although they can also be said to be common among all divorced parents, the level of intensity appears to be different for these people. Because both parents are fulfilling nontraditional roles, we believe that their adjustment process as divorcing couples and as individuals is tougher and, therefore, that the feelings that emerge are harder to resolve. These parents have fewer role models of how to handle the custody arrangements and their own personal relationships successfully.

None of the specific relationships we found fit neatly into one of the three categories. Instead, they all fall somewhere on a continuum between the two extremes of hostile and cooperative. Also, the relationships may shift from one type to another as the family members grow and change. And the children certainly play a role in the parents' relationship. A new developmental stage in a child may result in a more hostile relationship between the parents. For example, raising a teenage girl may have been easy for her parents before she wanted to have a car. Just as married parents enter into struggles with each other and their children when the children begin to go out, so do single parents. Such normal developmental changes, though, can stress a carefully constructed parental relationship. Hostility may appear where none had existed before. Using the conceptualization of a continuum where there is fluctuation seems the most appropriate approach in attempting to characterize the shifting relationships.

Conclusions

The mother's relationship with the father is shaped by the events in the marriage, by the way it ended, and by what evolves after the breakup. Money, access to the children, the changing needs of the children and the parents, and the mother's impressions of the father can be important factors in understanding the course the relationship takes. Many mothers viewed the fathers favorably as parents but remained ambivalent or angry in their relationships with them. The relationships can be conceptualized as spanning both the roles fulfilled by the mother and father, as ex-spouses and as parents.

8

Life as a
Noncustodial Mother

W HEN the dust has cleared, when the battles have been won
or lost, how does the noncustodial mother feel? This chapter
looks at a number of different areas of the mother's life. How do
other people treat her? What do people say when they learn that she
is noncustodial? How much guilt does she feel? Is she satisfied with
her job and her social life? How helpful have others been to her?
These mothers must navigate through a world that may be truly
hostile to them. Some feel like ancient warriors who, stripped of
their sword and shield in the heat of battle, must fight on. Their
protection has been their identity as full-time mothers living with
their children. Without this, they have none of the security that most
mothers have. These mothers have experienced a radical change in
their lifestyles. Besides dealing with the loss of daily contact with
their children, they also are often dealing with the loss of their
marriage and, with the problems of a reduced income.[1] In only 16
percent of U.S. marriages are wives earning more than husbands,
and these are frequently women who do not have children in the
home.[2]

Noncustodial mothers are in role conflict. There are few role
models for them. They are not clear about what the expectations are
for their behavior—nor do other people know how to treat them.
They are sometimes treated with disdain. Herrerias (1984a), in an
interview illuminating her own role as a noncustodial mother, described meeting a man who was completely turned off to her when

he learned that she was noncustodial: "He looked at me real disgusted, then he said I must have been a real [expletive deleted] to give up my kids" (p. 365).

Some mothers can overcome this kind of negative reaction or encounter very little of it. They view their noncustodial status as a relief from years of parenthood and as a chance for the children finally to get to know their fathers. Other mothers find being noncustodial a comfortable arrangement because they consider it best for all concerned. These mothers adapt to the situation because they feel that the children are content.

How a noncustodial mother adjusts is integrally related to a number of factors: the children's adjustment; the fathers's parenting ability; her job situation; her social life; the reactions of her friends, coworkers, and relatives; and how she came to be noncustodial.[3] At the same time, and because of the systemic nature of families, the way the mother adjusts has an impact on the other people in her family.

If the mother is seen by the father and children as doing well in the noncustodial role, it may reduce the father's sense of guilt both about the breakup and about having custody of the children. One father who was interviewed for the study of custodial fathers was acutely aware of the difficulty his ex-wife was experiencing. "I feel sorry for her," he said. "She grew up hearing one thing about how women are supposed to act, and now she hears something else."[4] If the mother is viewed as doing well and stays involved, it may make the situation easier for everyone.[5]

We must add a caveat to our discussion of adjustment, though. Many of the family situations are in constant flux. It is not uncommon for the mother to feel good about herself and her status one week and then, upon learning the following week that the children are having problems, regret her decision. In turn, as a bad situation with a child improves, so might the mother's view of her own situation. Changes in finances, a new career, or a new marriage can have a similar effect. Custody often goes back and forth, making a parent's situation seem less permanent. One's identity as a noncustodial parent may not be so well cemented in such situations. We must keep these shifting factors in mind when we discuss how the noncustodial mother is adjusting.

Review of the Literature

Past research has found that noncustodial mothers experience stigma, guilt, depression, dissatisfaction, loneliness, anxiety, and lowered self-esteem as a result of their noncustodial status. How prevalent are these feelings among mothers? Todres (1978) reported feelings of emotional upset and guilt in more than half of the mothers he interviewed. Slightly less than half of the mothers felt rejected by significant others in their lives. They also felt shame. One mother said, "I told lies. I did not want anyone to know what I had done" (p. 20). The other half of the sample, though, felt quite happy and relieved about being noncustodial. This was tied to having moved from an unhappy marital situation and to having resolved any ambivalence about the custody arrangement. Once the decision was made, the mothers could cope with the reality more easily than when it was hanging over them. Seeing themselves as successfully independent also boosted some mothers' self-image.

Fischer and Cardea (1981; 1982) found that noncustodial mothers were treated more negatively than custodial mothers by friends, family, and the church. They also reported that noncustodial mothers tended to describe their relationships in greater extremes. The implication was that they felt more strongly about their relationships than custodial mothers did because they had experienced more extreme reactions. People were either very helpful or very negative to them.

Herrerias (1984a) uncovered a link between depression and being treated negatively by others because of being noncustodial. The mothers who regretted giving up custody were also the ones with the lowest self-esteem (nearly a third of the sample).

Paskowicz (1982) described most of the mothers in her sample as "haunted by guilt." Over a quarter of them attempted to keep their noncustodial status a secret. A few committed suicide. Sixty percent were in therapy or were described as feeling the need for professional help. Forty percent were described as being "happy" and having no emotional problems. In striking contrast to the findings we are about to present, Paskowicz suggested that mothers who were coerced into giving up custody have the best chance for emotional health later. The reason she gave for this is that she believes that some of these mothers unconsciously manipulated their husbands to bully them. Thus, their real desire to be noncustodial could be masked by the husband's behavior. Paskowicz also suggested that the mothers who do the worst are the ones whose children chose to live elsewhere, a finding similar to ours.

Meyers and Lakin (1983) stated that the person who gives the mother the hardest time about being noncustodial is her own mother. This occurs, they believed, either because the mothers envy their daughters for doing what they wished they had done or because they are embarrassed by the behavior. Meyers and Lakin concluded, though, that it is really the noncustodial mother who is the hardest on herself. They found only a few mothers able to set aside guilt and ambivalence about their decisions.

What can be summarized from these studies is that although the reactions of others is often a problem, some mothers do live a satisfying life once they become noncustodial. Few mothers, though, seem to be free of guilt.

Building a New Life

When a mother becomes noncustodial, she has to start a new life. She needs to find a place to live if she is not staying in her old home. She has to find a job if she is not working. She has to put her emotional and social life in order. And she has to adjust to having more freedom and independence than before. A number of mothers spoke to this last point. Continuing with Bertha:

> Being a noncustodial parent, you discover you have more time on your hands than you did when you were raising your family. Especially if you are the "I hate housework" type. Since moving into my mobile home, I have become involved in ceramics and began making items for my children. I am basically a lady who hates housework. I can spend hours doing needlework, crocheting, knitting, or keeping my hands busy in other kinds of crafts. I am an avid reader and have a flair for writing poems and stories. Now I have time for all of those things.

Another mother told us:

> When the children went to live with their father, it was the first time I had been totally alone almost since I was a child. I had

married young and had children soon after. All of a sudden I could do things for myself and when I wanted to.

Yet with this freedom comes the feeling, for some mothers, of a great loss. Losing or even voluntarily giving up their children can be much harder than they ever anticipated. Henrietta, whose daughter chose to live with her father because she felt needed by him, wrote:

> Part of the terrible loss I suffered was almost unbearable for me except for the fact that my family (father, mother, and brother) and a few very close women friends gave me support. I also saw a therapist for a year and that helped a great deal. At the time (and still) I have no contact with other women in my position. My problems are unique to me as a woman and I have often found that I have more in common with divorced fathers, since they voice similar complaints.

The Reactions of Others

The reactions of others, whether wholehearted support or rejection, have an important impact on the way many mothers feel about themselves. Few people can live contentedly without the support of others. We asked the mothers two different questions about the reactions of others. In the first, 30 percent agreed that people had reacted negatively to them because they did not have custody, 36 percent disagreed, and 34 percent were mixed. Clearly, and no matter how the mixed group is interpreted, many of the mothers have experienced bias because of their parenting status.

The mothers were also asked to indicate whether it was difficult for them to deal with the reactions of others. For 39 percent of these mothers, dealing with negative reactions had been difficult; another 32 percent said that it was slightly difficult; and the remaining 30 percent said that it was not at all difficult.

The mothers who found the reactions of others the most difficult to deal with tended to be the ones who were the least satisfied with their relationships with their children and with how the children were adapting. When a mother is satisfied that things are going well with her children, this tends to reinforce her noncustodial situation.

Then other people's negative reactions to her tend to have less of an impact.

Another question sought information about how comfortable the mothers felt telling people they were noncustodial. Thirty-three percent felt comfortable with this, 26 percent were mixed, and 35 percent felt uncomfortable. Many of those mothers who felt uncomfortable had been noncustodial for more than five years, indicating that such feelings do not go away easily.

Some of the mothers' comments will help to illustrate their experiences with others. Sarah is in her mid-30s and lives in Chicago. She gave up custody of her son ten years ago, when he was 4. She has since had a second child while single, and she has custody of that child. She does not tell people about her first child. She believes that if people found out, they would not like her.

Another noncustodial mother offered this concrete advice: "When applying for a job I found interviewers asking me point blank why I did not have custody. I think the issue should be skirted if possible. If they find out, it may cost you the job."

A saleswoman wrote: "I feel there is a lot of negative reaction to mothers without their children."

One of the mothers who was interviewed had given up custody of a developmentally disabled child. She had raised her daughter for the first few years after the separation but felt the need for a break from the constant demands. The father was interested in giving single parenting a try. This mother told us:

> The social norm is that all mothers should have custody, and it is just not accepted when you don't. The attitudes are not positive toward you, though it's become more accepted in the last few years. Being sure that it was best for everyone has made it an easier situation for me to deal with.

Another mother, who had split custody, wrote: "Society lays guilt on you, 'What kind of mother would let her child go?' It's not really fair."

One mother, who had not had custody since 1969, wrote: "Custody losses can happen to the most fit mothers. The societal stigma is much greater for both the mother and the children than it is for a noncustodial father."

Some noncustodial mothers deal with the reactions of others in a positive way. One mother living apart from her two small children wrote:

> Let's educate society—noncustodial mothers are maligned. We are not tramps, unfit mothers, or dirt. We love our children, and it is this love which has given us strength to realize that we made the decisions based on what was best for the children (and at a great expense, sacrificing what may have been best for us)!

Guilt

Closely related to the way mothers are treated is the guilt they feel. Guilt feelings generally arise when someone feels bad about something they have or have not done that has had a negative impact on someone else. Guilt is common among parents who are divorced, whether or not they have custody. Parents may feel guilty because they have not been able to work things out for the benefit of the children. They may feel guilty because they have witnessed a great deal of distress in the children or in each other. Parents may also feel guilty if they think they were not good enough parents.

We can hypothesize that a mother without custody may feel a great deal of guilt because the role of mother is so closely tied in her mind, and in the minds of others, with being female. The mother is vulnerable to feelings of guilt and may find her feelings exacerbated by the reactions of others. Ironically, if the mother is not feeling particularly guilty, she may wonder whether she is normal in not feeling guilt.

Our questionnaire asked the mothers whether they felt guilty because they did not have custody. According to their responses, 37 percent did feel guilty, 38 percent were mixed, and 35 percent did not. Thus, although guilt was prevalent, a third of the mothers did not experience it.

Which mothers are the most likely to feel guilty? Generally, those most prone to guilt feelings are mothers who are unhappy with the situations in which their children are being raised. Mothers who are pleased with the living arrangements of their children have less reason to feel guilty. If the children are doing well, the pain is not as great for the mothers or their children.

We learned that mothers who had fewer children living elsewhere felt less guilty[6] and that mothers who were still raising at least one of their children (split custody) also experienced less guilt.[7] These two findings would be expected. If it is hard to relinquish custody—and we have established that for many mothers it is—then it would be likely to be even more difficult when there are more children. At the same time, a mother who still retains custody of at least one child would be expected to have less guilt because she still has part of her identity as a full-time mother.

We also found a relationship between the reasons for custody and guilt. Mothers who did not have custody because the children chose the father and because the mothers were acting in the best interests of the children felt the least guilty. The mothers who lost custody in court—because they were unable to parent or because of money—felt much more guilt.[8] The mothers who said that they gave up custody voluntarily also feel less guilty.[9] We will return to these issues later.

The way the mother feels about her life also clearly reflects the guilt she feels. Mothers who feel comfortable telling people that they do not have custody, mothers who are satisfied with their careers, and mothers who give themselves a high rating as parents feel less guilt than other mothers.[10] These feelings naturally go together. For instance, as a mother becomes more satisfied with her career, she may feel less guilty and she may feel better about telling people that she is noncustodial. Also, learning to deal with the guilt may help her feel better about herself as a parent and appreciate her job situation more.

One of the results was surprising. We had hypothesized that mothers would feel more guilty if they were living apart from daughters than if they were living apart from sons. The belief, here, was that the mothers would feel that their daughters needed them more. Also, we believed that the mothers could more easily rationalize that a son should be with his father. In fact, however, we found no differences between the mothers living apart from sons and the mothers living apart from daughters.

What we are seeing with these findings is that guilt is not free-floating; rather, it occurs in specific situations. It is not felt equally by everybody, and it is not tied consistently to being noncustodial.

Circumstances in the mother's life may mitigate it, and a significant portion of the noncustodial mother population is not bothered by it.

A few mothers conveyed their feelings of guilt to us. One mother, noncustodial for five years, wrote, "Guilt is the hardest thing to cope with. Much of the guilt is caused by our own mothers and the ex-husbands." Another mother, who had been away from her children for only a few months, said, "Sometimes I feel guilty that I could not be an effective mother."

One mother had lived apart from her three sons for seven years. She gave up custody after attempting suicide twice and because she was unable to manage her children. She told this sad story:

> I thought my ex-husband would treat my three sons better than he did me, as I blamed myself for his drinking and abusiveness. But without me to take out his anger on, he used the boys. Now one is in a Boys Home—I took him there when he was so mixed up neither of us could care for him. Another has grown up and moved away. The other is having difficulty adjusting to his new stepmother, as his father has remarried and is on drugs. I have a lot of guilt about this. I should have kept them with me.

Some mothers offer advice for fighting the feelings of guilt. One said, "Don't give in to guilt or peer pressure. If you feel you made a good choice on your own, stick to it." A second offered, "Non-custodial mothers should try to not feel guilty as long as they feel what they have done is best for the children."

Work

Part of the mothers' adaptation involves the workplace. Most of the mothers (85 percent) were employed or had an occupation at the time they took part in our study. Returning to work, continuing to work, or starting to work was a necessity for most of the mothers from both a financial and an emotional point of view. For many of them, work was one way out of a bad situation and into a better one. For some, it provided the first chance to be independent and to achieve a sense of identity that did not depend on children and marriage; they could be their own person. For others, it meant devoting more time to a career that, because of the time demands of marriage and parenting, had been put on the back burner.

According to recent reports from the Census Bureau, the number of mothers in the workforce with children under 18 in the home was well over 52 percent for married mothers, 54 percent for separated mothers, and 68 percent for divorced mothers.[11] Over the past few decades, women—whether married, single, or divorced—have been gradually taking greater part in the workforce. In 1970, less than half (43 percent) of the women 16 years old and over took part in the labor force. By 1980, the percentage had risen to 52 percent and the projection for 1995 reaches over 60 percent.[12] Between 1970 and 1983, the percentage of people who were not looking for work because—to use the Census Bureau's terms—they were "keeping house" shrank from 64 percent to 51 percent.[13] Clearly, the trend is toward greater involvement by women in the workforce.

This is a continuation of a pattern that has been interrupted in the twentieth century only by wars and the Depression. Prior to this century, the participation of women in the workforce varied. Before the Industrial Revolution, women's and men's work was centered primarily in the home. Rosen (1982) pointed out that as farms turned to the production and sale of cash crops, market imperatives intruded upon the family in unforeseen ways. Cash, rather than bartering for goods, became the goal of production. "As early manufacturing transferred some of women's work outside of the home, women's vital partnership in a traditional domestic economy began to diminish" (p. 7). In well-to-do families, the Industrial Revolution meant that the woman's role in domestic labor was reduced. There was more help available as well as labor-saving devices. In poor families, it meant that women and children were more likely to work outside of the home. In 1900, 2 million children between the ages of 10 and 15 and five million women over 15 were in the workforce. Together, they constituted almost a quarter of the total labor force. The numbers continued to grow until the Depression, which affected men and women alike. In some jobs, men replaced women; in others, women working in menial positions retained them while their more highly skilled husbands went unemployed.[14]

A number of studies have found that women who have stayed single or are married and child-free are more likely to work outside the home than mothers are. A mother's decision to continue in or leave the workforce when there are small children in the home may influence her later work experiences. Stay-at-home mothers are at a disadvantage in terms of income when they go to work in comparison with those who never left the workforce.[15]

Many of the mothers in our study were initially entering the workforce at a disadvantage. They either had a lack of work experience, had been working only part-time, or had been splitting their allegiances while at work between their children and their jobs. Some were going back to school and were experiencing culture shock in being the oldest in the classroom. Telling co-workers, employers, and fellow students about their noncustodial status was a problem for some of them. They felt vulnerable on these issues. Some women said that they were divorced and that their children were old enough to live on their own. Others told the truth and found no problem. One secretary said, "I never had any problems with it. Sometimes people came up to me and asked how I managed to pull it off. It was something they were thinking of doing."

Despite initial problems, a slight majority of the mothers (53 percent) described working as trouble-free, and slightly fewer (41 percent) said that they were satisfied with how their careers were going. As might be expected, satisfaction with career was related to higher income and occupational status. When compared with other areas of adjustment—such as starting a social life, arranging visitation, being single again, and dealing with a new financial lifestyle—work was by far the easiest.

Our impression from these findings is that when a mother becomes noncustodial, she invests more in her new identity as a working person than she had previously. This is partially out of necessity. She has lost part of her identity as a mother living full-time with her children and now has to derive her sense of self from her work experiences instead. The importance of work grows for her, as it is both a means for her to develop an identity and a means for her to support herself.

Financial Situation

A great deal has been written about the role of money in the mothers' decision not to seek custody or in their loss of custody. Finances also play an important part in their adjustment to their role of noncustodial mother. As noted in the first chapter, the average income of the mothers was over $16,000, putting them in a higher income bracket than the average woman.[16]

We asked two questions about the mother's financial situation. The first inquired about the mother's difficulty with her changing financial situation. More than half of the mothers (58 percent) responded that it had been difficult, 19 percent said that it had been slightly difficult, and 23 percent said that it had not been difficult. The second question asked the mothers whether they agreed with the statement: "I am not financially secure." Fifty percent agreed, 14 percent were mixed, and 36 percent disagreed.

Looking at the responses to both questions, we are able to get a general idea of how these mothers were faring financially. Somewhere between 23 percent at the low end and 42 percent at the high end (if we include people who said that their changing financial situation was slightly difficult) have not had a difficult time. This is validated by the range presented in the second question—36 percent who felt financially secure and another 14 percent who were "mixed" about their financial security. Roughly, a little less than two-thirds of the mothers (around 60 percent) felt they *had* experienced some financial hardship or were currently feeling it.

We can compare these findings with data available from the study of fathers with custody. It is important to reiterate that we are comparing fathers who have primary responsibility for the children with mothers who do not. Thirty-five percent of the fathers had said that their changing financial lifestyle was difficult, and another 27 percent had said that it was slightly difficult. When the fathers were asked whether they agreed with the statement: "I am financially secure enough to provide the basics for myself and my family," 82 percent agreed, and 7 percent were mixed, and only 11 percent disagreed.[17]

What we are seeing is not so much that these mothers without custody are having an overwhelmingly difficult time financially— although, clearly, more than half are—but that there can be a great discrepancy in the financial comfort of these two groups and that the fathers, with the financial burden of the children, say that they feel more comfortable. It is not only the financial situation of the father without custody that improves after a marital breakup while that of the mother declines. But relatively, the father with custody seems to fare better than the noncustodial mother. Even when the father has the children, there is a tendency for him to "feel" better off than the mother, though not necessarily better off than he would have been if he did not have custody or better off than he was before the breakup. (Child support payments from the mother are not a major contributing factor to this inequity, as will be discussed in chapter 9.)

Some of the mothers' descriptions reflect the impact of their financial situation on their lives. One mother, who is unemployed and receiving $400 a month alimony, wrote, "I have no money to join your group [referring to PWP]. I would like to if I could." Another mother, an unemployed factory worker, wrote, "Their father can buy them everything they want. I can't." Bertha, quoted earlier, wrote, "It was especially hard for me at Christmas time. I was working in a store where people were buying things for people and I could not buy anything nice for my children." Finally, a mother who was working as a teacher gave a different view: "I am on my own financially for the first time in my life. I love it."

Social Life

Establishing a social life after the breakup is one of the challenges that faces all divorced and separated people. Socializing becomes one way to cope with the loss of a marriage. More important, for many, it is a way to test out their relationships with others. Whatever the reasons for the termination of the marriage, the divorced person often wonders about his or her capacity for friendships and for intimacy. By getting involved with new people or reinvolved with old friends, the newly separated person has a way of testing the waters. The person can see whether he or she is still likable and attractive to others and can make attempts to change if the response is negative. People also socialize in an attempt to deal with loneliness. Being accustomed to having a spouse at home, a great sense of emptiness can set in when the spouse leaves. If there is pain from a divorce, it must be worked through both internally and through contacts with others.

For women who have been out of the social scene for a number of years, being newly single is a time of exploring and questioning. Many of the mothers in the study had married in the mid-1960s when the expectations for men's and women's behavior were quite different from the expectations after the impact of the women's movement was felt. The mothers often found themselves in a totally new social scene. They saw women calling men up for dates, offering to pay their own way, and having sexual relations without a marriage certificate in the safe deposit box. As will be shown, despite initial uneasiness, many mothers adapted quite successfully.

A variety of questions inquired into the mother's social life. For example, almost 80 percent of the mothers felt that involvement in social activities was helpful to their adjustment. (A similar percentage of the fathers with custody reported that social activities were helpful.)

Being single again was hard for almost half of the mothers: 47 percent said that it was difficult or very difficult, 21 percent said that it was slightly difficult, and 31 percent said that it was not at all difficult. The fathers with custody gave responses to a similar question that revealed a comparably high level of discomfort being single.

Loneliness plagued these mothers; 61 percent said that it was difficult for them to deal with. Mothers who stayed very involved with their children did not have an easier time dealing with loneliness. A fascinating finding turned up when we compared the feelings of loneliness on the part of the mothers with that experienced by the fathers with custody. Almost an equal percentage of the fathers (62 percent) said that loneliness was difficult for them, too. The presence of the children in the household did not mitigate these parents' needs for adult contact.

Once some of the initial tentativeness about dating had been overcome and the mothers' social lives began, they achieved a high level of satisfaction. More than half (54 percent) said that their social lives were satisfactory, 21 percent described them as mixed, and only 25 percent said that they were unsatisfactory. Two other comparisons are needed to put this information into perspective. Of the custodial fathers, a smaller percentage (36 percent) said that they were satisfied with their social lives, and a larger group (40 percent) described their satisfaction as mixed. Data had also been gathered previously from a group of 150 mothers *with* custody. These mothers had a slightly lower rate of social satisfaction than the custodial fathers or the noncustodial mothers.[18] Thus, of these three groups of single parents—mothers without custody, fathers with custody, and mothers with custody—we see that the first group had the most satisfying experiences. (See chapter 11 for our findings on noncustodial fathers.)

A comparison of three groups of single fathers, those with custody, those with joint custody, and those without custody supports this finding. Among those groups, the fathers with the least contact with their children had the most satisfying social lives.[19] Obviously, parents—male or female—who do not have children at home can pursue their social lives with greater ease.

Intimate Relationships

A final question asked the mothers whether they had had intimate relationships and, if so, how helpful these relationships had been to their adjustment. The majority of the mothers (77 percent) had had at least one intimate relationship since becoming noncustodial. Approximately 80 percent found it helpful and slightly less than a quarter did not find it at all helpful. Although we found that the number of years of being noncustodial was not a predictor of when someone would have an intimate relationship, we did learn that younger mothers were more apt to say they had been involved in intimate relationships than older ones.

Among the group of mothers who had had intimate relationships was a subgroup who went straight from marriage into a relationship that they had been maintaining during the marriage. In some cases, those relationships were the reason for the divorce and for the mother being noncustodial. Twenty-three of the mothers had remarried and, naturally, described their social lives as quite satisfying.

Getting Help from Others

Sixty percent of the mothers in the study sought help from a mental health counselor. The majority of those found that contact to be of great assistance. Some mothers added comments on the questionnaire indicating that their counselor had been very influential both in the decision to relinquish custody and in their adaptation to the non-custodial situation.

The support of relatives was described as helpful by 57 percent of the mothers; 25 percent said that it was not helpful, and 18 percent said that it did not apply to their situation. Contrary to Meyers and

Lakin's (1983) finding that the mother's mother was very critical, we found that to be the case for only a minority of the mothers. One mother did say, "My parents never understood how I could live without my children." But for most of the mothers, help was there when they really needed it. Carol (described in chapter 2), for example, received a good deal of help from her mother in her attempts to see her son.

Being with friends proved to be beneficial to the mothers. Ninety percent described those friendships as being integral to their adjustment. One mother wrote this advice to other noncustodial mothers: "Get lots of good supportive friends. They have helped me enormously!"

Support Groups

Joining support groups, such as Parents Without Partners and Mothers Without Custody, and finding other parents in the same situation was also mentioned frequently as helpful to the mothers' adjustment. Nearly two-thirds of the mothers who joined PWP, for example, described the group as helpful. Meeting other noncustodial mothers, though considered helpful, was less common; only half of the mothers knew anyone else in their situation. Many mothers had comments about support groups. One mother wrote simply, "Support groups badly needed." Another wrote, "Get involved in PWP, church groups, any social organization. Keep busy and you'll be happy. Make friends from these organizations."

Collette is a typesetter in a small community in the South. She lost custody when her son chose his father over her. She spoke highly of the benefits of being with others:

> If you have difficulty coping with being noncustodial, try to become acquainted with other mothers in such a situation. They are the only ones in our society who truly understand your pain. Join groups which advocate custody reform and give you support.

The idea of joining a group for support or for reform of the legal system was mentioned occasionally. Some issues raised involved protecting the rights of women seeking custody, assisting women in receiving financial support from custodial fathers, and increasing access to the children through visitation. One or two mothers mentioned joining fathers' rights groups, which often fight for equal custody laws and improved visitation rights. A few mothers believed that working with these groups would improve their own chances of getting what they want. One woman wrote, "One suggestion I would make is that programs for divorced fathers without custody be opened to moms with the same situation. We all need support with the terrible losses we suffer."

Bertha was one of the mothers who wrote about self-help groups:

> During the spring of this year I learned of the organization called Mothers Without Custody. In the deepest regions of my mind I wondered what people would think of me for giving up my son. I am sure many people judge me as "unfit" when learning I have given him up, but as I stated to my former spouse, I know in my heart, soul, and mind that I made the best decision for my child. I could never have been able to provide him with the clothing he needs nor purchase all the food a growing, teenage boy consumes, even with the most generous child support.
>
> I was hesitant to join MW/OC as I was dubious about being with other mothers who perhaps did not have a similar lifestyle to mine. The second meeting I met two ladies who had the court make the decision and I wholeheartedly agreed with the father raising their children based on their current lifestyle. Perhaps being in my 40s I cannot tolerate a woman living with someone and drinking to ease the loneliness.
>
> Yet most of the ladies are lovely. As we explained our individual situations, I learned they had all made the painful decision regarding their children primarily for financial reasons and the knowledge the father could give them a more secure environment. Despite the bitter feelings or the irreconcilable differences that lead up to the divorce, and the huge monster the father is at the proceedings, or kissy kissy to the judge to make an excellent impression, none of these were bad fathers.

Joining groups is not for everyone, though. Some mothers do not want to be reminded of their situation. As one mother responded:

> I never met any noncustodial mothers and I adjusted on my own. Didn't want to be around people feeling sorry for themselves or on guilt trips. I consider myself pretty well adjusted to it. My kids

turned out better than most kids in two-parent families. Top students in school and no emotional problems, drugs, etc.

Which Noncustodial Mothers Are Most Comfortable?

This chapter and the preceding ones have given us an overview of the noncustodial mother's life and how she handles various aspects of it. We have looked at the mother's relationships with her children, with her ex-husband, and with friends and acquaintances; at others' negative reactions to her; and at her work, financial situation, and social life. We can now try to determine which of these mothers are doing the best in their role of noncustodial mother. Who is most comfortable?

To begin to find out, we asked the mothers whether they agreed with the statement: "I feel comfortable as a noncustodial mother." The responses to this were as follows: 34 percent agreed, 34 percent were mixed, and 32 percent disagreed. The responses to many other questions related to adjustment also resulted in three equal-sized groups of mothers: those who were doing well, those who were having difficulty, and a mixed group. (See the stories of Carol, Barbara, and Wilma in chapter 2.)

The best predictor of the mother's comfort was whether the mother said that she gave up custody voluntarily. Those who did felt the most comfortable in their situation. Five other experiences were also associated with the mother's comfort:

1. The reason the mother gave for the divorce: Mothers who shared the responsibility for the breakup with their husbands felt more comfortable than those who considered the breakup to be the husband's fault. When a mother feels that she was partially responsible, she feels more in control of her own life.

2. The reason the mother gave for why she does not have custody: Mothers who indicated that they were noncustodial because it was in the children's best interest feel more confortable; mothers who lost custody in court felt the least comfortable. In part, altruistic feelings come to play here. Mothers who feel that their children are better off are more comfortable with their own role.

3. The stress at the time of the custody decision: Mothers who indicated that they did not feel a great deal of stress at that time

were more comfortable than those who said that giving up custody was very stressful. This confirms the obvious, yet it also points out something important about consistency. Many mothers were not shaken from their initial decision by later events.

4. The mother's religion: Respondents who said that they had no religious affiliation felt the most comfortable. Of those who affiliated with the three major religions in the United States, Protestants felt the most comfortable, Catholics next, and Jews the least.

5. Having to deal with a changing financial lifestyle: Although the mother's income was not significantly related to her comfort, those mothers who reported little or no difficulty dealing with a changing financial lifestyle felt more comfortable than those who experienced greater difficulty in this area. It is not one's absolute income that is important but the shift in one's situation that takes the toll. A mother who has always made do with less can continue to make do with less, whereas a mother who suffers a drop is more prone to discomfort.[20]

These findings also showed that many other variables—such as the age, sex, and number of the children living away from the mother; her income; and the number of years the mother has been noncustodial—are not related to the comfort the mother feels. These points are noteworthy. We had hypothesized that mothers who had been living apart from daughters or young children would feel a greater reluctance to be apart from them because they might have a closer bond to them and because society might have a greater expectation for them to be raising the children. This was not the case. Most surprising was that time did not help the mothers feel more comfortable. This finding may be counterbalanced by the strong influence that the voluntary nature of the situation has on comfort. What we can conclude about the mothers' adjustment is that early experiences concerning custody are not easily erased. If the mother goes into the custody situation feeling favorably about it, she is likely to maintain that feeling. By the same token, if she is unhappy about the custody decision, that feeling is not likely to change over time.

Current Factors in the Mothers' Comfort

We wanted to find out what a mother who wanted to improve her situation could do—that is, which experiences were the most highly associated with the mothers who felt comfortable. Clearly, some of those factors were present from the beginning of the custody situation, but we wanted to focus on the comfortable mother's current situation to see what she was doing correctly that was linked to her feelings of comfort. Three factors turned out to be particularly highly associated with a noncustodial mother's comfort:

1. Satisfaction with her relationship with the children living apart from her
2. No guilt feelings
3. The belief that the children are better off living away from her[21]

What is most noteworthy about these three factors is that two of them have to do with the children. The mothers who are most successful as noncustodial mothers feel that way, in part, because they are content with the status of their children. They are happy with their relationships with them, and they believe that the chidren's best interests are being met by living away from them.

Five other factors were less highly related to the mother's comfort:

1. Satisfaction with her social life
2. Experiencing less loneliness
3. Satisfaction with the children's progress
4. Satisfaction with her career
5. Giving the ex-husband a high rating as a father

Conclusions: A Broad Look

What we found among this sample of mothers were three distinct groups: one-third who felt comfortable being noncustodial, one-third who did not feel comfortable, and one-third who felt "mixed." This finding is important in that it supports the viability of the noncustodial lifestyle for many of the mothers. This viability is optimal when custody has been turned over voluntarily and when the mother is pleased with how the children are adjusting.

Many of the mothers' lives are *not* fraught with unhappiness, guilt, loneliness, mental illness, and victimization. They are satisfied with the decisions they have made, are pleased with their children's growth and development, and have active social lives and careers. Their marriages most likely ended on fairly good terms. Many of the mothers have found it easy to live with their decisions. Others have struggled over a long period of time to feel good about themselves, and most days they feel that they have succeeded. They have adopted a role for themselves that is more encompassing than that of "mother." Although they still see themselves as mothers, they also have identities that go beyond that role.

The mothers who described themselves as "mixed" are those who have characteristics of both those who are doing well and those who are not. They may have good days and bad days when they think about being apart from their children. They probably gave up custody reluctantly. Their relationships with their children and ex-husbands may fluctuate, as may their financial situation. They may have a good relationship with one child but not with another. They may be sensitive to the reactions of others but convinced that having their children living apart from them is the right thing.

At the other end of the spectrum are the mothers who are having difficulty with their noncustodial status. This would be a population most likely to be "at risk." Some of these mothers lost custody against their will—because their children chose the father, because they were unable to raise the children financially, or because of emotional problems. Their divorces were likely to have been particularly acrimonious. They may have had an especially tough time with friends, relatives, and their own parents. They may not be on good terms with their children. Their own lives may not have taken a positive turn. Finances, work, socializing, and their emotional well-being may still be problems. Many of these mothers have not let go of their identity as a day-to-day parent. They have not been able to mourn the loss of their parenting role effectively, and they remain bitter, often feeling victimized and out of control.

The Mothers' Own Words

Many of the mothers wrote about their current situations and offered advice to other mothers. In their own stories, we see the range of their adjustments. As expected, some stories are sad; others show

how the mothers are succeeding at living the kind of life they had hoped for.

A 49-year-old nurse living away from two sons wrote:

> There are many positive reasons for a mother to give up custody that are overlooked. I am pretty comfortable about my situation because I feel that I operated out of the principle of what was best for all concerned, no matter what other people might think.

A 35-year-old secretary whose son lived away from her for eight years now has a son from a second marriage. She wrote:

> I believe not having custody is like having a wound that will never heal completely. I am still remorseful it turned out this way and sometimes resentful my parents could not have helped me more through my difficult times. I missed out on raising him day to day. I now have a 1-year-old son and enjoy every minute that I missed with my first son. The baby's father and I broke up before he was born and I have only seen him occasionally since. I still see my son, but it's never been frequent. Truthfully, it was too painful to be reminded of my "neglect." Now I'm making more of an effort so he can be with his new brother. I really care about him and his welfare but have a conflict sometimes in that I know I won't be as close to him as if we lived together.

A 33-year-old divorced mother who is living apart from four children wrote:

> When I went to school I got a certificate in mechanical drawing and now I can't even find a job. It has been two years since I completed the courses, and I am afraid I have forgotten everything. My original plan was to let the kids live with their dad, go to school, find a job, and get the kids back. Being single has been so frustrating. If it hadn't been for PWP I don't know how I would have survived.

A 45-year-old separated mother who is a counselor and part-time student and living away from one son advised: "Take advantage of your freedom from the responsibilities of custody and improve yourself!"

A saleswoman in her 40s with two children living away from her wrote:

> Concentrate on you for a change. If you are relieved of responsi-
> bility it is OK to feel relief. Consider that you did the best you
> could for the children when they were with you. Remember, it is
> the quality of the time spent with them, not the quantity.

Another saleswoman, who is 37, noted: "You must find a reason to like yourself before anyone else can like you."

A 40-year-old student with split custody advised:

> Use your time well—in some ways being without custody is a
> relief and your time with the chidren can be better than it was
> before. Also, get to know yourself—through therapy, education,
> and relationships.

A 36-year-old woman, who gave up custody of three children because she could not afford to raise them, is working as a secretary. She wrote: "No woman should ever give up her children no matter what the circumstances are!"

A 39-year-old mother who is living apart from two children and working as a clerk wrote:

> The best advice to any noncustodial mother is find a support group
> of others in your situation because no one else can really understand
> what you are going through. I was in a group led by two noncus-
> todial mothers who were therapists, and that group got me through
> a lot of very difficult times.

A 30-year-old mother who has remarried and works as a teacher wrote: "It is very painful to be without my son. However, I got very involved in my career and with my new husband and friends, and that helps."

A 36-year-old divorced social worker who is living apart from her four boys wrote: "The best thing a noncustodial mother can do is find a support group with other women in the same situation. We help each other in many ways with support and coping strategies, socially, and other ways."

A 43-year-old divorced secretary who is living apart from one daughter and two sons wrote: "I feel that I reared the children without interference for sixteen years. Now it's dad's turn. Yet when I think about it, I feel I've been slapped in the face by the ERA. People just don't understand."

Finally, a 46-year-old separated nurse who is living apart from a teenage daughter advised: "Talk about your problems with a counselor and friends. Do some reading on the subject. Keep yourself happy and busy with things that you like. That will keep you most happy in the long run."

9

Child Support

C HILD support payments play a key role in the life of the non-custodial mother. One mother told us:

I do not know to this day what really brought Jerry, my son, to his decision. My ex was cited with a summons for owing me back child support on a Tuesday. My ex called up Jerry and I have yet to learn what promises he was given by his father so that he would leave me. My ex is a manipulator, and Jerry is very closemouthed. It always seemed like I was giving him the third degree when I asked him why he left, so I don't really know why. I do know that my ex did not want to pay back all those years of child support he owed me. He claimed he was laid off, but then I found out he was working. Anyway, my ex called Jerry on Tuesday, and by the weekend he had moved out. Most of the things in his room were gone, and there was a very ugly message on the phone recorder from my ex, "I have him and you are not getting him back." Needless to say, I got hysterical. He called me later and asked if I got the message. I asked to speak to Jerry, and he would not let me. Jerry's school work deteriorated for awhile and then got better. He seems very happy.

Months later we went to court to see about custody. I hired a good attorney who knew how much my money was tied up and how bad things were for me financially. After the trial my lawyer asked for his $300 at once. And to top it off I lost and had to pay child support! And then had trouble with the Bureau of Child Support because I was a woman paying a man. My lawyer said this was very common these days (1982) of women's lib, the woman paying the father child support, but talking to the people at the Bureau, I realized it was the first time for them making those kind

of arrangements and they looked up all these regulations. It was
just the icing on the cake for me.

Researcher Judith Cassety (1984) has written:

> The issue of child support—that is, the economic support of chil-
> dren by their natural or adoptive parents with whom they do not
> reside—is emerging as one of great concern to social scientists,
> public officials, social workers, and the average citizen. (p. 74)

Child support is not only, as Cassety suggests, an issue of vital
importance to professionals and lay people; it is also central to many
of the disputes between parents concerning custody. In the majority
of cases, child support payment issues pertain to the noncustodial
father, who is held accountable for the payment of support to the
mother. The first part of this chapter will explore this most common
arrangement before discussing our findings concerning the noncustodial mother.

The record of fathers paying support is not a good one. Nuta
(1986) reported that in 1983, the same year our survey was done,
approximately half of the fathers required to pay support paid the
full amount, one-quarter paid less than they were supposed to, and
the other quarter paid nothing. About 60 percent of all single mothers
were granted child support awards. The Office of Child Support
Enforcement (1984) reported that the nation's unpaid child support
bill reached $2.4 billion in fiscal year 1984. Nuta (1986) went on to
say that the payment of child support is an emotional issue that
represents one of the last links between people who are trying to
build separate lives.

For the mothers who took part in our research, the question of
their paying child support is often reacted to with ambiguity, ambivalence, and anger. Child support can be affected by what actually
happens in court or by what a mother fears will happen in court.
Payment can become one more bargaining chip in a battle over
custody, alimony, and property division.

According to a fact sheet published by Parents Without Partners
(1986), children are entitled to support from both parents; to get that
support, one must get a court order that is approved by a judge.
Few circumstances relieve a parent from this obligation. Moving out

of state or remarrying does not mitigate the responsibility. Parents who move out of state and do not make payment can be tracked down through state parent locator services.

The determinations concerning child support decisions usually begin at the family level and can eventually spiral into the city, state, and federal arenas. At the family level, the divorcing parents may attempt to come to an informal agreement concerning custody, alimony, property, and child support levels. As Weitzman (1985) pointed out, it is artificial to treat these issues separately, as they are often negotiated together. Nevertheless, whatever agreements the couple are able to reach on their own are not binding unless they are sanctioned by a judge.

Even after custody has been agreed on, child support can be a thorn in a parent's side because it is often linked informally to visitation. For years, members of fathers' rights groups have complained that fathers are denied visitation when they have refused to pay what they consider to be unfair support payments. Horowitz and Dodson (1985) suggested that the states should pass legislation that would separate issues concerning visitation from those concerning child support.[1] In some states, this is happening. It was recently ruled in California, for example, that visitation should not be dependent on child support. The ruling stated that visitation was as much a right of the child as of the noncustodial parent and that failure to pay should not remove that right.[2] In North Carolina, a different type of ruling supported the separation of visitation and support payments. According to that ruling, a parent was not freed from the obligation to pay child support even though the child refused to visit the parent.[3]

Determinations involving child support can eventually spiral into the various levels of government when disputes arise or when there is nonpayment. For example, a mother who receives public assistance because her ex-husband is not paying the child support he has been required to pay is a burden on resources and the taxpayer.

Increasingly, governments are shifting the responsibility back to the errant parent when possible.[4] Getting the noncustodial parent to pay relieves the taxpayer and makes more money available for other governmental needs. Congress, with the Child Support Enforcement Amendments of 1984 (P.L. 98-378), has taken the initiative in the delinquent collection process by requiring that states pass laws by 1987 that allow the delinquent parent's wages to be attached through a variety of methods if support payments are more than thirty days in arrears. This legislation builds on earlier legislation that was put in place in 1975 by Title IV-D of the Social Security Act. The thurst of that act was to help offset the burden placed on the taxpayer and to help keep mothers off Aid to Families with Dependent Children (AFDC). The states have many avenues to follow in collecting unpaid support, including wage withholding, liens against real and personal property, posting of bonds by the absent parent to ensure payment, attachment of income tax refunds, and notifying credit bureaus when delinquency surpasses $1,000.[5]

These methods of collecting back payments are not without their problems. Krause (1983) raised the question of the costs versus the benefits of some of the proposals to get back payments. Programs to collect payments can often cost more than what is received, especially if the program is not managed effectively. Hope is beginning to emerge, though, that programs can be cost-effective. According to figures released by the Office of Child Support Enforcement (1984), an average of $3.29 was collected for every dollar spent in fiscal year 1984. A host of other criteria have to be considered when weighing the costs and benefits of recovery programs. These include, on the plus side, the possible psychological benefits to society, to the custodial parents, and to their children of pursuing delinquents. On the negative side, such programs may result in less frequent contact between the noncustodial parent and the child if the parent wants his whereabouts or identity unknown.

If a custodial parent is persistent enough, he or she can often get back payments. In one case, fourteen years after the divorce and the husband's four subsequent marriages, a mother received overdue child and spousal payments from the father.[6]

The methods used to decide on the proper payment of child support are generally agreed to be in need of reform. Issues of equity make determination extremely complex. At least three methods have been used. Cassety (1984) cited the approaches of cost sharing and resource sharing. With a cost-sharing approach, the noncustodial parent matches with support payments the standard of living of the custodial parent. There are problems with this approach, as the custodial mother's standard can be difficult to determine if her standard of living is determined by support and alimony payments, as it often is. In a resource-sharing approach, the assumption is that the total costs of child rearing are to be shouldered proportionately on the basis of the parent's ability to pay. This can be a fairer approach, but it means that a downturn in a noncustodial parent's income can have a debilitating effect on the lifestyle of the custodial parent and the child, as perhaps it should. Haskins et al. (1985) cited a third method—having the noncustodial parent pay a fixed percentage of his or her income for the support of the children. When this approach is worked out fairly at the outset, it has potential for equity.[7]

A number of studies have looked at the issue of child support and the noncustodial father. Haskins et al. (1985) reviewed data from a random sample of 120 AFDC and 120 non-AFDC fathers living in North Carolina. Ninety-four percent of the non-AFDC fathers claimed that they paid child support, a figure much higher than the norm and one that, upon cross-checking with court records, was found to have been inflated by the respondents. These fathers were found to be making other types of in-kind payments in addition to money. For example, many of the fathers helped out with health insurance, transportation, household repairs, and babysitting. The fathers were also asked their beliefs about why fathers (though not necessarily they) do not pay child support. The reasons deemed the most important were that the mother was not spending the money on the children and that the father was unemployed.

Weitzman (1981) looked at child support payments in California and discovered that many fathers with the ability to pay do not. The nonpaying fathers were rarely pursued by the authorities (at least in the 1970s), and the mothers were put in the position of being the one to do the chasing.

Tropf (1984) discovered increases in voluntary support payments by 101 divorced noncustodial men upon their remarriage but decreases if the ex-wives remarried. Such variables as geographic distance and the continuing relationship between the father and child did not have an impact on voluntary payments.

When the Mother Is the Noncustodial Parent

We have discussed some of the issues concerning child support from the noncustodial father. But what happens when the situation is reversed? What happens when the mother, especially one who earns less than the father, is the noncustodial parent facing child support obligations? Suppose that the mother is on welfare and is barely making ends meet for herself? Is it fair for her to pay money to a father who may earn more than an adequate income? It is these questions that lead to the ambivalence, ambiguity, and anger that many of the mothers we interviewed felt when they described their child support situations. Some were frankly amazed by the questions, feeling that the reason they did not pay was obvious—they earned less money. Nuta's (1986) work with Parents Without Partners revealed a similar reaction among the noncustodial mothers she had contact with. She wrote:

> One of the most striking characteristics of the noncustodial mother
> who is not paying child support is the refusal to acknowledge that
> there may be an obligation to do so. While fathers may make
> excuses, the mother denies that she should support the children at
> all. (p. 179)

Yet according to unpublished data from the Census Bureau (U.S. Department of Commerce, 1986a), 60,000 fathers (about one in ten) were receiving child support payments in 1984.

The perception of whether a mother should pay has been complicated by the changing view of women's roles and the 1984 congressional legislation. In previous chapters, we established our view of women as victims as a result of both societal expectations and lower earning capacities. Therefore, expecting them to pay child support to men who are often earning two to three times their income would seem ludicrous. At the same time, women clearly have more opportunities than ever before. They have made great inroads in the workplace and in educational attainment. Many women earn at least as much as men. Between 1960 and 1984, the percentage of men in the workforce declined slightly, while the percentage of women increased by nearly 50 percent. Between 1950 and 1980, the number of women with college degrees grew by nearly 450 percent while the number of men increased by less than 50 percent.[8] With the women's rights movement and laws spelling out requirements for child support, women are being held increasingly accountable for payments, even though they earn less money, on the average, than men. Thus, there is a conundrum. On the one hand, people believe that it is inexcusable to ask that a mother pay child support she can ill afford. On the other hand, she is expected to pay just as a man would. These issues are not easily resolvable. They are further complicated by visitation agreements, the couple's history, and the proliferation of stepfamilies.

Despite legal rulings concerning the separation of visitation and child support payments, many noncustodial and custodial parents fudge on their obligations because they know they can get away with it. For example, a noncustodial mother who is required to pay $100 a week may realize that she can get by with paying $80 a week for a long time without being taken back to court by her ex-husband for the extra $20. It often would not be cost- or time-effective for him to pursue it. Similarly, a custodial father could deny a mother's visitation occasionally without being punished.

As will be shown later in this chapter, the family history can also play a part in how child support payments are handled. Some noncustodial mothers base their payment decisions on whether or not they were paid when they had custody.

Findings from Our Study

On the questionnaire, we asked the mothers the amount of child support they paid per week (if any.) No question asked whether or not payment was court-ordered or whether the respondent was paying the full amount agreed upon, formally or informally. Seventy-one mothers (14.3 percent) said that they paid some child support. In breaking down the respondents into those who belonged to Parents Without Partners and those who belonged to Mothers Without Custody or were unaffiliated with any self-help group, we found some differences. Despite the fact that PWP members had a slightly higher income than members of the other group, they were less likely to pay child support—12.1 percent as compared to 21.4 percent.[9]

One possible reason for this difference between the groups in child support payments is the identification that members might feel. We believe that PWP members are more likely to have joined their support group to meet other single parents and to socialize both with and without their children. Although both groups offer support, Mothers Without Custody is viewed as less of a social group and more of an issue-oriented group. The payment of child support is likely to be one of the issues discussed. If that group's norm is to pay child support, the individual member's behavior will be affected, and payment will be more likely the norm than if the topic never comes up.

The amounts that the mothers said they paid in child support ranged from $1 to $125 per week, with $50 being the most common amount paid (1983 figures). The mean payment the mothers were making per week was $40.37. When the number of children being raised elsewhere is factored in, the mean amount being paid per child is $28.67. PWP members were paying slightly more per child than mothers in the other group—$31.13 as compared with $25.32.[10] Among the seventy-one mothers paying child support were nine who had split custody. The majority of the mothers with split custody were raising fewer children than the father. For example, a mother who retained custody of one child may have been paying some child support to a father who was raising two of their children.

Looking at the percentage of mothers who are paying support and their incomes, we can make a few tentative comments. It is note-worthy that, given the changing role of women, only 14 percent are paying support. It must be mentioned, though, that, in many cases, other forms of "payment" are being made. Although they are not giving money, mothers could be helping out with the purchase of clothes, gifts, education, and health care plans and still claim they are not paying any actual child support. These in-kind payments can be quite helpful to the custodial father.

The 14 percent of noncustodial mothers who are paying child support can be compared with census data from 1983 (U.S. Department of Commerce, 1986a) showing that about one-third of the mothers with custody receive some child support payments from the fathers. (Remember that not all single mothers are awarded child support.) To compare further, the noncustodial mothers in our study were earning an average of $16,298, similar to the amount earned by all men in the United States[11] and more than $2,500 above the earnings of the average working single mother in 1983.[12] The mean amount paid for child support was also virtually the same—an annual rate of $2,099 paid by the mothers in our study versus $2,340 received by the custodial mothers in the Census Bureau report.

The points we wish to make from these comparisons (allowing for differences related to sample bias) are (1) that fewer women than men pay support when they are the noncustodial parents and (2) that, at least for this group of mothers, mothers who are paying support are paying roughly the same percentage of their income as fathers who pay support. Hence, although fewer mothers than fathers pay support, when mothers *do* pay, they often pay roughly the same percentage of their income. We hypothesized that one explanation for this could have been that the mothers who were paying support were those who had most recently become noncustodial and that recent legal changes had affected them. Yet when we factored in the number of years that mothers who were paying child support had been noncustodial and compared that number with mothers not paying child support, we found no differences. We believe one explanation for this payment pattern is that it is a reflection of our society's dichotomous view of women: on the one hand, women are protected (from paying); on the other, they are held strictly to a man's standard.

Mothers Who Pay versus Those Who Do Not Pay

We were able to compare characteristics of mothers who pay support and those who do not. We found the following:

1. Mothers who paid support were earning a higher income than those who did not. The payers earned an average annual salary of $19,210, versus $15,670 for those who did not pay support.[13]

2. Mothers who paid support were less likely to have split custody than those who did not pay support. Approximately 14 percent of the payers had split custody versus 36 percent of those not paying.[14]

3. Mothers who paid support tended to describe themselves as more involved with the children living away from them[15] and said that they were consulted more frequently by the children's caretaker (usually the father) than the mothers who did not pay support.[16]

We had expected that mothers with higher incomes would be more likely to pay support. They have greater means and also are more likely to be asked to pay by judges and by husbands. We had also expected that a mother would be more likely to pay if she did not have custody of any children. When children are being raised in both homes, it would be unlikely to expect the mother, who is probably earning less money, to pay the father.

The third finding has to do with the amount of contact the mother has with the children. The finding that mothers who paid support felt more involved and were consulted more is probably a reflection of a more positive toned relationship that developed at the time of the marital breakup. Yet there was no link between the reason for the divorce and the custody decision and payment of child support. Thus, this relationship may have developed for different reasons, not as the result of an evolving relationship beginning at the time of the breakup. Rather, payment in and of itself may set off a relationship that is characterized by more involvement but may not necessarily be characterized by better feelings.

Some variables that we found were *not* related to the mother's paying support were the reasons for the divorce; the reasons for custody going to the father; the number of years of being noncustodial; the age, sex, and number of children living elsewhere; the mother's marital status, whether a stepmother was involved in parenting, and the mother's attitudes about herself. We were surprised that the reasons for the custody decision were not related. We had believed, for example, that mothers who gave a court decision as a reason for not having custody would be the most likely to pay support, as they would have been asked to pay at the time of the custody decision. The characteristics of the children were also not related to support payments. Mothers who were living apart from a large number of children were no more likely to pay support than those who were living apart from one child. Also, younger children were no more likely to be the recipients of child support than older ones. Finally, the marital status of either partner had no effect. Mothers who had remarried were not more likely to pay than mothers who had not. The reason might be that even though these mothers had higher family incomes when their new husbands' incomes were added, some may have felt that their incomes had to be used for the new family and perhaps for children that their new husbands brought into the marriage. Even more surprising was the finding that the father's remarriage was not related to whether the mother paid child support. Apparently, the presence of a second potential wage earner in the father's home is unrelated to whether the mother pays.

The Mothers' Reasons for Paying or for Not Paying

The foregoing discussion centered on the amount of support paid and a comparison of the characteristics of mothers who pay and mothers who do not pay. We gained further insight about support payments from our interviews with the mothers. The reasons the mothers gave for paying or for not paying tended to fall into broad categories. At times, more than one reason applied in one situation. Generally, most of the arrangements that have been reached, amicably or otherwise, have not involved the courts.

Reasons Why Mothers Pay Support

Some mothers pay support because they are required to do so by the court. Increasingly, the courts are holding noncustodial mothers responsible for making child support payments. Some of these mothers resent paying support and would not do so if they had not been forced to; others accept it as part of their responsibility, although they might not pay if they did not have to.

One example is Louise, who is now 34. She lost a custody battle to her husband and was subsequently ordered to pay child support. At the time, she was earning much less than her husband. The judge, without giving an explanation, set the payment level at $20 a week. Now, seven years later, she is paying the same amount, although her income as a secretary has nearly doubled to $18,000. Her ex-husband and his new wife have a combined income of more than $60,000. Her ex-husband has never taken her back to court or asked for more, and Louise has never taken steps to change the payment level. Although Louise hates paying, she claims that she has never missed a payment: "It really hurts having to write a check every week. I know my ex-husband doesn't need it." Louise understands the rationale behind her paying support but at the same time feels that it should not have to be done unless her ex-husband needed the money.

Some mothers pay because they consider it the "fair" thing to do. In this group are mothers who believe that they should make at least some payment to the benefit of their children whether or not they were ordered to do so by the courts. They see payment as part of their continuing responsibility to their children. A few see it as a way of helping out the father. Some mothers feel that it is fair for them to pay because their ex-husbands made payments to them when they had custody. There are mothers in this group earning less than $10,000 a year and making payments of one or two dollars a week as well as mothers earning much more and making substantial payments.

Josie, a 41-year-old store manager, earns $26,000. She had custody of her son when she first separated. Her husband was "fanatical" about making his child support payments, always making them on time. When Josie's oldest son became a discipline problem, he went to live with his father, who had remarried. Josie said, "It is only fair that I pay him now that he has our son. He always paid me. I send $40 a week." Josie does not know how much her husband earns as a salesman but believes it is higher than her income.

Some mothers pay so that they can stay involved with the children. They feel that it entitles them to greater involvement in the children's life. These mothers are keenly aware of protecting their own rights. They know that child support payments are one tool they can use if they wish to stay involved with their children or if they wish to contest custody. Occasionally, it is the ex-husband's behavior that forces a mother to use money as a lever. The ex-husband may have threatened to withhold visitation unless payments were made.

Alice, 43, has worked at a variety of jobs. She is currently earning $18,000 as an export manager. She gave up custody of her daughter when the daughter developed academic problems. Alice worried that she would lose her influence in her daughter's life, so she insisted on paying $40 a week in child support. Her daughter's behavior and age were part of the motivation. "She is 16 and 16-year-olds know where money comes from. I did not want her to forget that I could help her out, too." The support arrangement was written into the custody agreement. "When I pay, I feel I have a right to know what is going on with her. I can see how some [noncustodial] fathers feel about paying now. I am never really happy about how the money is spent." The arrangement is working well for Alice. She describes herself as being very involved with her daughter.

Reasons Why Mothers Do Not Pay Support

Most mothers are not paying for financial reasons. As mentioned earlier, many mothers feel either that they cannot afford to pay support or that there is no justification for them to pay someone who has a higher income than they do. This is the most frequently given reason and the one that stirs up the most controversy. Among this group are mothers who are in contempt of court for nonpayment as well as mothers who are receiving alimony from their ex-husbands. A few of the mothers were mentally incapacitated and had no visible means of support other than their parents or relatives.

Jan, a 41-year-old mother of two, worked part-time as a nurse's aide when she and her husband divorced. Her current income is $17,000 a year. Concerning payment of child support, she said, "He earned more money than me and I was just scraping by when he took custody. He never asked for it and I never offered it."

Some mothers are not paying support because the judge and/or the father did not require it or request it. This reason can be subsumed under the first reason and is frequently related to the mother's lack of financial resources. In one case, there was no law in existence at the time of the custody decision that would require the mother to pay. It has been noted elsewhere that, in the past, judges have sometimes been reluctant to ask a mother to pay child support if she is relinquishing custody.[17] The impression was that a judge may feel that the mother has suffered sufficiently in losing custody in court and that asking her to pay child support would be pouring salt in her wounds. It was also noted that fathers are sometimes reluctant to ask for child support payments. They may believe that it is not "masculine" for them to accept payments from the wife they supported during the marriage. Some fathers may not ask for payments because they believe that the mother might some day use her payment of support as a sign to the courts that she has remained responsible for the children and thereby gain custody.

Roberta, 51, has worked sporadically as a waitress. As primary custodian for the first four years after the breakup, she received most of the support payments she was owed as well as alimony. Her daughter now lives with Roberta's ex-husband. When the new custody arrangement was approved by the court, Roberta was not aked to pay. "My husband was a professional man. We went to court. The judge never said anything to me about paying."

Sophie, 37, is a counselor. Her husband would not accept the child support payments that Sophie sent. The checks were always returned. Sophie is not sure why he will not take the money but believes it is related to Sophie's remarriage. She has stopped sending the money.

Some mothers are not paying support because their ex-husbands did not pay them when they had custody. The mothers in this fairly large group had been owed money from a few months to the whole time they had custody. Some had even lost custody because the father never paid support. Now that the father has custody, the mother has no intention of paying him money that she is still owed from when she was the custodial parent.

Lindsey, 34, is a government employee earning $22,000 a year. She had sole custody of her two children originally and then split custody. More recently, the child living with her has moved out of the house, but her 14-year-old son lives with her ex-husband. She does not pay any support because her husband still owes her $10,000 from when she was the primary caretaker. They have not gone back to court yet on this matter, but she vows "never to pay a cent until I get paid what I am owed first." She has not seen her son in the six months since he left.

Some mothers do not pay child support because they are angry with their ex-husband or their children. A few of the mothers were abused or harshly treated during the marriage, and they feel no obligation to pay anything to someone who treated them so poorly. One or two mothers were not on good terms with their children and had not seen them for long periods of time by either their choice or their children's choice.

Susan, 39, is a waitress. Her response to our question about child support was, "Pay that bastard? Are you kidding? After what he did to me?"

Another mother, Rosemary, had similar words for her ex-husband. She left the marriage and took her daughter with her, leaving her son with her husband. Five years later, he remarried and won custody of the daughter in a court battle. "The court mediator gave my daughter to him because he was married. I spent $5,000 on the case, lost it, and then they expect me to pay child support to him in addition? Forget it."

Conclusions

The debate around child support payments by noncustodial mothers will continue to be heated. More research is needed to determine how successful our present methods are for deciding support levels. We have learned that mothers earning an average of $19,210 are paying approximately $2,000 a year of that income in child support. We do not know how much the custodial fathers who receive these payments are earning, but having that information might help in establishing the wisdom of these mothers' paying slightly more than 10 percent of their income in child support.

Further discussion is needed about whether noncustodial mothers should pay approximately the same percentage of their income as noncustodial fathers do. We question the fairness of this. We believe this situation has evolved from our society's ambivalent view of women. On the one hand, the mother may be protected, rightly or wrongly, by not being expected to pay. On the other hand, when she does pay, she may be held to the same yardstick as the father. These decisions are most often made by judges or by court-appointed mediators on a case-by-case basis, and they may take the relative financial position of the mother and the father into account. More often, though, the position of women in society may be ignored in an attempt to treat women "equally." Because noncustodial mothers who pay support are rare, there are few models to follow. Thus, when their cases come up, they are either held to no standard or to the same standard that is used for fathers.

Holding women to the same standard as fathers ignores some relevant issues concerning the financial history of women in general and of these mothers in particular. In addition, it ignores the income of the father. When noncustodial fathers make payments, it is often to mothers who are earning significantly less than they. For example, if a noncustodial mother pays $2,000 of her $16,000 income to a custodial father who earns $50,000, it will add some but not a great deal to the children's lifestyle. Yet that percentage of her income will certainly affect her lifestyle. When a mother makes payments, she is often paying "up the line" to a man earning more than she. If women are to be held accountable for support payments, a payment schedule should be worked out that is relevant to the financial positions of the noncustodial mothers *and* the custodial fathers, rather than applying the same measures that are used for noncustodial fathers. At the same time, the yardstick must be sex-neutral—that is, taking into account the financial situations of the custodial and noncustodial parents.

Working out such sex-neutral formulas, as the states have attempted in 1987, is quite difficult. Some issues that muddy those formulas are medical insurance, the cost of a lawyer for the less well-to-do parent, college tuition costs, and stepparents. For instance, how do you factor in the income of a stepfather if he, in turn, is paying money to his ex-wife, who is raising children from *that* marriage? And what if one of the items in the stepfather's last divorce settlement is contingent on another stepfather's payments? We can see that concentric circles of child support settlements could stretch across the country. Moreover, even when guidelines are established, they can be set aside by a judge who has additional insight into the case.

The issue of child support payment can place an additional burden on an already stressful relationship. In addition, it has social and political implications that affect legislative policy and collection processes. Furthermore the issue has implications for the way women and mothers are treated and the way they treat themselves. Thus, it is not just the issue of money that is being debated but the broader issue of how women and mothers are going to be viewed in the future.[18]

10

Experiences with the Court System

I do not have custody because my ex-husband gave false testimony in court and made radical efforts to divide and alienate the children from me.

The judge went against Friend of the Court recommendation to give custody to me. There was a long, bitter fight over custody which frightened the children. My husband's attorney pulled several dirty tricks to get custody. Recently he started a lawsuit against me to get child support for my son. He and his new wife earn three times my income, but again it is a revenge tactic to make me pay for embarrassing him. If I had not asked for a divorce, no one would have known the mental anguish he put us through. Also, there is a psychiatrist's report on file, required by the judge, stating that, without extensive therapy, he would not be able to be a good father and husband. Where is justice when you need it?

After an ugly legal battle involving charges that my boyfriend took liberties with my daughter and then my daughter's pregnancy and abortion (she was impregnated by her boyfriend, not mine), the judge, a Roman Catholic, awarded the children to my ex in a fit of moral outrage.

T HESE stories come from women who lost custody of their children in court. In chapter 5, we cited court battles as one of the ways in which mothers can lose custody. In this chapter, we wish to discuss some of the court-related issues in greater depth, as it is in the courts that these mothers experience some of their greatest defeats. As Chesler (1986) asserted, mothers who are good enough to parent have been denied custody. Stories abound among the mothers we interviewed of their being denied custody when they were the most fit parent, the parent who had spent the most time with the children, and the parent who could least afford adequate representation. Fathers have also lost custody when they were the most fit parent and because they were male. Atkinson (1984) noted that the " 'best interest of the child' is the universal standard for deciding child custody when custody is initially determined at the time of dissolution of marriage" (p. 4). What actually happens in court in a custody dispute is sometimes just and sometimes fickle. It can vary from state to state, from county to county, from judge to judge, and from case to case, and it can work against either parent. Before it seems that we are condemning the court systems, it is important to add that making custody decisions can be an incredibly difficult job. There are laws intended to make custody decisions more equitable and predictable, but no amount of legislation will be able to cover every situation with which a judge is faced. And these problems are not going to go away. There are strong indications that the number of custody disputes is increasing.[1]

Atkinson (1984) cited several criteria that have been used in deciding disputed custody cases: maternal preference, which parent has been the primary caretaker, which parent will be more available to spend time with the child, who has been with the child since the original custody decision was made, stability of the environment which refers to how well the child has been doing where he is, the child's preference, and visitation availability. Polikoff (1982) found that the earning power of each of the parents has also been used as a criterion.

When there are disputes about custody, one possible solution is shared, or joint, custody. More than half of the states now have provisions for joint custody.[2] In some of those states, there is a joint custody presumption; that is, the guidelines indicate that a cause has to be given in the custody agreement for why custody of the children is *not* being shared.

Once a custody decision has been made, the ease with which it can be changed varies from state to state. A recent New Hampshire decision ruled that a child of "mature age" can decide if he wants to live with his noncustodial parent.[3] (The child in the case was 13.)

The child does not have to be at risk for a change to be made in custody. In Illinois, the opposite may be true. In a case tried in the same year as the New Hampshire decision (1986), modification of custody within two years of the original custody decision was prohibited, except in emergency situations or when there is clear endangerment.[4] Atkinson (1984) stated that most states require a "substantial and material" change in the custodial parent's or the child's circumstances before a custody order can be modified. Improved financial and emotional conditions of the noncustodial parent are usually not sufficient.

About 10 percent of the mothers in our study lost custody in court battles. One of four reasons was usually given: (1) they were found to be unfit, (2) they could not afford to raise the children, (3) the children chose the father, or (4) the father was the more qualified parent. Sometimes, although a mother may want to do battle with the father, she is either too financially or emotionally drained to undertake the long and expensive process. Some mothers avoid a battle because they feel they cannot hire as good a lawyer as their husbands can. They withdraw without actually going to court.

It is important to highlight another reason why mothers do not go into court. We asked the mothers whether they agreed with the statement: "My pursuing custody would have been hard on the children." Almost two-thirds (62 percent) of the mothers agreed. Thus, many mothers may avoid court battles because they are aware of the toll such a fight can have on their children.

How the Courts Decide

The procedure followed when a case does come to court varies according to the mechanism in effect in that court system. Some counties have personnel on staff who routinely deal with cases that are being adjudicated; other counties have consultants who are hired on an as-needed basis; and many have no procedures in place to help the family or judge arrive at a decision.

One example of how the courts can work cooperatively with mental health professionals can be found in Baltimore.[5] When a custody dispute comes into the city court system, it is assigned to the staff psychologists for evaluation. The procedure used for evaluating which parent should have custody is usually the following:

1. All of the adults involved in child care are interviewed. This includes not only the parents but also the grandparents and any other significantly involved people.

2. The parents (assuming that they are the ones contesting custody, though it could be a parent and a grandparent or some other combination) are given a battery of psychological tests to help determine their "fitness" as parents.

3. The children are interviewed individually to learn about their interactions with their parents and their wishes about custody.

4. Depending upon the age of the child, the child and each parent may be observed playing together.

5. Depending upon the circumstances, someone from the courts may visit the homes.

6. Records from school personnel and pediatricians are reviewed.

Besides taking psychological tests, the parents are interviewed extensively about their own families, their work history, the reasons for the divorce, their plans for allowing visitation, their prior involvement in raising the children, whether they have a criminal record, their future plans for marriage, whether they are dating anyone, what they see as the role of a parent in raising the children, and anything else deemed relevant.

The stability of the prospective households is a major factor in deciding where custody will reside. A parent with permanence at an address and the presence of a long-term adult–adult relationship would be valued over a parent in physical and emotional transition. For example, if a gay parent is seeking custody, sexual orientation would not be held against him or her if the relationship of the gay parent is consistent and enduring. The nature of the parent's home life is what is considered important.

The relative incomes of the parents can be a factor, but it is always weighed against other considerations. An example of a custody battle in which income was considered but was not an overriding factor was a dispute over a 12-year-old girl. The father was making a very good income and was willing to send the daughter to a private school. The mother was living in a very small shore community and was on welfare. Despite the advantages that the father could buy for the daughter, the court personnel determined that the daughter should stay with her mother. The reason was simple: She had formed a much better relationship with her mother than with her father.

The Baltimore courts appear to be as willing to give custody to the father as to the mother. Decisions are based on the merits of the case, not on the sex of the parent. There are a variety of ways in which a mother may become noncustodial. In a common scenario, a mother leaves the home, her husband, and the children for a variety of reasons, many of them honorable. She works to improve her position financially and emotionally and, a few months to a few years after leaving, sues for custody. By this time, she may have a stable job and a stable relationship, none of which she had when she first left the marriage. During her absence, though, the children have formed a strong bond with their father, who is parenting competently. It would be difficult for the mother to get custody under those circumstances.

In one situation, a dispute arose over custody of an 8-year-old girl. Following the divorce, the mother got custody, and both parents remarried. The mother then separated from her second husband and began living with her boyfriend and receiving welfare. The father, who had married a schoolteacher, had liberal visitation rights and took his daughter on the weekends. Very often, the daughter did not want to return to her mother's home. She told her father that she did not like taking care of the boyfriend's 4-year-old daughter. She also complained about being examined physically every day by her mother. (No sexual abuse charges were leveled). The daughter was not doing well in school and was displaying many signs of depression. The father sought to have custody reversed.

The mother was interviewed and agreed that the physical examinations were taking place and said they were being performed for health reasons. The mother displayed no insight about her daughter's discomfort with the procedure and had no idea why her daughter was depressed. During the course of the custody evaluation, therapy was recommended by one of the court-appointed evaluators to help alleviate the depression. The therapist noticed a marked improvement in the girl after she had spent time with her father. The recommendation was for the father to have custody. The judge interviewed the daughter in his chambers and agreed to the change of custody. One year later, the child was doing much better.

Once a recommendation for custody is made to the judge, it may include such specifics as how much visitation should be allowed, the way the visitation should be scheduled, whether the visitation should be supervised, and whether parenting courses are advised for either the custodial or the noncustodial parent. Sometimes the recommendations concerning visitation arrangements can be quite specific. For example, they might state that one parent should give the children breakfast in the morning before they are picked up by the other parent or that visitation time should commence at exactly 7 o'clock in the evening. Joint custody may also be a recommendation.

Divorce mediation is sometimes used by divorcing parents to help settle their differences without hiring lawyers. A divorce mediator can be hired by the court or by the parents before they get to court. Divorce mediators are considered less expensive and less likely to engender ill feelings than lawyers.

A divorce mediator, whose training could be as a lawyer or as a mental health professional, might help resolve such common issues as child care, property division, child support, alimony, the resolution of debts, how income taxes will be filed, health insurance, pets, and child visitation. Where children are concerned, in addition to custody and visitation, such issues as medical care, religion, discipline, and education may be negotiated.

Our Research in the Courts: 400 Cases

To learn more about the trends in the court system in Baltimore County we examined the court records of 400 cases.[6] Baltimore County (which borders the city of Baltimore) has a population of over 650,000. The racial composition of the county is similar to, though slightly more white than, that of the United States; 90 percent of the population is white, 8.2 percent black, 0.8 percent Hispanic, and 1 percent other. In 1980, the average income per household was $24,800. In the United States in 1980, the average family income was $21,023.[7] Baltimore County is slightly more affluent than the U.S. average and probably closely approximates the average income of families involved in PWP.

We reviewed courts records: (1) to see if there was a clear trend away from mothers getting custody; (2) to learn more about what happened to mothers who lost custody in court; and (3) to learn about patterns of child support payments. Because the original questionnaire had been published in June 1983, we chose that month as a starting point and reviewed the first fifty decrees of divorce that were filed in the county in that month. Using June as a benchmark, we looked at more recent cases, those filed in June 1984, June 1985, June 1986, and June 1987. The next time period we selected was June 1978, a year in which many of the mothers in our survey either were getting a divorce or were considering such action. We then chose two earlier dates, of June 1968 and June 1973, in further search of trends. Only cases in which minor children were involved were counted. Table 10–1 presents a breakdown of the cases.

Before discussing our findings, a brief review of the legal climate over the time period covered is necessary. Five changes in Maryland between 1973 and 1978, most of which improved a father's position, may partially explain what has happened to mothers in court. One change that worked to the mother's benefit was the change in the adultery presumption. In the past in Maryland, if a mother committed adultery, it was presumed that she was unfit as a mother. The burden of proof was on her to prove her parental competence. This presumption was tossed out in 1977. Another change involved no-fault divorce. No-fault divorce, which had been creeping onto the books in Maryland since the 1930s, became easier to achieve with a new law in 1978. With its passage, if a couple agreed to separate for three years (a reduction from the previous five-year requirement), they could then have a no-fault divorce. Cause was no longer needed for a divorce. Three other changes occurred that did not help the

Table 10–1

CUSTODY AWARDS IN BALTIMORE COUNTY IN
SEVEN SELECTED YEARS

(n = 400; 50 cases/year)

Year	Mother	Father	Joint	Grandmother
1968	41 (82%)	8 (16%)	1 (2%)[a]	
1973	44 (88%)	6 (12%)		
Laws changed				
1978	46 (92%)	2 (4%)	2 (4%)	
1983	45 (90%)	2 (4%)	3 (6%)	
1984	42 (84%)	2 (4%)	6 (12%)	
1985	40 (80%)	5 (10%)	5 (10%)	
1986	36 (72%)	6 (12%)	7 (14%)	1 (2%)
1987	35 (70%)	5 (10%)	10 (20%)	

[a]The term used in this case was "shared custody."

mother seeking sole custody. First, the ERA was passed in Maryland in 1972, which meant that women and men were going to be held to a more equal standard. Second, in 1974 the Maryland General Assembly disavowed using maternal preference in custody cases. Finally, joint custody came into fashion.

Since 1978, we can see a clear trend away from mothers getting sole custody and toward fathers being more involved.[8] This may be due, especially in the most recent years, to the father's improved legal status and to the increase in joint custody. We found a high percentage of fathers getting custody in 1968 and in 1973, which was most likely due to the bias against the mother if she committed adultery. In looking at the complete court records of five of the 1968 cases, we found that four of them included charges of adultery against the mother. The statistics also showed that, despite the media attention given to fathers recently if they are sole custodians, fathers have been raising children alone for a long time, at least in Baltimore County.

Noncustodial Mothers' Court Battles

We looked in depth at thirty cases in which the mother did not have custody to see whether she had fought for custody or had voluntarily given up custody. Often, in reading through an actual case record, it was difficult to determine the point at which custody of the children was decided. If there was any mention of the mother wanting custody, either in the court transcript or in any written document from the mother or her lawyer, we considered that she was fighting for custody. It should be noted that court records do not provide a complete picture; they usually include only the statements of the parties involved, with no indication of whether the judge or the master hearing the case believed either party's charges. No insight is given into how a judge ultimately made a decision. As mentioned elsewhere, we are aware that many of these decisions are made outside of the court and may involve a good deal of coercion or manipulation on either parent's part. A father may threaten to withhold alimony if his wife attempts to gain custody. A mother may threaten to sue for custody unless she receives a certain settlement.

Thus, a custody battle may occur even if a parent does not want the children and is using the children to gain something else.

Of the thirty noncustodial mother cases, custody was apparently uncontested in twenty-three (77 percent) of the records. In one of the remaining seven cases, both parents agreed that the maternal grandmother should have custody. In the other six (20 percent), the mother fought for custody at some point in the divorce proceedings and lost. A number of the thirty cases also contained lengthy records of child support disputes. No trend was found in terms of awarding custody of boys to their fathers. Split custody was not awarded in any of the cases. In a few cases, child custody was reversed later, about half the time without a fight. Some of those reversals were among the twenty-three in which there had been original contest.

In one case, for example, two years after a father had been granted custody without a battle, he was sued by his ex-wife. She charged him with sexually abusing their daughter. He fought her in court and lost. She now has custody. In another case, a father who originally had won custody without a battle later gave it up without a battle. His daughter chose to live with her mother instead of him. The mother wanted custody legalized, took the father to court, and sued for child support, which she eventually won.

Many of the mothers who did not contest custody never showed up for the court hearings. Either they ignored the court date or sent a letter stating that they agreed that the father should have custody. In some of those cases, according to the testimony of the father and his witness, the mother deserted, often with a lover. When mothers did come for the court hearing in an uncontested case, they usually stated that the father was the more fit parent.

Examples of reversal of custody against the mother can also be found among the six cases in which the mothers fought and lost. One mother who originally had been given custody was sued by her husband, who charged her with physically abusing two of their children. She fought the charges but lost. One case in which the mother never had custody involved a series of allegations and counter-allegations. The mother charged the father with physically threatening her, throwing her out of the house, changing the locks on the door, and barring her from visiting the children. The father charged the mother with having sex with her lover in the house and in front of the children. The father won custody but was not awarded child support; he sued for it and lost.

Child Support Payments

We looked in depth at the pattern of child support payments for the month that the survey began, June 1983, and also for a more recent month, June 1986.[9] One of the two mothers who was noncustodial in 1983 was held accountable for child support of $25 a week for one child. In the three cases of joint custody, the father was held responsible for child support in one of the cases ($40 a week for two children), and expenses were shared in the other two. The mothers were never held responsible for support at the time of the divorce decree when there was a joint determination. In thirty-nine of the forty-five cases in which custody went to the mother, the father was held responsible for support at the time of the divorce decree.[10] The amount of child support the fathers paid varied from a low of $20 a week for one child to a high of $212 a week for two children. The most common award was $25 a week per child; $50 a week was the second most common award. The average amount of support paid by the thirty-nine fathers for the sixty children living with their mothers was $60 a week, or a little over $39 a child.

In June 1986, none of the six mothers without custody was ordered in the divorce decree to pay support. This was surprising to us because of the case that had turned up in June 1983. We randomly searched through the early months of 1986 and found twelve more cases in which fathers were granted custody. Only one of the twelve mothers was ordered to pay any specific amount. In addition, in the seven joint custody cases, none of the mothers was ordered to pay support. In those cases, both parents were held responsible, the father was ordered to pay, or it was not specified.

Of the thirty-six mothers with custody in 1986 whose decrees we examined, child support awards were made in twenty-eight cases. The range of payments in this group went from a low of $25 for one child to a high of $300 a week for two children. The average support paid by the twenty-eight fathers for their forty children was $73.50 a week, or approximately $50 per child. An award of $50 per child was by far the most common amount.

What we found from our review of the records was a surprisingly low number of support payments awarded to custodial fathers at the time of the decree (two in twenty). As noted in the preceding chapter, this is not to say that some sort of financial or in-kind payment was not forthcoming, just that it was not court-mandated at the time of the custody decision. Thus, in comparing outcomes at the time of the divorce decree, we can see that many more noncustodial fathers were being ordered to pay than noncustodial mothers.

Conclusions

The court systems have been shifting increasingly in favor of fathers and in favor of joint custody awards. Mothers are now much more likely not to have full custody. The gender of the parent is less of a consideration than before when cases are disputed, although the outcome in these cases may be decided idiosyncratically. Many cases in which the mother becomes noncustodial are not disputed. In the nondisputed cases, the mother may have struck a bargain with the father, may not have wanted custody, may have been threatened by the father, or may have believed that a battle would be detrimental to the children. Despite increasing equality of the sexes, the vast majority of noncustodial mothers are absolved of paying child support.

The financial position of women in the United States puts them clearly at a disadvantage in many cases. Money plays a part in some mothers' decision not to pursue custody and in their losing custody when it is pursued. Custody and child support cases can cost thousands of dollars and can take months to resolve. The mother, because of her lower income, is often the underdog in many of these situations.

We have a court system that is often trying to make impossible decisions. At times it succeeds for all concerned, but at other times it may work against those whom it is intended to serve.

11

Noncustodial Mothers and Noncustodial Fathers: A Study in Contrasts

T HROUGHOUT this book we have been relating the experiences of noncustodial mothers to those of custodial fathers who were studied in 1982. Those comparisons have provided a counterbalance—a way of looking at the situations of the mothers from the fathers' perspective and a way of getting a more systemic view of the life of the noncustodial mother. This chapter compares the noncustodial mothers with a different population—noncustodial fathers. The purpose of the comparisons is to show the differences and the similarities among fathers and mothers when they are noncustodial. As will be seen, there are few areas in which the fathers' experiences are much better than the mothers'. This might be expected when comparisons are made between parents in a traditional role (noncustodial fathers) and parents in a nontraditional role (noncustodial mothers). In no areas do the fathers fare significantly worse than the mothers, and in some areas there are striking similarities.

The Noncustodial Fathers

Our sample of forty-seven fathers was gathered in 1986 from PWP social functions in the Baltimore-Washington area. Fathers without custody of a child 18 or younger were asked to complete the same questionnaire the noncustodial mothers had completed with minor word changes on the questionnaire to allow for discrepancies between asking questions of mothers and fathers.

Any conclusions from comparisons of the sample of 517 mothers with these 47 fathers must be drawn with caution because of the way the studies were carried out. The fathers were approached as they were going into a social event whereas the mothers received their questionnaires in a magazine (the PWP sample) or at a meeting (the Mothers Without Custody or networking sample) and could fill them out in the privacy of their homes. In addition, the fathers could ask for clarification on the purpose of the study or the meanings of certain questions, an option not afforded the mothers.[1] Despite these limitations, however, we believe that the opportunity to compare the responses of these male and female parents is valuable in helping us understand the effect of being female or male on the noncustodial parent.

Backgrounds

The fathers' average age was 40.25. On the average, they had been noncustodial for a little over four years—about the same length of time they had been separated or divorced from their wives. The average length of the marriages was nearly ten years. Some of the fathers had only recently separated; others had been single for up to thirteen years.

The forty-seven fathers were living away from sixty-nine children 18 or under, over 60 percent of them female. The children's average age was 11.7. Seven fathers had split custody, and five of the seven children living with the fathers were male.

What most obviously separated this sample of fathers from the sample of mothers was income. These fathers had an average income of $31,794, whereas the mothers had an average income of $16,298 in 1983. This great difference proved to be consistent with other samples. The single custodial fathers interviewed in 1982 had an average income of $28,325, whereas a comparison sample of 150 custodial mothers in 1983 had an average income of $15,642.[2]

Occupations among these fathers varied from U.S. Marine, student, and welder, to letter carrier, engineer, and attorney. Their education also ranged from one man who had completed ninth grade to a few who had master's degrees and one who had a doctorate.

Slightly more than half of the fathers had not completed a four-year college. Of those giving a religious affiliation, Catholics were the most highly represented, followed by Protestants, Baptists, Jews, and others.

Thirty-three fathers (65 percent) reported that they were paying child support. The average amount of child support paid was $98 a week. About a quarter of their ex-wives had remarried.

Reasons Given for the Divorce

Two main reasons were given for the divorce by the thirty-two fathers who answered the question. Nineteen fathers (59 percent) linked the divorce to shared reasons—communication problems, incompatibility, growing apart, and boredom. This was a higher percentage than we found in the mothers' study, where the figure was about 45 percent. The second reason, given by seven fathers (22 percent), tied the divorce to the wife's infidelity. Virtually the same percentage of the noncustodial mothers blamed their divorce on the husband's infidelity. The other reasons were scattered and were mentioned by no more than two fathers. Thirteen fathers said they initiated the divorce, twenty-four said the wife did, and ten said it was a mutual decision. These figures are consistent with other findings that wives are more likely to end a marriage than husbands.[3]

Reasons Given for the Custody Decision

The reasons the fathers gave for custody going to the mothers were markedly different from those given by the noncustodial mothers. In fact, the whole orientation of the responses exemplifies the differences in many people's view of the importance of a mother to the children. Sixteen of the thirty-nine fathers who answered said that they do not have custody because they believe that children should be with their mother. The responses included: "Mothers are better," "Children need their mother," "Young children need their mother," and "She is a good mother." One father wrote that it had never occurred to him to seek custody. The implication in many of these answers was that the mother was more competent to parent than the father because of her sex. Virtually none of the noncustodial mothers gave this type of reason why the father had custody, whereas 40 percent of the fathers gave it. With this response, in its baldest sense, we have the primary difference between the orientations of the non-custodial father and the noncustodial mother. A significant per-centage see custody of the children as the mother's province.

The reason given second most frequently, by ten of the fathers, was that it was in the best interests of the children to stay with their mother in their own home and neighborhood. These situations tended to emerge when the father was leaving the home following a marital breakup. The father believed that the children should stay where they were rather than go with him into a smaller apartment or a new neighborhood. One father wrote, "My son is better off with his friends, schoolmates, family, and relatives. It would be too traumatic to remove him from this environment and subject him to my current single lifestyle." Two fathers mentioned that they did not attempt to gain split custody because it was best for siblings to stay together. Approximately the same percentage of the mothers (24 percent) gave the best interests of the child as the reason they did not get custody.

Two reasons were each mentioned by four fathers: the children chose the mother and custody was decided by mutual agreement. Two fathers lost court battles, and a third said he did not attempt to get custody because he was convinced he could not win a court battle. One father had custody for three years, felt it was not working out well for the child, and turned him over to the mother. He described his situation this way, "After three years in my custody, I felt I wasn't doing right by him. He was only seven years old when I gave up custody. I got the distinct feeling he needed his mother more than me."

The issues surrounding custody are obviously different for moth-ers and for fathers. One stands out. Many men agree that the mother should have custody because she is the mother, and the question of getting the children never arises. For those who do consider getting custody, their reasons for not having it are similar to those of the noncustodial mothers.

Like the mothers, some of the fathers were clearly angry at the custody outcome. One father wrote, "The children made their own choice. They were brainwashed by their helpless mommy." Another wrote, "The courts historically favor maternal custody. The judicial system is not fair or just."

Two fathers talked about their guilt. One father who ended the marriage said, "At the time I never thought of having custody. I was only feeling guilty for leaving." Another father wrote, "It is lonely and I do feel guilty about not seeing the children more." (He spends eight nights a month with them.)

Visitation

The fathers visited their children fairly frequently. Nineteen of the forty-seven reported visits once a week or more, and another fourteen said that they saw their children at least every other week. Thus, almost two-thirds of the fathers saw their children at least every other week (whereas only 51 percent of the noncustodial mothers said that they visited that frequently.) This amount of visitation by the noncustodial father is consistent with findings of other researchers (see Koch and Lowery, 1984). Three fathers visited their children once a month, and four fathers saw their children only in the summer or for holidays. Two fathers said that their ex-wives were withholding visitation, and another father said that he saw his children about once a year. The fathers said that their children spent an average of 2.5 overnights a month with them on a regular basis. One-third of the fathers said that their children spent no overnights with them. This pattern of visitation shows greater involvement than the noncustodial mothers described when they were asked the same questions. Another way to consider these responses is to compare the frequency of visitation with the responses given by the 1,136 fathers and 150 mothers with custody reported on elsewhere. Approximately 45 percent of each of those sets of parents said that the noncustodial parent visited at least once every two weeks.[4]

Comparisons of Responses

We selected for comparison eighteen key items from the questionnaire that tap into a variety of the fathers' and mothers' experiences. In half of the cases, the answers were significantly different.

Relationships with the Children

We examined the responses to several questions that looked at the fathers' relationships with their children. These questions covered the father's involvement with the children, the satisfaction he felt about the children, a rating of himself as a parent and a rating of the mother, and whether he was content with the custody situation.

When we asked the fathers how involved they were in the lives of their children, we found that they felt significantly more involved with their children than the noncustodial mothers did.[5] This did not necessarily mean that they *are* more involved, but only that their impression of their involvement was greater.

We also asked the fathers if the children's caretaker (in all forty-seven cases, the mother) consulted them about the children. Thirty percent said that they were consulted frequently, whereas only 11 percent of the noncustodial mothers said that they were consulted frequently.[6] As discussed earlier, visitation is sometimes related to better feelings between the parents and, hence, more contact concerning the children. Therefore, where there is more visitation, there is often more consultation. Other explanations are possible. The fact that more of the noncustodial mothers' than the noncustodial fathers' custody decisions were decided adversarially could lead to less contact between noncustodial mothers and custodial fathers.

When we asked the fathers their level of satisfaction with their relationships with the children, we found that the fathers were more satisfied than the noncustodial mothers were.[7] This difference could reflect a number of things. It could be that because the noncustodial mothers are in a nontraditional role, they are more prone to feel dissatisfied with their situation. It could also reflect the processes that led up to the custody situation. For example, it is possible that, in some cases, more problems may have existed between mother and child, leading to the mother's becoming noncustodial, than would have existed in the more common situation of a father becoming noncustodial.

The fathers were asked their level of satisfaction with the children's progress in most areas of their lives. As in the previous question, there was a difference between the answers of the two groups, with the fathers clearly more satisfied.[8] Again, this could reflect the more common situation of the fathers versus the mothers.

The fathers were asked whether they agreed with the statement: "My ex-wife was a more competent parent than I when she first got the children." Twenty-six percent agreed, 27 percent were mixed, and 47 percent disagreed. Here, the mothers were much more likely to disagree with the statement (67 percent disagreed), perhaps pointing out the difficult circumstances under which many mothers give up custody.[9] Even though the mothers generally felt more competent, they still ended up without custody for financial, legal, and personal reasons, or by choice of the children. Nevertheless, 20 percent of the mothers did feel less competent than the fathers. It is important to note that the question forces the respondent to make an evaluative decision about the other parent's competence as compared to his or her own. Therefore, respondents who agreed that the other parent was more competent would not necessarily believe that they, themselves, were incompetent.

The fathers were asked whether they agreed with the statement: "The children are better off where they are." This item attempts to tap into the parents' satisfaction with the custody arrangement. Twenty-four percent of the fathers agreed, 50 percent were mixed, and 26 percent disagreed. We had hypothesized that the fathers would be more likely to agree with the statement because many fathers believe that children should be with their mothers. In fact, a slightly higher percentage of mothers agreed (32 percent) although the differences are not significant. Many noncustodial mothers were convinced that the children were better off with the fathers, although an almost equal percentage (33 percent) were not convinced. The fathers, on the other hand, were less sure about this, as evidenced by the large number of "mixed" responses.

We pressed the fathers further on this issue by asking them whether they agreed with the statement: "The children would prefer living with me." Fifteen percent agreed, 54 percent were mixed, and 31 percent disagreed. Here, the fathers continued to express ambivalence, while admitting that the mother was the preferred parent. Both sets of parents had similar views of themselves in terms of the children's preferences. We were suprised by this finding, as we had believed that the mothers would be much more apt to think that the children wanted to be with them.

Two more questions asked each father to rate the custodial mother as a parent and then to rate himself as a parent. Nearly half of the fathers (49 percent) gave the custodial mothers a rating of excellent or good. The mothers were much less positive about the custodial fathers—34 percent rated them excellent or good—though the differences are not significant. This finding was surprising given that the mothers' situation was more rare. We were expecting the fathers to give higher ratings to the custodial mothers. Our impression is that many more of the mothers are angry with the fathers than the reverse. Although this may be true, such anger does not have a great effect on the rating. In fact, what might have made the ratings more positive was some mothers' need to idealize the fathers' parenting skill in order to make their own noncustodial status more acceptable. That is, the better she feels the father parents, the easier it is for her to be noncustodial. This need to idealize the custodial parent applies to some noncustodial fathers, too. In addition, these mothers, though still angry, were able to separate issues about the marriage from those about the father as a parent. Thus, the anger the mother may have felt did not always influence her perception of the father as a parent.

The self-ratings of the noncustodial fathers and the noncustodial mothers were quite similar. This points out one of the central points of this book—that many noncustodial mothers have adjusted well to their role. Many of them believe that, despite their status, they remain good parents, and their self-esteem as a parent is not inexorably related to society's negative view of a noncustodial mother. In certain cases, their self-rating may even be improved by being noncustodial, as they are acting, in their own eyes, like a good parent by not holding on to custody.

These nine items have afforded a close look at some of the differences and similarities between noncustodial mothers and fathers concerning the rearing of their children. In five of the nine questions, the differences between the groups were significant. The fathers reported a higher level of involvement and satisfaction with the children. The mothers were less likely to feel that the father was the more competent parent. The two sets of parents did not differ on their ratings of themselves or in their beliefs about the children's preferences or about where the children are better off.

At least two different, though not necessarily conflicting, interpretations are possible. The noncustodial father's relationship with his children and his more positive evaluation of it may be due, in part, to the possibility that the children being raised away from their father are adapting better than the children being raised away from their mother. They may be doing better, in part, because of the noncustodial father's greater involvement with them or because they are in a more traditional living situation than that of children with noncustodial mothers. These are important points that are not easily answered by this type of research.[10]

A second interpretation is that the evolution of these custody situations makes them more likely to be satisfactory for the father than for the mother in that it is more common. In addition, many noncustodial mothers suffer more anguish at the hands of society than noncustodial fathers do. This is likely to strain their relationship with the children from everyone's perspective. Furthermore, one manifestation of the mother's nontraditional role is that satisfaction may be harder for her to achieve than it is for the father in the more traditional role.

Becoming Noncustodial

Two questions were chosen that dealt with becoming noncustodial. One asked about the amount of stress associated with giving up custody and the other asked about the voluntary nature of the custody decision. The answers to these questions tell us a great deal about the noncustodial fathers. Custody decisions were stressful for this group. In fact, they were as stressful for the father (64 percent found them very stressful) as for the mothers (77 percent found them very stressful). Apparently, many fathers, like mothers, give up custody reluctantly (28 percent said it was not voluntary) and feel ambivalent about it. It is difficult for them to separate from their children, even though it is the norm. We may need to rethink many of the normative views that we have about men suffering less than women when they are separated from their children. Just because their noncustodial status puts them in a fairly large group with other fathers, this does not mean that it is a comfortable role for many of them.

Social Life, Work, Finances

We compared responses concerning the social lives, the work lives, and the financial situations of these two sets of parents. The noncustodial fathers and noncustodial mothers reported remarkably similar degrees of satisfaction with their social lives (57 percent and 54 percent, respectively, were satisfied). In contrast, when custodial fathers and custodial mothers were asked a similar question, much less satisfaction was expressed (only 30 to 35 percent were pleased with their social lives).[11] Although it is not surprising that noncustodial parents generally have more satisfactory social lives than custodial parents do, it is interesting to see the extent of satisfaction felt by both groups of noncustodial parents. This may be an outgrowth of the women's movement. The noncustodial mothers, while expressing more unhappiness than the noncustodial fathers about many aspects of their lives, are able to enjoy their social lives.

Comparisons of the fathers' and the mothers' satisfaction with their careers indicated that the fathers were slightly more satisfied (52 percent satisfied versus 41 percent of the mothers satisfied). The responses of the mothers could be slightly misleading, as it is hard to know how a mother who was not working would answer the question. (All of the fathers, except for one who was a student, were working.) Our impression from interviews, though, is that many of the mothers were experiencing a number of problems with their careers (see chapter 8). The fathers had been on their career paths longer, so it would be expected that they would have achieved a greater level of satisfaction. Many of the mothers had recently entered or reentered the workforce after having spent years in the home. A few were in training programs or schools. These mothers had a greater distance to climb to reach the career heights of the fathers.

Income and the financial arrangements made at the time of divorce are also important variables related to career satisfaction. Not only do the fathers earn more money than the mothers, they also are more satisfied with their financial situation overall. Fifty-seven percent of the fathers said that they were financially secure, as opposed to 37 percent of the mothers. This major difference is most likely linked to the severe financial shift that many of these mothers have experienced.[12] For the mothers, the feeling of financial insecurity is pervasive.

Feelings about Being Noncustodial

The most significant differences that we found between the fathers and the mothers involved their feelings of guilt about their situation and their impressions of the reactions of others. The mothers were much more likely than the fathers to feel guilt about not having custody.[13] Nearly 60 percent of the fathers are guilt-free, as compared with only 35 percent of the mothers. With this single comparison, we see one way in which the socialization process works against these mothers. Perhaps fueling the guilt are the mothers' perceptions of others' reactions to their noncustodial status (see table 11–1).

Essentially, the fathers did not perceive any negative reactions because they are noncustodial, whereas 65 percent of the mothers felt that they received some negative reactions. As an outgrowth of these negative reactions, the mothers naturally have more difficulty dealing with people's reactions to them. The fathers, in experiencing little that is negative, have less to contend with.

Despite these great disparities in what the fathers and mothers experience, little difference exists between the groups in the comfort they feel as noncustodial parents (37 percent of the fathers and 34 percent of the mothers felt comfortable). This finding was particularly unexpected. Given the nature of the differences that we found in other areas (satisfaction with the children, financial security, and the reactions of others), we had expected that the fathers would feel more comfortable than the mothers. In fact, however, their levels of comfort were very similar. We know, though, that the primary predictor of comfort as a noncustodial parent is whether the custody arrangement was voluntary (see chapter 8), and the voluntary nature of custody did not differ significantly between the groups (although it is a better predictor for mothers than for fathers).[14]

Conclusions

Being a noncustodial parent is different for these 47 fathers than it is for the 517 mothers. The most notable differences are the guilt

Table 11–1
FATHERS' AND MOTHERS' AGREEMENT WITH THE
STATEMENT: "PEOPLE REACT NEGATIVELY TO ME
BECAUSE I DO NOT HAVE CUSTODY"

(percentage)

	Fathers (n = 46)	Mothers (n = 512)
Agree	0	30
Mixed	7	35
Disagree	93	35

$t(556) = 6.876; p < .01$

the mothers feel, the reactions they experience from others, and their financial situations. Economic factors can have a major influence on the lifestyles of these parents. The mothers' relationships with their children are less satisfactory than the fathers', and they feel less involved with the children. Yet, ultimately, the level of comfort in being a noncustodial parent, the extent to which their situations are voluntary, and their satisfaction with social lives and careers are similar.

We learned a great deal about the fathers, too. They are also experiencing a great deal of pain as noncustodial parents—in some areas, as much pain as the mothers. For example, the decision to give up custody was as stressful for them as it was for the mothers. When these two groups are compared, then, we do not find that fathers without custody are better off across the board than mothers without custody. Ultimately, however, the mothers do have more difficulties because of their gender.

12

Help for Noncustodial
Mothers

O NE of the major points that emerges from our findings is that
a mother's being noncustodial does not mean that she is im-
moral, incompetent, or mentally disturbed. We wish to reemphasize
this point at the beginning of a chapter in which we discuss the
clinical applications of our findings. Not all noncustodial mothers
seek mental health services, nor do they all need mental health services. This chapter is directed toward those who do seek help. Such
services are sought out by many mothers and can be extremely
beneficial. Approximately 60 percent of the mothers in our study
did receive counseling, and the vast majority (88 percent) found those
services either helpful or very helpful. This level of satisfaction in
counseling stands in stark contrast to another frequently used service,
legal help. Only 53 percent of the mothers sought out the assistance
of a lawyer, and over 60 percent of them found the assistance not
helpful.

Our purpose in this chapter is to give mental health practitioners
who serve this population of mothers our impressions of the issues
that may need to be addressed in treatment and a framework in
which to address them. At the same time, we are aware that many
readers of this book are not mental health practitioners but are other
interested parties and the mothers themselves. For them, the issues
we identify here may be of value in understanding these mothers or
in structuring discussions for self-help groups. We do not view help-
seeking as necessarily related to pathology or mental illness. With
these mothers, such help is often sought for assistance with the

difficult life change from married parent with children to single parent living alone.

Therapeutic Framework

We have noted that the feminist perspective informs our understanding of what mothers experience living away from their children. Feminism, as Collins (1986) suggested, is an awareness of sexual inequalities and of possible directions for change. It is vitally important to apply a feminist perspective to clinical work because, until recently, the male model of how the world should work was applied to females. Beginning most notably with Freud, developmental theorists used the behavior and physical attributes of males as the standard against which females were judged. A body of professional literature grew that supported this approach. For example, Howell (1981) wrote, "According to Freud, penis envy is the beginning and the crux of what is the matter with women" (p. 4). These views were fused in the social changes the family was undergoing at the beginning of the twentieth century. During this period, men increasingly began to work outside the home in factories. Women were left with the responsibility for the home and the children. Whereas, in an agrarian society, men, women, and children spent a great deal of time together, in an industrial society, the separation of family members became the norm. Thus, the prevailing view of the mother was that she was subordinate to the father but, ironically, was in charge of the children.

This view of "acceptable" behavior for women did not die (nor did it begin) with Freud. Recent studies have shown that sex-role differences still exist. In a report published in 1970, Broverman et al. (1981) asked seventy-nine mental health professionals to identify characteristics of healthy females, healthy males, and healthy adults. The researchers hypothesized that the mental health professionals' views of what was healthy for men and women would parallel the sex-role stereotypes held by society. Their hypothesis was upheld by both the male and the female professionals. Healthy women, for example, were seen as more submissive, more dependent, less aggressive, more emotional, and more concerned about their appearance than men. The researchers considered this an odd way to describe a well-functioning individual.[1] More recently, attempts have been made to construct developmental theory that applies specifically to women.

We certainly found differences between men and women in our research on noncustodial mothers and fathers. The mothers believe that they experience much more recrimination than the fathers do. Whereas the fathers perceive that others have no negative reactions to their noncustodial status, the mothers have nearly the opposite impression. Is this purely the perception of the mothers and the fathers? We believe that it is one more sign of the different behavior expectations placed on mothers and fathers.

The role of women in society is connected to the role of women in the home. As Goldner (1985) asked, if men and women do not function equally outside the home (in the workplace), how can they be expected to function equally in the home?

A feminist perspective sensitizes us to the values we apply in looking at mental health issues and the behaviors of men and women. Noncustodial mothers approach their role as mothers and as women, and an appreciation of both is needed in order to build a framework for intervention as the two roles intertwine. Some of the issues faced by the noncustodial mothers are related to being a single parent. But, as our research has shown, there are definite points of departure. Mental health professionals cannot ignore the status of women in society when they work with their female and male clients.

This is important because values are an important part of doing therapy.[2] How health and illness are defined will affect the way women who seek help will be treated. If mental health professionals believe that a mother should be with her children, the treatment has to be geared in that direction. If they believe that there are other healthy options for women, treatment becomes a way to help a mother make choices about her own life. Such a perspective does not always make things easy. Even for a feminist therapist such as Kim Stoll (1985), the stigma against noncustodial mothers was strong. She recounted this internal dialogue between her three different personas when she was considering relinquishing custody herself: "Therapist: 'You must keep cool. Don't get angry.' Mother: 'How can I let my baby go—I'm her mother.' Feminist: 'There is nothing wrong with a father having custody'" (pp. 54–55).

Throughout this book, we have applied a systems perspective to help show that behavior does not occur in isolation—that our actions affect as well as are affected by others. It is not enough to describe a mother as having lost custody in court. Other parts of the family, the courts, and society were involved in that outcome and must be considered. We favor a systems approach to understanding the interplay between family members and recognize that the roles of males and females in the family are often inequitable and that these inequities cannot be ignored in family work.

Treatment Models

Family therapy is both a method and a way of thinking about people that views people in the context of their family, not as isolated individuals. It is one approach to use with noncustodial mothers. Historically, family therapy has considered an inappropriately involved mother to be the root of the child's and often the family's problem. In the early years of family therapy theory, it was believed for example, that a child became schizophrenic as a result of poor parenting, usually by the mother. Where was the father during the family's psychological downspin? He was usually depicted as being distant from the family—immersed in the evening newspaper or in his work. He was viewed as the disciplinarian who would keep the children in line. In this view, the responsibility for nurturing and, often, parenting continued to be placed with the mother. Since the mother was seen as the expert with children, she became the obvious target for attack when problems arose.[3]

The therapeutic goals with this type of family—if, for instance, the mother was seen as being overinvolved—would be to remove the mother from her position in the family and encourage the father to become more appropriately involved. One often-cited danger of using systems theory in family work is that it ignores the social and political context and focuses merely on the interactions in the family.[4] When a feminist perspective is applied, however, different considerations flow into the treatment process. If we begin to shift our view of the mother to one that is cognizant of women's status in society, a different picture emerges. It is too simple to say that she is overinvolved. A more accurate picture may show her to be embattled—trying desperately to hold the family together while attempting to provide the children with some nurturance and to keep her marriage intact. This shift in view brings with it a shift in treatment goals for the family.

How does this approach work in treatment? In the past, the mother would have been told to take a "vacation," thus stripping her of her identity and importance in the family. A different perspective was offered by Papp.[5] In a case in which a child had been misbehaving and things improved when the father was moved into the picture, Papp chose to compliment the mother for all the love and caring she had lavished on the child over the years. Papp indicated that it was that affection that had made it possible for her husband to do a better job with the child. Here, the mother's behavior was praised, not derided. She was not removed from the family scene but praised for making the family work. This represents an important shift in family work, as it positively reframes the position of the mother.

When a noncustodial mother seeks treatment, the mental health professional may involve the children in the treatment process if they are available and if their inclusion is indicated. The permission of the custodial parent may have to be acquired first. Often, treatment centers on problems in the relationship between the mother and the children. Like many forms of therapy, the goal when working with the family may involve making the mother feel more competent when she has the children, clarifying commmunication among the family members, and helping the individuals adjust to their situation. Having a perspective that supports the strengths of the mother can be vitally important in this process.

Debate continues about the wisdom of bringing the custodial father into the treatment session. Walters (1985) argued that it is unhealthy for the children to be in the same room as their divorced parents because it stirs up the usually unrealistic fantasy that their parents will get back together. Others argue the opposite view.[6] They believe that having all members of the family present is the best way for them to assess what is going on in the family and to move to correct miscommunication. We believe that, with families, it is best to withhold a decision until the therapist has had a chance to talk with the parents. Then decisions about inclusion or exclusion can be based on the relationship between the parents and the needs of the family members. Meeting with all family members when it is a family like the one discussed in chapter 14 would not be a problem. But with many other families, the anger existing between the ex-spouses could be sufficiently intense to make it a painful experience for the children.

There is also debate about whether the therapist should be male or female. Although it is difficult to argue in favor of a male or a female therapist for working with a two-parent family, a case can be made for the therapist being the same sex as the primary client. For noncustodial mothers, this can be especially important. Hare-Mustin (1981) believes that women need successful women as role models. She disagrees with the argument put forth by some male therapists that males are the therapists of choice because they give women the chance to relate to healthier males than they are accustomed to. What can benefit a woman, wrote Hare-Mustin, is not a "special male re-inforcing traditional stereotypes by assuming that the female client needs a special male who will treat her differently. . . . What a woman needs to learn is . . . how she can become a different woman" (p. 566). The female therapist provides this by modeling competence as a woman in a variety of areas.

Many of the mothers we interviewed had a great deal of anger. They felt that they had been victimized by many of the men in their lives—their husbands, lawyers, judges, or sons. Even with an understanding male therapist, therapy can be slower if this anger toward men affects the therapeutic relationship. Perhaps as important, the therapist–client relationship can become a replication of other power relationships the mother has experienced in which she has been in a one-down position. A female therapist, more easily than a male therapist, could help a mother work through transferential issues surrounding that mother's own mother. As mentioned elsewhere, the mother's mother can be particularly harsh about her becoming noncustodial.

The Support Group

Another valuable model of treatment and help for the noncustodial mother is the support group, which has been an integral part of the women's movement since the 1960s. Getting people together who have a common goal or need has proved to be an effective endeavor in the United States since the nineteenth century. Group techniques have ranged from social action and cognitive to psychoanalytic and leaderless.[7] Most recently, self-help groups have emerged as a popular method of both encouraging change and giving support.

We cannot overestimate the importance to many of the noncustodial mothers of meeting other single parents in the self-help groups they have joined. People often join self-help groups to be with people with whom they identify. A newly separated parent may suddenly feel out of place in the community if she or he knows few other single parents. Joining a group in which the concerns of single parents are the focus can provide the parent with emotional support, information about single parenting, and a chance to socialize. Members of PWP have described the benefits of hearing other single fathers and mothers talk about their experiences, and members of Mothers Without Custody have felt that they have benefited from the more homogenous membership and the greater focus on emotional support.[8]

A Mothers Without Custody Meeting

The following is an edited account of a Mothers Without Custody meeting. No meeting is typical, but the topics discussed are frequently similar, regardless of the region of the country or the number of members present. This meeting was attended by five members.

The five members are at different stages in their lives. Some are just beginning as noncustodial mothers, while others have had more experience and have resolved many of the issues that are raised.

Amy, at whose house the meeting is being held, begins by making sure everyone has met and by offering coffee and cookies. The first ten minutes are spent exchanging names with the one new member, Jennifer. Carole, Maggie, and Maureen give brief introductions, telling a little about their custody situations, their work lives, and where they live.

Jennifer starts the discussion by describing at great length and in considerable detail her continuing struggle to regain custody of her children. Her children and her ex-husband moved out of state two years ago, and she has been trying to find a trustworthy lawyer to represent her. Recently, she has found a woman lawyer. Jennifer is bitter because her ex-husband's income is substantially higher than hers. Working part-time, she is worried that she will not be able to afford to wage a legal battle against her ex.

Looking very determined, she says, "I cannot give up the fight. We mothers have to stick together. We need each other and we need to advocate for each other." She then wonders whether the group is interested in getting involved in legislative and legal issues, or just in providing emotional support. She notes that chapters in other states have pulled their membership together to advocate for changes in the legal system that will increase equity for noncustodial mothers, "Why can't we do the same?" she asks.

Amy responds:

> I've been at this for a long time. Change happens very slowly on the state level. I was once where you are now. You try and look for any course to pursue that might be of help. These are your children you're fighting for. You're thinking, "How and why should I be deprived of access to them? Who has the right to do that?" I understand how you feel. I don't think anyone can understand how a mother without custody feels except another one.

Carole says, "I don't know how I lost custody. It just happened. I am trying real hard to visit my children as often as I can. I really do miss them, though [she laughs] my daughter can be quite a problem sometimes." (The others smile in response.) Carole's husband had recently obtained a court order to deny her the previously agreed upon visitation schedule. She seems confident that this is a temporary obstacle, but it is nonetheless a hassle for her. Carole says, "I'm in a comfortable place. I don't want to keep fighting for everything. That can't be my focus anymore."

Maggie supports her by saying, "Your kids are not your focus now, Carole, so your job is." Recently, Carole started a new job in which she travels a great deal. She loves the work, and the income is just beginning to pay off the mountains of legal bills that have piled up over the years from past custody battles.

Agreeing with Maggie, Carole continues:

> There are other things in my life now, though they don't take the place of having my children with me. I have a great support system. My ex's family is on my side. They often act as a buffer between my ex and me and help lessen the impact of some of the bad comments he makes about me to the children.

The conversation focuses next on upcoming holiday plans and then returns to Jennifer, who cannot understand how a mother could stop battling for her children. This is followed by a discussion of others' impressions of noncustodial mothers and their own feelings about their situation.

Maureen says:

> There are different steps. It's kind of a psychological process of elimination to get to the point that you don't have to feel guilt anymore and realize that you're not an unfit mother, or person for that matter. It's similar, I guess, to going through a mourning process.

(Maureen's children are living with their father because they did not want to move out of their house when the parents divorced.)

Maggie then talks about the material enticements that her husband had used over the years to attract her child's attention.

> It's a real issue when your ex is making $50,000 a year and I am making a third of that. It's not just the luxury items. He can offer the staples like clothes, access to a car, and enough money just to do the normal things kids like to do. I can't offer that because I don't have enough money to do it myself.

Silence follows for a few seconds.

Maggie speaks again: "But my kids tell me, 'Mom, we have everything from Dad, but love is the thing we have with you.' " This statement is followed by silence. Everyone seems moved by this, and a few mothers wipe tears from their eyes.

Amy brings up a new topic. She is at a point in the relationship with her children in which her concerns center on their day-to-day needs and how those needs change over time.

> My daughter is being forced to leave the school where she is because she is learning-disabled. My ex is fighting the school—he can't deal with the fact that his child is having problems, but she is. The school has asked for my help to convince him, because they think I am a sympathetic ear. I feel pretty confident we'll win this battle and she'll get the school placement.

Jennifer interrupts, "But of course you have some say in her education. She's your child."

Amy answers, "But Jennifer, I'm the noncustodial parent. The court has determined my jurisdiction. I can accept that now. Believe me, I did not and still don't like it but I have to direct my energies elsewhere."

Carole interjects, "Jennifer, you might get angry at me for asking this, but do you really want your children back?"

Jennifer responds, "Yes, because I am the better parent."

Carole says, "My position with my children is stronger with me being away from them. I'd be warden, teacher, cop, and so on. Now. I'm their emotional support. That would change if they lived with me. I'm a more effective parent with them away from me."

Maureen nods in agreement:

> My kids want to see me get married. They say, "But Mommie, make sure you don't go out with anyone we don't like." [She laughs.] I tell them, "Whoa! You live with your father now. That doesn't mean that I stop loving you or being concerned about you, but I do what I want now. And when you come to visit me, you abide by the rules in my home."

Maggie notes that if she has plans one of the nights the children come to visit, she leaves them with a sitter. "I try to be home as much as possible when they are there, but I can't do somersaults to please them."

Amy adds, "I don't do anything special when they are over, either."

Maggie says, "I don't do anything special for them, even if they expect it. I am not here to entertain them, even though that is what their father tells them I'm supposed to do. He can't lay that guilt trip on me."

Conversation drifts among the mothers as they talk about how they spend time with their children. Carole introduces a new topic:

> I never used to be able to say that my kids do not live with me. You tell people you're a mother without custody and it's a label. Now, I can tell them because I am not living away from my kids because I am a bad mother. I know that now.

Jennifer, supporting Carole, says, "I find people don't ask. If they do, I tell them it's part of my life I left in Philadelphia. It's really none of their business."

After a lull in the discussion, Amy looks at her watch and, in concluding the meeting, says, "It's not the worst thing that could happen not to have your children." The mothers slowly put on their coats and continue to talk animatedly as they leave.

Such groups provide a balance between support for the mothers' positions and confrontation. This dual focus is typical of many self-help groups in which people can discuss their feelings and find that they are not alone in them. The supportive atmosphere enables the mothers to feel safe bringing up things that they may never have discussed before.

Areas for Intervention

We have been discussing family and group approaches. During our research, a number of areas emerged that are possible foci for clinical interventions. It may be appropriate to consider these areas when working with mothers individually, in groups, or in families. Suggestions for change are based on the successes we saw in many of the mothers. If we look at those mothers who have adapted to being noncustodial, ideas emerge regarding how to tailor our interventions. Most important for the mental health professional is an awareness of any negative stereotypes or feelings of countertransference he or she may hold about noncustodial mothers. Mental health professionals often hold the same values as society and may be conditioned to believe that a mother's place is with her children.[9]

The following are possible areas of clinical focus:

1. Many noncustodial mothers suffer from low self-esteem. They are carrying a great weight that has been placed upon them by their conditioning. It is not easy to quiet the internal voice that has told them for so long that children belong with their mothers. They also hear about their status from others, and the comments can be quite negative. They worry about the impression they make. Some feel guilty about living away from their children. They hesitate to tell people they do not have custody.

It is not only living away from their children that may affect their self-esteem. Preceding many of the negative feelings that come with being noncustodial are those that come from a divorce. Divorce is a painful experience that makes one question competence as a spouse and as a person. Divorce also forces many women into the workforce on a full-time basis. Returning to work or starting work outside the home for the first time can be exciting if success is found or disheartening if an enjoyable job is hard to locate. The poor financial situation of the divorced mother is frequently a problem area.

Thus, a series of events can combine to hinder the development of the mother's self-esteem. The divorce, the assumption of the non-custodial mother role, the vagaries of the work world, and an impaired financial situation leave many mothers in a downward cycle, questioning their self-worth. Helping the mother to recognize this cycle, to see that some of her reactions to it are normal, and to see that she may not be to blame for some of her experiences is a beginning point. As a further way to help counteract this downward cycle, attention should also be given to helping her appreciate the areas in which she is competent. A support group can be particularly helpful for a mother in sorting out what she has experienced in the past and may continue to encounter.

2. As illustrated in the account of the support group meeting, some mothers may need assistance in defining themselves in a role that is broader than that of "mother." Carole and Maggie talked about their jobs being their focus now instead of their children. They have begun to see that they have other facets to their existence that do not involve their children. Some mothers cling unrealistically to the hope of regaining custody of their children. Others are unable to see other options for their lives that do not involve the children. When the children and the marriage have been the focus of their existence, it is hard to look elsewhere. One goal of treatment can be to help them explore the positive aspects of moving on with their lives, of pursuing activities that they never had time for, and of finding new ways to define themselves.

3. Many mothers have issues to work through that are related to the way they were raised. These issues often have to do with parenting and their perceived failure at it. A natural point of departure for the therapist is to explore the mother's own experience in being parented (family-of-origin work). A mother may find herself re-

peating dysfunctional patterns of behavior that can best be understood by exploring her early experiences. The therapist must be careful not to buy into the prevailing societal view that a mother is incompetent if she is noncustodial. The mother may have this view herself. If the therapist has this view, she or he may begin looking into the mother's past for the roots of the incompetence. Was the mother abandoned as a child? Was she raised in a single-parent family? Did she receive an insufficient amount of nurturing? And so on. Such an inquiry from the therapist may ignore the status of women in society today, which may have contributed to the mother's seeking treatment in the first place. At the same time, the therapist must not gloss over early experiences of the mother if they are relevant to her case and if they are a contributing factor. Dealing with the mother's past constructively requires a balancing of the past and the present and a commitment to being open-minded.

4. Helping the mother with her feelings about the divorce and custody decision can also have a beneficial effect. The mothers who have adapted the best to being noncustodial are those who are least likely to blame the ex-husband for the divorce and most likely to have relinquished custody voluntarily. Sometimes the anger the mother feels toward her ex-husband is appropriate. But it is still anger that needs to be worked through. Mothers who share the blame for the breakup tend to do better. When appropriate, helping the mother see her part in the breakup may help her resolve some of her anger. The mother may be able to shift her perception of herself, for example, from that of victim to that of active participant in her own life. Such a shift can help her feel more competent in changing her situation.

When the mother was abused, an opposite approach may be called for. She may feel that she deserved the punishment she received, and she will need help in not blaming herself. With past or present abuse, referral for legal action against the abuser may be indicated.

When custody goes to the father, some mothers are left feeling powerless. Some deny that they had anything to do with their children ending up with the father. Again, helping the mother to see what her part was in the custody arrangement can be a mobilizing force. If she was victimized in the situation, she will need help in mourning her loss so that she is not left crippled by it. Once the mourning process is complete, she may need support in taking steps to reverse the victimization. Again, making referrals for legal counsel and advocating for the client can be appropriate steps. Referral for legal aid should also be considered if there are inequities in child support payments, visitation, and alimony.

5. One major area of concern is the mother's relationship with her children. Many are in great pain because of the enormous loss of daily contact. The majority of the mothers in our study were not satisfied with their relationships with their children. Most wanted more contact. The mothers may need assistance and support in arranging visitation, telephoning, and writing letters to children with whom they are out of touch. If there has been a complete break between the mother and her children, reestablishing contact can be an especially painful process for all concerned. Letter writing can be a good beginning point for the mother if she wants to reestablish a relationship.

The mental health professional can help the mother interpret the communication she gets from the children and the father. This can provide the mother with a more objective view of her situation and can help her sort through some of the roadblocks to more frequent visitation if that is what she seeks. Those mothers who feel the most rejected by their children will have the hardest time interpreting communication from the children.

6. Including the children in treatment has also been suggested. The therapist should consider seeing the children without the mother, as there may be issues the children would feel uncomfortable discussing in front of her. For example, they may be feeling angry and rejected because of the divorce or because of their separation from the mother. The children may feel protective toward their mother and may be afraid to say anything negative about her. Some children worry that they will push the noncustodial parent away from them if they express anger or disappointment to that parent. Therefore, instead of expressing those feelings, they brush over them. This may heighten their feelings of pain and loss and can add to their sense of vulnerability. They may also feel "put upon," or they may feel that they are "crazy" because they are coming to a therapy session. Allowing the children to discuss openly these feelings can be helpful both in dealing with them and in clarifying the mother–child relationship. Boundary issues are often a fruitful area to focus on. Helping the children remove themselves from any parental triangulation

that exists can reduce tensions.[10] Abelsohn (1983) suggests working with divorced families to restore parental nurturing and to correct distortion about the divorce process. The therapist must be sensitive to the issues that living away from the mother raises for the child.

7. The issue of child support payments, frequently an area of great concern, must be handled with care. Many custody arrangements currently in effect are by-products of a period when mothers were not expected to pay as frequently as they do now. Although a mental health professional would naturally avoid taking a position regarding whether or not the mother should pay support, she or he should be aware that the issues around payment are often quite complex. Merely raising the question may set off a chain reaction. Most of the mothers in our study do not pay support. If the mother is being sued for payment by the father or is questioned about it in a treatment situation, it may add to her feeling of victimization. On the other hand, if the mother is exonerated from payments and is not asked about them, she may feel that she is being protected from her responsibility as a parent or actively shut off from it. No easy answer exists for many of the mothers. Many are bound to feel conflict about their situation.

We can hypothesize that because mothers who pay child support tend to be more involved with their children than those who do not, making payments is one of a number of options to be pursued by the mother who desires more contact. Some mothers want more contact but are in difficult financial situations. The mother may need help in recognizing that even a payment as small as a dollar a month can be a symbolic gesture of her interest in the children's welfare. It may be a gesture that the children, who are satiated by their father's financial support, will not recognize or appreciate immediately, but they might remember it when they are at an age to appreciate such gestures.

8. The mental health professional should not assume that the mother wants or needs more contact with her children. Some mothers are content with the level of involvement they have with their children. For them, living away from the children is an opportunity for a fresh start. A mother who married at a young age and immediately started a family may never have had the chance to be alone. Some mothers see turning over the children to the father as a way for the father and the children to get to know each other for the first time.

Since many of the fathers had not been very involved in child care during the marriage, having the children live with them allows their relationships to develop.

9. The changed financial situation of many of the mothers must be considered in the treatment relationship, also. Usually, the mother's income goes down following the divorce. Some of the mothers we interviewed described living on very little income. Others were quite comfortable. We found, especially among those mothers who are scraping to make ends meet, a great deal of anger about not being able to buy things for their children and themselves that they could afford when they were married. A lack of early success in the work world added to many of the mothers' dissatisfaction with their financial position, as did legal costs and therapy bills. The therapist should be sensitive to the status of divorced women and women in the workplace. The mother's precarious financial position is often not her own doing but is what she is left with after the marital dissolution. Referral for financial counselling may be appropriate.

10. Some mothers "burned out" trying to be "supermoms." They could not pursue a full-time career and be a full-time parent and a full-time wife. Something had to give and, in their cases, it was the role of full-time parent and wife. These mothers may benefit from insight into what led them down the path to overload. Because they had such high expectations for themselves when they were married, they may continue to demand a great deal from themselves as non-custodial parents. Working with them on these patterns can help the mothers establish their priorities more realistically.

11. Issues concerning the custodial father are also relevant. Many fathers get a great deal of praise for raising the children alone. Such support for them, if heard by the mother, can heighten her sense of incompetence. She may wonder, "Why is he getting all that praise when I received nothing when I had custody?" This may add to her sense of role ambiguity; she is unsure of how to act and does not know what is expected of her. The way the father is raising the children has a strong impact on the mother's perception of her own situation as does the way he gained custody. His parenting can stir many different reactions in the mother. If the father is doing a good job, she may feel relieved that the children's needs are being met, or she may feel unneeded. Conversely, the mother who feels the father is not parenting well may feel upset for her children. The

more resolved the mother is about her own situation, the more joy she is apt to take in her children's well-being and the more upset she will be if the children are having difficulties.

Consciously or unconsciously, children can add fuel to the smoldering flames between the father and the mother. They may play one parent off against the other, may go from one parent to the other when they are not happy with their situation, or may report back to one parent the behavior of the other. Often the fire is so hot that instead of fueling the flames, the children get burned, too. Whatever the situation is, the therapist needs to be clear about where the boundaries should be drawn. The children should not be in the middle, and an attempt should be made to reach consensus about child-rearing issues. If consensus cannot be reached, both parents should at least be made aware that it is not helpful to the children for the parents to be mixing unresolved problems from their marriage with their continuing parental responsibilities. The two relationships must be separated.

The presence of a stepmother in the children's life is sometimes a red flag to noncustodial mothers. With a stepmother, the potential is there for one more person to be pulled into any triangulation that is going on among the father, the mother, and the children. The stepmother may be trying to build rapport with the children and their father while also trying to figure out the noncustodial mother's relationship with her new family. Sometimes confusion about who is in charge of the children in the custodial father's house adds to the noncustodial mother's feelings of frustration.

More often than not, the mothers in our study viewed the stepmother as a competent parent. With such a view of the stepmother, there is hope that a viable arrangement between the family members can be worked out and that a therapist could assist in that process.

12. Grandparents—the mother's own parents or her in-laws—may have legal rights to visit their grandchildren. When grandparents are actively involved with the children, another layer of complexity is added to the therapeutic situation. In ideal situations, grandparents provide the children with a supportive and stable relationship that is not affected by their parents' conflicts. In less ideal situations, grandparents may be pulled into taking sides. If the mother sees the grandparents' involvement with the children as interference, it may be that they actually are interfering or meddling, or it may be that

their presence is stirring up feelings that the mother has not resolved about her parents. These issues must be attended to so that the mother does not feel conflicted whenever her parents visit her children.

Conclusions

We have tried to provide a number of specific areas of exploration that apply to the situation of the noncustodial mother. Clinical work can include working individually, in groups, or with the whole family. Advocacy on behalf of the mothers and referral to appropriate resources should be considered. Many self-help groups are available that are designed for singles, for single parents, and, in many regions, for mothers without custody. Public and private agencies and groups are available to help people with the specific problems of child support payments, child custody, child-snatching, emotional support, legal aid, social contacts, economic concerns, and education. Referral to these resources can be a vitally important addition to any contact with the mother.[11]

It is our clinical impression that the mothers who have adjusted well are those who have come to accept being noncustodial. These mothers have worked hard on moving ahead with their lives and are not dwelling on the past. The therapeutic process should be geared toward mobilizing the internal strengths that will enable the mother to continue on this path and toward enhancing the mother's external sources of support. Whatever course is taken, the feelings that come from living apart from their children must be addressed.

13

The Voices of the Children: A Three-Decade Perspective

My mother says that no matter what I do, she will still love me,
and I have finally accepted that.

As we discussed in the first chapter, noncustodial mothers are not a phenomenon of the 1980s; they have been around for generations. Many children who are now adults were raised away from their mothers at a time when the stigma connected to such a situation was much greater than now. These children perhaps suffered more than children today because divorce and father-headed families were much more rare. Their mothers also suffered more— not only because of the rarity of divorce but also because women had fewer options in life. The employment opportunities pursued by many of the mothers described in this book did not exist for women in the 1950s, 1960s, and early 1970s.

While writing this book, we met people who had experienced a noncustodial mother arrangement firsthand, either as a child or as a mother. We believed an important counterpoint would be provided if we included their perspectives. We asked them about their lives then and what impact their experiences had on their current lives. What follows are interviews with and letters from David and his mother Lois, Jim, and Ellen. David, 35 years old at the time of the interview, moved out of Lois's home in the 1950s. Jim, in his late

20s, describes his life away from his mother, which began in the 1960s. Ellen went to live with her father in the early 1970s.

David's Story

David, an artist living in New York, recently married for the first time. He has a 9-year-old daughter from a long-term relationship that did not include marriage. He shares custody of his daughter with her mother.

David wrote:

> I'm so sorry that it's taken so long to respond to your letter. I have been busy, but it is also characteristic of my relationship with my mother that we talk infrequently. We don't have that kind of guilt-induced contact often found with parents and children. I think partly she does not feel she can lay that kind of thing on me—but I also think she genuinely doesn't want to manipulate people in that way. We often say to each other that we feel "connected" without having regular contact. We don't do any of the obligatory holiday things or birthdays. Some times (almost always) I'll call her on Mother's Day. I see this as very much a product of not living together while I was growing up. There is a certain intimacy and forthrightness to our relationship. We don't have a tremendous amount of day-to-day baggage and we can be very frank with each other.
>
> In some sense something is missing. And, of course, I missed her tremendously while I was growing up. The fact of the division has profoundly affected me. In relationships with women it was always my experience that it wouldn't work out. Eventually they would be gone. So, of course, I would leave first.
>
> But a lot of what is missing with my mother may be beneficial in its absence. We are not emotionally "knotted," which is partially due to our personalities, but also must have resulted from the circumstances of our lives. We treat each other as adults, because basically that is when we got to know each other. All the resistance to my individuality was provided by my father. Of course, he was my primary parent—and this exacerbated the primal father/son conflict. My mother, who is still very angry at my father, came down very firmly on my side, partly in defiance of him. Defiance is the wrong word actually, because they have no contact whatsoever. But she is definitely on my side against him.

We were able to interview David's mother, Lois. Her story provides the early details that help put David's response into a context. Now in her late 50s and also living in New York, Lois described a path to becoming noncustodial that was similar in many ways to the other stories in this book.

Lois was married at 18 and had two sons in quick succession; David was the second. "In our church that was normal. But looking back on it now, I know I married too young and had not experienced enough first." Her marriage to Richard was a rocky one. Twice she left him but was convinced by her parents that she should return. She almost did end the marriage when she tried to commit suicide by putting her head in the oven. "I obviously didn't succeed," she laughed. "One of my friends called and I went to answer the phone, and while I was talking to her I passed out. She called my husband, who came home from work and asked me why I had tried to do such a stupid thing. Then he went back to work. I pulled myself up by the bootstraps and tried to work at the marriage again."

Lois began seeing a psychiatrist.

> As part of therapy he was giving me some kind of gas that was supposed to help me recall my early childhood. Twice when I came off the gas he raped me. I was too embarrassed to tell anyone about it or to think about suing him. He also encouraged me to meet a man and have a love affair. I did meet someone and did have an affair that went on for a while. I became pregnant just before the man moved to Chicago. I was still married to Richard and can't remember if I ever told him about the affair. But somehow he was convinced that child [a daughter] was not his.

The marriage continued to deteriorate, and Lois decided that the only way out was to make elaborate secret plans to leave with the children. When Richard learned of Lois's plan, he packed up his two sons and left first. The baby daughter stayed with Lois. "He couldn't handle a baby, and he didn't think she was his anyway."

At that time Lois had no place to go and no job.

> I stayed with friends for six weeks and then Richard and I began meeting with lawyers about getting a divorce. Richard said he would not give up the two oldest. He said if I fought him in court, he would tell my parents that I had been unfaithful to him. [During

the 1950s, charges of nymphomania and infidelity were common
allegations leveled against mothers as a means of getting custody.]
He was fighting so hard, and in the church the man has the rights
over the family, that I just decided it was best if I did not fight it
anymore. He had been a very good father, so I did not have any
qualms about him as a parent. But I did want them.

I was very emotional for a long time after that. I would cry and
cry for days. He threatened to not let my parents see the children,
but they put their foot down. When the children would visit them,
I would see them—about once a month.

The 1950s were a difficult time to be a noncustodial mother. "I
didn't tell anyone where I worked that I had two other children—
only my friends knew. My mother and aunts did not approve of
divorce or of giving up my kids."

About two years after the divorce, Lois remarried. She and Carl,
her second husband, had two more children. With a new family,
her relationship with David and his brother began to slowly improve.
Richard allowed more visitation, although it was still infrequent, and
all the children would get together at Lois's house. Then David and
his brother moved to New Jersey and contact nearly ceased. Letters
would go back and forth, but there was no visitation. Lois said:

> I would see them only very occasionally. Then they moved back
> to New York and I began seeing them a little. Things really im-
> proved between us when they each invited me to their high school
> graduation. That's when I really got to know them.
>
> Now things between us are exceptionally good and have been
> for years. I look back on those times and know I couldn't have
> made it raising them. I didn't think about welfare and I didn't have
> the money to go it alone. The thought that has kept me alive is
> that although I had no choice, I was still better off without them
> and they were better off with Richard. That kept me going.
>
> With David, we don't see each other a lot but we talk on the
> phone. We can pick up just where we left off. There is a deep
> feeling there. The cementing of the relationship really came as they
> grew up. They realized what I had been through and that I had
> no choice. I'm me and we have this mother–child love that is more
> adult–adult now.

Jim's Story

Jim is 29 years old, married, and the father of a newborn child. He works part-time in construction and part-time in human services. He has moved around a great deal during his life and is currently living in Atlanta. One of Jim's earliest memories is of his parents having a big fight and his mother being pushed down. When his parents separated in 1960, Jim began a life in which it seemed that his suitcase was constantly packed—moving from his aunt's to his father's to his mother's to boarding schools and back to his mother's again. Jim told us:

> Following the big fight, my parents separated and I went to live with my mother's sister while they tried to decide on custody. She nearly physically abused me. She used to hold me over the toilet and force me to have bowel movements. I began soiling my pants, which was a problem for years. My father saw my brother and I weren't happy there and took me to live with him and his mother, where I stayed for two years.

Jim left his father's and grandmother's home when his mother won custody of him in a court battle.

> She won the case because the judge said children should be with their mother. I was very frightened of her, though. She instilled in me all these fears that I still have today. She is paranoid and very litigious. About a year after she won custody, she tried to commit suicide. I am not sure if it was a serious attempt or if she wanted us to find her. She turned on all the gas in the house, but she did not turn off the alarm clocks. So when we heard the alarm go off in the morning, we saved her life and ourselves. It made all the newspapers. [He pulls out a folder and shows the clipping.] She wasn't working at the time and had poor occupational skills. She probably felt she couldn't do anything right.

The next day, Jim's father took him and his brother away and placed them in the first of many boarding schools in which they would spend the next six years. Jim's mother visited him at the boarding school.

It was awful. She would visit and spend the whole time constantly berating my father. She wanted me to change my opinion of him in order to help her next custody case. I feared her whenever she came. I was happy to be in boarding school and happy to be away from her. My father would visit every weekend, which I liked.

When their first boarding school closed, the two boys moved to a different school, which had a much rougher student body. "It was where a lot of juvenile delinquents were being sent." When his father learned that Jim was not happy there, he removed both boys and he and the boys moved into an apartment together. "That was the first time I recognized what a single-parent family was. I really liked it." Six months later, his mother was suing for custody again.

I did not want to move out of my father's house, but I did not know how to confront my mother with that. She had me caught in this emotional bind. She once said to me, "If you don't want to live with me, just tell me." When I started to answer that I did not, she quickly added "It would break my heart if you didn't." She was very manipulative. I just couldn't tell her. I lied to the social worker doing the investigation about where I wanted to live because I was being interviewed in front of my mother. Off the record, though, I did tell the judge that I wanted to stay with my father, so I was able to.

Despite Jim's preference to be with his father, the picture there was not always rosy.

He was an hysterical personality, always overreacting. I was embarrassed to be seen with him in public. He lived away from his own father a lot when he was growing up because of his father's alcoholism and work schedule as a salesman. He was always screaming or hugging us in public. Everything was blown out of proportion.

When Jim graduated from high school, both parents were present, as well as his mother's new husband, a half-brother from his mother's new marriage, and his brother. He went to college out of state, partly to get away from his mother, and found his life improving.

I began to feel more normal in college. I had already done my rebelling from my parents, and here were all these other kids also rebelling from their parents. My separation from my mother was nearly finished; they were just beginning it.

Over the next few years, Jim maintained only minimal contact with his mother. He would call or visit, but he never felt that any of the contact was initiated by her. He did keep seeing his father, who had married a woman whom Jim liked very much. Jim's last meaningful contact with his mother was in 1982, when his father threw a party to honor Jim's marriage.

I did not have any contact with her for a long time after that. I guess getting married I did not need her anymore. [Jim's brother has not had any contact with his mother for years.] But after no contact with her for all those years, I spoke with her last month. I was doing a paper on my family history for a course I am taking, and I called her up. I did not know anything aboout her family because I had identified with my father's family when growing up. Apparently, she was raised by her father after her mother died and she had also spent time in boarding schools. It took a few phone calls to her second husband [from whom she is now divorced] and her son until I found her. We talked for a little bit. I couldn't tell if she was happy to hear from me or not. Her affect is so restricted it is hard to know where she's at. She's working as a domestic now.

I don't know if I'll see her again. I'll play it by ear. I don't feel I need her. Other people became my community and my family. Being a parent myself now is a difficult role for me to be in. If I did not feel I was always running from my own family, I would probably feel more comfortable with my wife and child now. My image of my mother is of someone who has an appreciation for beauty but can never quite get it right. I think back to my parents' big fight and I see bright colors on fine china on the dining table. But all the china is tipped over and everything is spilling out.

Ellen's Story

Ellen, 27 and single, lives on the East Coast and is currently pursuing a career in the helping professions. She wrote:

When I was asked to write about how I felt about my noncustodial mother, I assumed it would be easy. However, I quickly discovered that it was difficult to put those feelings into words. My parents divorced when I was six, and both of them had lots of courage to give my father custody. I admire my mother for being able at that time to know that giving up custody was the best thing to do for all concerned. This doesn't mean that I didn't have ambivalent feelings about my mother or her leaving while growing up, but I do realize that her decision was quite difficult for her.

At present, my mother and I have a close relationship, which seems to me to have occurred in only the last eight years. It amazed me that my mother is so attuned to what is going on in my life; she knows if I am sad or upset, can spot any slight change in weight, and can usually calm me down if I'm angry with someone else. There are times when she, like all people, doesn't seem to understand what is going on with me, but she is able to ask me. I find now that there are some things I will tell my mother because I know that she will only give me support, not lectures or pity. My mother says that no matter what I do, she will still love me, and I have finally accepted that.

I still have some problems figuring out the roles my mother and I have in relationship to each other. I guess that seeing her only once a week while growing up didn't allow me to really understand our boundaries. There are elements of friend and motherhood in our relationship. One of the problems I had was feeling cheated because I seemed to have missed out on some of the bonding other women had with their mothers. I'm still trying to figure out how to be angry with my mother without feeling our relationship will end (and it won't) and how to be supportive of her when she really needs it. I am pleased that we have learned to communicate. There are still problems between my parents which make it difficult for my mother to attend events like graduation, and I need to learn to not let this hurt me since it doesn't have anything to do with me but rather my parents' feelings for each other. Both of my parents are important to me, but my relationship with my mother still takes some work for both of us.

Conclusions

As we look at these family situations, we see more turmoil than that described by many of the mothers who took part in our study. Two of the three mothers attempted suicide, although their attempts may not have been serious ones. David and Jim moved a great deal and lost contact with their mothers at one point. In addition, they were often aware that living away from their mothers was a unique situation. We can contrast this with the feeling we received, for example, from Mark in the next chapter, who felt that living with his father rather than with his mother was quite ordinary.

Although it is difficult to draw conclusions about other children in similar situations a generation ago, what David and Jim describe fits with that period of history. In the 1950s and 1960s, fewer mothers were working outside the home than now. The prevailing image of mothers coincided with what we saw on television—the mother who was at home all the time. This translated to a very powerful message to women, linking them inexorably with motherhood. When Lois, for example, broke with that image of motherhood, she felt ashamed. She felt that she had to keep her noncustodial status to herself when she went to work. Lois probably felt alone in her situation. Supportive self-help groups did not exist then.

With Ellen's story, we see less recrimination and a smoother transition than David and Jim had. This could be idiosyncratic to Ellen's family or it could be a reflection of the early 1970s, when women had more freedom.

These adult children are ambivalent in their feelings toward their mothers. Their relationships with them have been intensified, perhaps because of living in a one-parent family or perhaps because more extremes in the mother's behavior were needed in the 1950s for her to become noncustodial. Notwithstanding their early experiences, or maybe because of them, David, Jim, and Ellen are working very hard to resolve many of the issues surrounding their upbringing. They are also working on their adult-adult relationships with their mothers. Success in this last endeavor, has varied, but they all choose to continue pursuing it. That in itself is a good sign.

14

When Custody Decisions Work Out Well: An Interview with a Noncustodial Mother, Her Son, and the Custodial Father

W E found a number of what we considered exemplary custody situations. They usually had four basic characteristics: the mother had adjusted well to living away from her children and felt comfortable with herself; the mother and father were on good terms and were able to parent without letting past differences get in the way; the father felt comfortable being the sole custodian; and the children were progressing well. By this point in the book, we hope that the reader will not find it surprising that many of these custodial arrangements have worked out well for everyone. As we reported in chapter 8, one-third of the mothers in our study felt comfortable about their situation, and another third had mixed feelings. This is a large pool of potentially well-adjusted noncustodial mothers to pull from.

We interviewed the members of one family in depth, a noncustodial mother, her ex-husband (a custodial father), and their son—to get their impressions of how custody came to reside with the father and what life was like for them three years after the custody decision. Since the parents' divorce, the mother has remarried, but for purposes of discussion we will still refer to them as a family. We chose them because they seemed to be a good model of how family relationships can work out when a child is living with the father. We wish to emphasize that the term *model family* does not imply that they are problem-free. Many families, with single parents or two parents, struggle with the same issues with which this family is struggling. We consider them a model family because, to a large extent, they have the four basic characteristics described at the beginning of this chapter.

We interviewed the family in four stages over a one-year period. The mother, Susan, was interviewed first over the telephone. The second interview, which also involved only Susan, took place in an interview room, and a videotape was made. Following further discussion with Susan, she agreed to bring in her ex-husband, Joe, and their son, Mark, to be videotaped as a family. Because of some of the possible contraindications of reconstructing a family that has gone through a divorce, we took special care to ensure that the interview with all three family members was not an unusual event for them. In fact, this family had gotten together within the previous year at a holiday celebration, and they felt comfortable discussing their family history. Each viedotaped interview lasted between one and two hours. Because Susan had been interviewed individually first and had had a chance to tell her story, she tended to speak less during the family interview than she might have if we had just met. Finally, we conducted another telephone interview with Susan a year later. What follows is partly description and partly a transcript of the interviews. Susan, 42, works in public health education. Joe, 43, is an administrator in a hospital. Mark is 15.

Background

Susan was raised in the Midwest in a close-knit Catholic family. She described her upbringing and that of her two siblings as normal, consisting of "everything you would expect a Midwesterner to do." She was a high achiever and the first one from her family to go to college.

> My father knew I would be good at whatever I did. He was very
> supportive and gave out the hugs. My mother was not a warm

person—where my father would hug, my mother would just smile. So my reinforcement came from my father. I am a lot like him. He is real comfortable with what he does. If something goes wrong, you fix it. And that is the way I am.

Susan's father was a salesman who was on the road a lot. "He was more cosmopolitan than my mother because he traveled, and I related to him better than my mother, who stayed home." Her parents are still happily married after forty-seven years.

Joe was also raised a devout Catholic and attended Catholic school. His midwestern upbringing, with his parents and three siblings, did not give him any indication that he might become a sole custodian someday. "My family was close," Joe said. "There were some interesting personalities, but nothing out of the ordinary." Joe's mother is retired. His father, a teacher, died several years ago.

Susan met Joe in college, two years before she received a degree in education.

I wanted to teach and he wanted to go into business administration. I was attracted to him because he was a nice guy, funny, and bright. We got married in 1967, with a church wedding and both our families there. We put off having children for a while so we could both pursue our careers. He got his master's degree and we moved to the East because he got a job in a hospital.

Shortly after the move, they had a son and then a daughter. Susan said of this period:

It was not always a good marriage. There were problems. Some of the problems came from the housework and child care. A lot of that was my fault. I thought I was there with the children and so I knew what was best for them, and I stopped him from disciplining sometimes. I thought the way I was reared was better than his background, so I thought I knew what was best. So we had some real discipline disagreements. I was working at the time and was also with the children more. Joe had a very good knack of being able to read a book, the newspaper, and watch TV simultaneously, so when the children needed attention, they came to me. On the nights when I worked, I would come home and the children would not be in bed. I would have to do it. That was not his forte. It was mine. So here I had worked all day long and then would come home and have to work to put the children to bed. There were problems like that, but it never spiraled into open conflict. It was just different perspectives. The roles were traditional. When I went to work full-time, I knew that I would have to do all of the work at home, too. I knew I would have to do that because he did not want me to work.

Joe agreed that when the children were first born and Susan was not working, he was an uninvolved father. That was because of the way he had been raised and because he was struggling to get his career off the ground.

> But when Susan went to work, I became the daddy and the mommy, because I had the kids three days a week. I was cooking and cleaning. We even had this special thing where we made dinner for mommy and cleaned up the house for her. Our conflict was that on weekends she wanted to do things together, but I was exhausted after working around the house and having a job. There were other things pulling us apart, though. The silence was deafening.

At this point, although the marriage was difficult for Susan and Joe, it was acceptable. Then a tragedy occurred. Susan told us:

> When our daughter was 6 there was an automobile accident and she was killed. That was the final straw in the marriage. We grieved totally differently, which all of the literature says happens. We were different people. We agreed to stay together for one more year to try and make a go of it. After a year, we separated, and I stayed in the house with Mark, who was 9 at that point. The agreement was I would stay in the house for three years with Mark and then see what happened. I would not get child support or alimony, and Joe would pay the mortgage. There was no crisis money-wise, it was just an emotional issue. I was just doing okay dealing with the loss of our daughter, meaning I was doing healthy things, and my husband was not capable of doing that yet.
>
> So we separated and grew to be the best of friends and much better friends than when we were married to each other. When we were dating other people (after the divorce), we would always share our experiences with each other. It was fun.

The Change in Custody

Susan described the reasons for her becoming noncustodial:

At age 12, this child [Mark] was not fit to live with. [She smiles.] The three years that we had spent together I think were just normal developmental things for him. I had been a teacher and was supposed to know how to deal with all these things but was not happy with our relationship and with my son. I did a lot of planning things for us. I joined PWP to have a social outlet for us both. Sometimes he resented that. He thought because I got so involved in PWP I was planning for others but not for him. Mark did not like the people I was dating. Yet there were never any problems when he visited his father. Joe was a typical weekend father. These two are probably known in every restaurant in the city because they ate out a lot. Mark also got a lot of material things from Joe. He came home with more clothes than I had. That was fine. Joe was happy to be in the noncustodial role. One night at dinner, when things were at a low point between Mark and me, Mark announced that he thought we should get a divorce, that this was not working. [She laughs.]

At the end of the three years, my husband and I sat down and we talked about what we were going to do. I did not want to stay in the house or buy Joe's share of the house, and he wanted to move back into it. We talked about his taking custody of our son. He was eager to do that. It had been a three-year period of growth for him and he had come out on a real success pattern. Mark was agreeable to wanting to live with Joe, so I moved out and he moved in. It took some getting used to for Mark. He was used to running rampant over me and all of a sudden his father was putting his foot down. But they adjusted and have lived that way for three years."

Susan explained part of the reason she had not put her foot down:

I had been very lax. I did not give my child a chance to be a 10-year-old kid or an 11-year-old kid. Instead, he was a 10-year-old adult and an 11-year-old adult. When I started dating after the breakup, I sat down and talked with him like he was an adult. I said, "You'll always know where I am and who I am with," and he did not have to know those things but I gave him the benefit of knowing everything. After three years I realized that I did not have a kid anymore. I had an adult who is talking about getting a divorce. We did not have a mother-son relationship anymore. When his father moved back in, he could put his foot down at the beginning.

Mark and I did try therapy because things were just really bad. I could not do anything right for this child. Anything he could find to criticize he would. Therapy was horrible. The therapist met with us for the first couple of times together. Mark just dumped on me during those sessions, saying I never bought anything for him even if we had just come from the Mall where I had bought him a sports coat. The therapist just let us talk and gave us nothing back. So it was like open warfare on me. After a month he began separate sessions with us. The therapist even met with Joe. The therapist did not see anything wrong with Mark. Well, he was not living with Mark and did not see how I was being dumped on. It got to the point where I called the therapist and said he was not giving us anything and that we were going to stop. He said, "You have my number and you can call back if you need anything." Well, I can't even think of his name now because I know I will never call him. I think what was going on with Mark was that I was treating him like an adult. He was doing well in school, but he was in a new school, and there also might have been some self-imposed pressure to do well that could have added to his feelings.

Just before Mark went to live with Joe, Susan did begin putting her foot down.

About a week before I was going to leave and Joe was going to move in, I was having dinner with Mark. Mark said to me, "You know, Dad can be pretty tough to live with." I said that I could be pretty tough to live with, too. Mark said, "I don't think it's going to work." I told him he was going to have to give it a try. He said, "Maybe I'll try it with Dad for a week or two." I said, "No, you'll try it for six months." I think Mark was worried because his father was dating someone at the time whom he did not like. Two months after Joe moved in, Mark said he was going to go live with me again. I was living with a girlfriend at the time and had not met my present husband. We all had a big talk and decided he would continue to go back and forth unless we did something, so we told him he had to stay with Joe for the six months. There were a lot of things like this but they were not major things. I think part of the problems between Joe and Mark were that they are the same type of person and they rubbed on each other.

Joe's impressions about the divorce and custody provided a slightly different perspective:

> When we broke up, I think for expediency sake I left. That would leave more continuity for Mark with his home and neighborhood. Also, we had just lost our daughter the year before, and that was enough of a disruption, and it was better to have something stay the same. The state in which we live and society see the mother as the primary custodian, so it was just accepted.
>
> Over time, Mark was becoming unmanageable for Susan. We discussed a custody change, but it never came to anything. We were doing taxes together one year and Susan was talking about being tired with the house and the cat [Susan laughs], so we began to think about if I got the house I would have to take the cat and Mark, too. [More laughter from Susan and Mark]. About a year later we decided, given the circumstances, that it would be better for me to become the custodian. We did not go through any soul searching. It really became a practical matter. Mark did not change anything. He stayed in the house while his parents moved in and out.

Joe later added that the custody decision was made not only because of the difficulty Susan was having raising Mark but also because of finances.

> Susan had been unemployed for a period of time and it was a rough period for her. He did not help by saying things like, "Dad bought me this and you bought me that." That playing us off against each other may have made it a little more difficult.

When asked about that period, Mark said:

> Living with my mom was okay, but I think whichever of them I lived with there would always have been conflicts. My mother was more easygoing than my father. Things would have to get done but not as fast. I wanted a change to be with my dad for awhile. I grew tired of living with my mother. I did not see my father as

much as I wanted. I decided to switch for a while and see how it was.

Joe stepped in at this point in the interview and said:

I don't know if you are looking for these subtle psychological reasons. They just aren't there. They are there but they are not that important. The decision was more a practical one of finances. Susan and Mark went through a tough period when there was no heat in the house and food had to be bought sporadically. With our trading, there was stability. My perception is that Mark and Susan became better friends because I became the ogre just as she had been.

Susan noted: "After Mark went with Joe, he could escape to me." Joe went on:

He could escape to Susan just as he had escaped to me. One of the reasons we never fought that much about Mark is that when our daughter died, we overcompensated trying to make things easier for him. While other couples fought, we did whatever we could to get along to make it easier on Mark. Even after the divorce we never got into battles about things like a chair or the china.

Susan, laughing, interjected: "But he now has all those things." Joe, also laughing, replied: "But you got married. That was the problem. After a while she did not want those things. I guess after a while, if we don't fight over those things, we weren't going to fight over Mark."
Mark spoke:

I think when they first broke up I got a lot of attention and got spoiled. It seems they were both getting along well, too, and were agreeing on things and then I began to wonder why, if they are getting along well, they got separated in the first place.

(A long silence followed this statement.)
We asked if that was a feeling he had now, too, or just at the time. He responded: "It's still. . . I think now they are probably better apart. It's still good for me as I can get along better with them as people now that I'm more grown up."

After the Change

Two years after Susan moved out she remarried. Initially, Mark was troubled by the changes. When we saw Susan alone, she told us,

> For Mark, my marriage meant that his parents were not going to get back together again, and my son did not have a good relationship with his stepfather. Mark liked him as a person but did not always like his rules and regulations. So when he came to visit in our house every other weekend, he was not always happy with what went on. So the day I remarried was a very happy day for me but was a very sad day for my son. He did not come to the wedding. He was very angry. He did not want to be in any pictures or anything. It was not a carryover from Joe. Joe was very happy with the marriage, and I almost invited Joe to the wedding. But I did not know who would be comfortable with whom.
>
> Over time, Mark continued to visit us. At that point we had one of my stepchildren living with me who was 17. [Hence, there was another noncustodial mother involved in the family—Susan's husband's ex-wife.] He did nothing to include Mark in any activities, so when Mark visited, it was like it was Mark and me doing one thing and my stepson and his father doing something else. So I worked very hard at having a good relationship with my son. A few months later, my younger stepson, who was Mark's age, came and lived with us, too. Well, he and Mark got along famously and still do, and that relationship has made it much more enjoyable for Mark to visit and has helped my relationship with him. As a matter of fact, some weekends Mark and my stepson stay with Joe. It got to be a big joke. What should my stepson call my ex-husband? So this stepson has added a great deal to our lives.

What Makes The Relationships Work Now

We asked Mark how he felt being with his parents at the interview: He replied: "It's always funny. You guys [his parents] were sitting out in the lobby making jokes before we came in here."

Susan commented:

> We do all talk at least once a week. Mark has matured a lot, and that makes things easier, as it is three adults getting together. It is

not us trying to figure out how we are going to deal with this child. If we had more children, it would be more difficult. Despite everything that happened, we always remained in communication with each other. We never had long periods of not talking.

Joe responded:

Even though we were having difficulties at the time, after a while it got to be easy. When it got to that point, there was a great deal of acceptance of each other. We never argued about money. Our attorneys could not believe when we drew up the divorce decree that we did not fight. I am surprised when people of means fight about these things. I can understand if you do not have enough you fight over the little that is there. But for us it never made sense. I can't understand when a father who has the money does not support the kids or see the kids. They were a part of his life. It is beyond my comprehension. Yet I see it with people who are educated and have money. Maybe I could see arguing about the big stuff, like college tuition. But it is the little stuff that people fight over.

We asked where the family got its strength. Mark replied:

My parents were always involved in things. Being around them and seeing them doing things, I got a sense of what's right and wrong, and I think their image comes across in a pretty strong way, and that is where I got it [strength] from.

Susan also responded:

Both of my parents were strong people. I think we have learned a lot from having lost a child. We don't worry about the same things as we did before the crisis hit. We are all people-oriented, and certain things seem more important than before and others less important.

Joe's response was as follows:

I think for a while after our daughter died there was not a day when I did not think about it. I think my religion helped with that and helped us with the divorce. It has given me the faith to deal with things. Our time is so short, we better get on in dealing with people. Whether we were together or not, that death put our lives in a different place.

Susan went on: "Also, I don't think we were afraid to reach out to others. We never isolated ourselves, and we sought help in both instances from self-help groups and from therapists." And, finally, Joe said: "Some of therapy really helped me to get rid of the anger. The anger does not get you anywhere. So we get along so well because of communication. We are honest with each other about what we want."

How Others Respond

Mark said that he was never questioned about why he was living away from his mother.

A lot of my friends come from divorced homes, and no one thinks anything about it. I know one other person down the street and one from school who live with their fathers, but most are with their mothers. My parents got divorced when divorce was really becoming common.

Joe has been questioned about the custodial arrangement.

Someone comes up to me and says, "How did you manage that?" Strangely enough, I get most of the questions from women. They come up to me and say, "You're the custodial parent? Where's the mother?" The older generation has the hardest time with it. I think they think less of Susan because of it. But it is also thrown at me, like how could you raise a child? Then they ask how many children I have and how old is he. I would think that a father raising a daughter would have a much harder time. Some of them are very impressed that I am doing it, because it is tough raising kids.

Susan, when interviewed alone, mentioned some rough times when she first moved out on her own.

People tried to make me feel guilty because my son was not living with me. They would say, "How could you do that? When will you see him? How do you know he will be well taken care of?" Well, I knew my ex-husband and knew Joe would do a good job and not abuse him or ignore him. Many of the singles I met were angry and had had rough legal battles. Here I was, quite comfortable with my situation, and they resented it. They could not understand how I could be so positive when they fought so hard to do the opposite. One woman had fought tooth and nail to prevent her husband getting custody. She even hired a private detective. She had spent all her anger on this, and she was one person who came to me and said, "How could you do that?" I told her I was tired of being a custodial mother. Parents in intact families get a break, and that was what I was looking for. I had been through a hellish year of a separation and the death of my daughter. I am a very strong and determined person and a very comfortable person with most of my decisons. I was comfortable knowing I would see Mark a lot. But there were many questions from people who could not find anything positive in their situations, so they looked for something in mine.

I met a few mothers without custody in PWP and elsewhere. Most of them were noncustodial from the start. The fathers without custody I met in PWP had an interesting perspective. They felt they weren't getting the fun things out of parenting. They were only being asked to pay up, to give money for clothing and school, and then to only see their children for two hours on the weekend. Their reactions were different than the mothers. They did not want their children full-time, but they did want to have a comfortable relationship with them.

My friends were fine. They did not look down on me or anything like that. My parents were fine, too. They were very supportive. We [Joe, Mark, and Susan] were all very healthy in what we wanted. We weren't trying to get back at each other. I never lost any sleep and never lost my appetite because I was noncustodial.

Looking Ahead

We asked if they foresaw any difficult times in the future. Joe replied, "I think driving is going to be an issue. Access to either car, Susan's or mine, will be a big one." They all laughed, and when Mark said, "I have to pass the driver's test first," they laughed again.

Susan said: "I think in the long run college will be an issue. Mark wants to go to college. I think there is no problem with that, and we will support him in that, but driving is the next issue."

Joe commented:

> He can be a beach bum if he wants to be. [Laughter] Seriously, Mark does very well in school, and he would like to go to an ivy league school, but that is beyond our joint means unless we get a scholarship. We read the cost of the top schools as being almost $16,000 a year. So that could become an issue. But the car issue is going to come first. Even when we are splitting things, that is a lot of money.

We asked about the daily schedule at home for Mark and Joe. For ten minutes they bantered good-naturedly back and forth about house chores, allowances, taking care of the dog, dating habits of father and son, and so on. Mark and Joe were able to match one another's wit. Susan sat back during most of this and did not interrupt the pleasant flow of conversation. Joe added at one point, "I don't think these issues around housework and rules have anything to do with us being a single-father family. Two-parent families have the same hassles with the children. That's normal stuff."

The only recent conflict that they could remember that resulted in a punishement was when Mark stayed out past curfew and did not call home. His penalty? He was grounded for five days.

When we asked for any final comments, the good communication between the family members was emphasized again. Mark said that he got along well with Susan's stepson. Joe wondered whether he pressured Mark too much about academic issues. Susan said that she was happy they had stayed friends through all of the divorce and custody arrangements.

Susan had said when we interviewed her alone:

> One thing that scares me is that the children of divorce are more likely to get a divorce. I don't want Mark to think that it is easy to get out of relationships. I hope he does see that very important things can come from a relationship. I was the first person in my family to have a divorce. It was very painful for both Joe and me because we are Catholic. Even though we get along quite well, it

does not mean that there was not a great deal of pain. Getting a divorce was actually harder for me than giving up custody. It forced me to look at a lot of termination issues. I knew I was not losing my son, but the divorce meant an end to a lot of other things, including security.

One Year Later

One year later, we interviewed Susan again, this time by telephone. The driver's license issue had passed. Mark had turned 16, and Susan had taken him for his driving test. Joe was very generous at first in giving Mark the use of his car. But when Joe bought a new car, he became much more reluctant to share it. Susan said, "When Mark is here, I let him drive my car, but I bite my lip and pray all the time he is gone."

They are focusing on colleges now. Joe and Susan have divided up the trips to visit schools: Joe takes Mark for visits to northern colleges, and Susan takes him for visits to southern ones. Mark is only interested in a small college. Susan said:

> I am very proud of him. He is doing very well and seems to want a small school where he can have an identity and play sports. Joe and I and Mark have all gotten together a few times to discuss visiting schools and how we are going to work out costs. We are actually communicating more now than usual because of these college-related decisions. Joe and I continue to get along better not married to each other than we did when married.

Joe is single and continues to date a woman he had been seeing off and on for a year.

Conclusions

Susan, Joe and Mark provide an example of how a family can successfully work out many of the difficult problems that can follow a divorce. This family had more than its normal share. Suffering the death of a child was an enormous tragedy and was, to quote Susan, "the final straw" in an already weak relationship. Because of their Catholic upbringing, the divorce was particularly difficult for them.

Yet many factors were working in their favor. The strengths that Susan and Joe brought into the marriage helped them face many of the crises. They shared similar outlooks on life. Eventually, they came to deal with the death of their daughter in the same way. They adopted the belief that death trivializes many daily concerns. Fighting over joint-owned household goods became distasteful. At the same time, this belief may have helped them to look at the humor in life. Both parents felt that their educational backgrounds made it easier for them to work out the issues between them. They faithfully worked on their communication, which they see as the reason they get along so well now. The family's income has been a variable. When Susan worked, it was sufficient. When she was unemployed and having trouble paying for heating, her lack of income became a contributing factor, at least in Joe's mind, to his getting custody. The other factors were the rift that had developed between Mark and Susan and Susan's frustration and exhaustion with being a single parent. Had Joe been a less competent parent or had Joe not desired custody, Susan and Mark would probably still be together. The option of switching custody to Joe was there, however, and it was amenable to everyone.

Susan has adapted well to the role of noncustodial mother. This might be partially because of her remarriage or because of the good relationship that developed between Mark and her stepson, which improved things between her and Mark. But she believes that she was doing well before her remarriage and that her involvement with her second husband actually drove a wedge, at least temporarily, in the mother-son relationship. To her benefit, Susan avoids intruding on the father-son relationship, a sign that she understands and respects the boundaries that naturally develop after a divorce.

Joe enjoys being a custodial father. He demands certain things from Mark at home and will usually pursue Mark until he gets them. There is a fighting spirit between the two of them that has a fun side to it. When Joe and Mark bantered back and forth about their life together, it was like watching a well-rehearsed TV sit-com or a father-son version of the "The Odd Couple." Joe feels that he has come a long way in dealing with his anger over his daughter's death. The desire not to let things fester in his current relationships governs how he handles them. He is quick to speak when he is unhappy with something.

For Mark, the death of his sibling and the divorce of his parents were events that would be hard for any child to deal with. As his parents have struggled openly with the pain, he has, too, and he is stronger for it. He has also picked up some of his parents' humor and feisty manner. He and his parents are likable people. His departure from the family for college promises to be a successful one.

Is this a perfect family and a perfect adaptation following a divorce? Far from it—but they are a normal family who are doing well.

15

Follow-up, Conclusions, and a Look to the Future

W HAT does the future hold for the noncustodial mother? Although we do not own a crystal ball, we can surmise from our research that a number of things will happen.

First, there will be more mothers in both joint custodial and noncustodial arrangements. The rate of divorce has risen sharply and has only begun to level off. With the legal climate no longer favoring women to the extent that it has in the past, fathers who seek custody will have a better chance of getting it. In addition, there is the chance that one by-product of improved child support enforcement will be that some fathers may believe that it is financially beneficial for them to have custody. This may further increase the number of noncustodial mothers. Yet something else may stem the tide of mothers becoming noncustodial—their income. As women continue to close the wage gap with men, the mother's weaker financial position may not work against her as much as it has in the past. The ability to spend time with the children as a custodial parent may become an even more important variable if the parents' incomes are equal.

When we consider the impact of these social and child support–related changes on never-married and teen mothers, the future becomes harder to predict. There is a current push among welfare reformers for workfare, whereby mothers must be in training or employed to receive assistance. If the mother must work outside the home, that may encourage the father (whether he is married to the mother or not) to take a more active role with the children, as he may feel more needed. Also having an impact on the father's involvement is other legislation that is being considered to reverse the laws that have made it difficult for a family to receive assistance if the father is in the home and unemployed. If the father is not a financial liability, he may stay more involved. These changes may dovetail with improved child support enforcement that is geared toward establishing paternity when the parents were not married. When a legal connection is established, it could further cement the father to the family or, as discussed in chapter 9, it could push him away. Optimistically, if these trends hold true, the fathers, perhaps in the next generation, will be taking a more active role in these families, which could lead to greater participation in child rearing if the parents separate. We say optimistically because current research has not shown a great increase in the father's participation in the home even when both parents work.[1]

The increase in the numbers and percentages of divorced mothers without custody should make it easier for the noncustodial mother. As this role becomes increasingly common, she should have more models available to help her fulfill the role of noncustodian. The ambiguity associated with the role should diminish. In addition, as it becomes more common, mothers may be more willing to give up custody voluntarily, and we found that voluntarily giving up custody is a good predictor of adaptation to being a noncustodial mother. Although greater comfort may be anticipated, it is not assured. We are currently in a period when many women are refocusing on the family. Child rearing has been delayed by some women, who have chosen instead to pursue careers. Now many of those mothers are putting their careers temporarily on hold and are showing a renewed interest in child rearing. A backlash may be developing against mothers who are not the primary parent. The question is whether this current trend of working mothers having babies will result in a general feeling that women should be with their children. We don't know the answer, but we believe that the mother's status will generally improve.

A noncustodial mother should not anticipate being able to regain custody once it has gone to the father. This point was supported by the lack of custody changes found in the court records of noncustodial mothers that we discussed in chapter 10. The courts are not likely to make a change without good cause.

We wished to pursue this point further to learn what happened to the mothers over time. In early 1987, we contacted fifty mothers who had taken part in the survey and who, according to information on the questionnaire, still had a child 18 or under. These contacts yielded information three to three and a half years after the mothers had initially responded. The information we sought concerned the permanence of the mother's residency and whether custody or the mother's marital status had changed. We did not attempt to contact mothers whose youngest child living away from them would be over 18 in 1987.

We made approximately ninety five phone calls (forty-five were unanswered) before we gained information on fifty mothers. Of those fifty, only eighteen were still at the same number they had given on the questionnaire. Thus, thirty-two (64 percent) of the mothers had moved and either had wished not to leave a forwarding number with the telephone company or had moved so long ago that calls were no longer being forwarded.

Of the eighteen mothers we were able to reach, all agreed to answer our questions. Their ages had ranged from the early 30s to the mid-40s in 1983, and the ages of the youngest children living away from them in 1983 had ranged from 5 to 15. The sex and number of the children living away from the mother varied. The mothers had been noncustodial in 1983 for periods ranging from three months to six years. Two of the eighteen mothers were married at the time of the 1983 survey and were still married in 1987. Thus, the eighteen mothers were similar in a number of ways to the general sample. Two more mothers had married since 1983, and another mother was engaged. Thus, fourteen of the sixteen mothers who were single in 1983 were still single in 1987.

Custody had not changed significantly. Fourteen of the eighteen mothers (78 percent) reported no change; the children were still living with the father or elsewhere. Two said that they had gained custody. One of these two had remarried and had gained custody of three boys because of the remarriage. The other mother had gained custody of a 15-year-old daughter but had not remarried. In the other two cases, custody had shifted back and forth over the period. One mother now had custody of an 18-year-old son who had been institutionalized for juvenile delinquency. He had not wanted to return to his father's home when he was released from a detention center. The other mother stated that her 15-year-old son had gone back and forth a number of times and that he currently was living with his father.

Although we are aware that changing residences is not uncommon in this country, especially among the divorced population, we had not anticipated that so high a percentage would have moved. This pointed out to us the variability in lifestyles of the mothers. For example, one landlord that we reached told us that the mother we sought to interview had rented a room for only a few months before she had moved elsewhere. We also had thought a higher percentage would have experienced some custody changes. Further interpretations must be done with care, as we tapped into only a small subgroup of the sample. We reached only those mothers who were available. We do not know if those who moved did so because they received custody and remarried or because they moved away from their children. For example, it is likely that if a mother had remarried, she would have moved away from the residence she had when she was single. It is also possible that a mother who regained custody would have moved back into the old family home or would have found a larger residence. We would not have been able to reach such mothers. At the same time, mothers who remained in their homes over a long period might be most likely to regain custody, as they would present a more stable environment. It is difficult to determine the direction of the bias from this sample.

Giving us a different perspective on these issues, we do have follow-up information from the custodial fathers who took part in the 1982 study.[2] These fathers were also telephoned approximately three years after their participation in that study. Of the 105 fathers about whom information was gained, 61 (58 percent) were contacted (the phones of 44 (42 percent) of the fathers were no longer in service). Twenty-three of the sixty-one had remarried. Only five of the sixty-one had given up custody, and three more had changed to a joint custody situation. Approximately 87 percent of those still living at the same residence had custody. Thus, using either the mothers' or the fathers' figures, and allowing for the lack of information from those who had moved, we see that between 78 and 87 percent of those reached say that custody has not changed. We also see that it is much more likely for a noncustodial mother than a custodial father to have moved within a three-year period (64 percent versus 42 percent). Given that the fathers may have obtained custody in the first place on the basis of a promise of permanence in the neighborhood, this is not surprising. This residential stability would also improve the father's chance of retaining custody.

Finally, in the future, as seems to be happening already with the currrent generation, the children of noncustodial mothers will feel more accepted. Divorce is an accepted, though unwelcome, part of children's lives today, and the sex of the custodial parent does not seem to be an issue. Mark (in chapter 14) summed up this point when he said, "A lot of my friends come from divorced homes, and no one thinks anything about it. I know one other person down the street and one from school who live with their fathers, but most are with their mothers." This is different from Ellen's statement (in chapter 13) when she discussed the "courage" that it took for her parents to have her live with her father. The atmosphere has changed, and that should make it easier for these children now.

Whereas the future is hard to predict, the present is much easier to describe. Our purpose in this book has been to bring to light what we have learned about these often-misunderstood mothers. As a way of concluding, we will recount some of the major findings.

We found no strong link between the early childhoods of the mothers and their path to becoming noncustodial or their adaptation to that role. A few mothers who had had good relationships with their own fathers and weak ones with their mothers may have found it easier to have their children live with the father. The marriages of the mothers tended to be traditional, and marital incompatibility was the reason most often cited for the breakup. The husband's infidelity and physical and emotional abuse of the wife were also cited as factors. The reasons the mothers gave most frequently for becoming noncustodial included money, the mother's inability to parent, the children's choice to live with the father, the best interests of the children, the court's decision, and the mother's desire to pursue a career. Over half of the mothers in our study gave up custody voluntarily. Some mothers were victimized during the process and understandably remain angry about it. How the custody arrangement was arrived at has an impact on how well the mothers adapt. The path to becoming noncustodial can be conceptualized as a winding path that must be understood systemically. The roles of the father and the children in the process are key. Furthermore, the status of women—the way women are viewed and treated and particularly their financial position—must be considered.

Once a mother becomes noncustodial, she tends to find satisfaction with her social life and her work life. The relationship with her ex-husband tends to be mixed. Most troublesome to her are her feelings about her children. The mothers we studied wished that they had more contact with their children. They were not satisfied with their relationship with them and were ambivalent about the children's living situation. Many mothers were most vulnerable when it came to their children. They were sensitive about the children and wondered whether they had done the right thing. Because of the nontraditional nature of the arrangement, we surmise that the relationships between mother and children tend to be more tension-filled than those of a noncustodial father and his children. Nevertheless, a full third of our sample were content with their lives. They felt comfortable in their role, had chosen it voluntarily, did not feel guilt, had not encountered criticism for living away from their children, and felt at ease telling people they were noncustodial. Another third of the sample was mixed about many of the issues, and the final third experienced difficulties in all of these areas.

In comparing these noncustodial mothers to a sample of noncustodial fathers, we found that the differences were most pronounced in the areas of finances, the guilt feelings experienced, and the reactions of others. In all of these areas, the mothers fared worse than the fathers.

We did not encounter any mothers who had not experienced pain. Being separated from their children was difficult for all of them to various degrees. The desire to "mother" remained in many. Some mothers bitterly resented their status. They were in a great deal of inner turmoil and were immobilized by feelings of guilt, concern about others' opinions, and doubts about the future. Others had moved on with their lives. These mothers believed that what had been done either was best for everyone or was something that needed to be put behind them.

There were differences among the experiences of these mothers. The turns that their lives have taken indicate that each of them is unique. Common assumptions about a mother who lives away from her children need to be reexamined. So long as we do not understand her, it will be harder for her to adapt to her situation, and she will feel pressure to make it on her own.

Our contention is that these mothers are harshly judged and that that judgment comes from a lack of understanding regarding how mothers become noncustodial and from the common belief that children need to be with their mothers. It also comes from the belief that a father cannot be an adequate parent, a perception that is harmful to all family members. Although the information in this book can help erase the lack of understanding, it is much more difficult to change ingrained beliefs about the roles of a mother and a father. We hope that the current generation of children, who have had more exposure to divorce and to father-custody arrangements, will not grow up holding such beliefs.

Appendix: Additional Variables and Statistical Tables

Mothers with Custody of at Least One Child

One variable that was not discussed in depth in the text was the effect of split custody on the mothers' experiences. We compared the responses of the mothers with split custody (26 percent) with the responses of those who did not have split custody. Mothers with custody of at least one child:

1. Described themselves as being less involved with the children living away from them ($\chi^2 = 19.109$; $p < .001$)

2. Were less likely to see the children living away from them weekly ($\chi^2 = 10.566$; $p < .001$)

3. Spent fewer overnights with the children living away from them ($\chi^2 = 13.146$; $p < .001$)

4. Were less satisfied with their involvement with the children living away from them ($\chi^2 = 5.251$; $p < .05$)

5. Were consulted less by the children's caretaker ($\chi^2 = 5.195$; $p < .05$)

6. Felt less guilt ($\chi^2 = 7.091$; $p < .01$)

7. Were most likely to say that custody was determined by the children's choice ($\chi^2 = 8.900$; $p < .07$.)

No statistically significant differences were found between the groups regarding satisfaction with career, the reasons for the divorce, feeling financially secure, difficulty dealing with loneliness or establishing a social life, satisfaction with the relationship with the children living elsewhere, comfort in the role of noncustodial mother, self-rating as a parent, satisfaction with the children's progress, stress of the decision to have the children live elsewhere, difficulty experienced in living away from the children, voluntarily giving up custody, and income.

The meanings of these findings vary from one mother to the next and must be considered in light of some mothers' only having one child. The major differences between the groups occur in two areas: guilt feelings and amount of contact. Mothers who retain custody of at least one child feel less guilty about being away from their other children than mothers who have no children with them. Yet that reduction in guilt is not great enough to change their overall comfort as a noncustodial mother. Or it may be offset by the other major difference, the amount of involvement and contact between the mother and the children living away from her. What is clear is that there tends to be less involvement between the mother and the children living away from her when there is split custody, than when she has no custody. The reasons for this may be that the mothers with split custody feel needed by the children they are raising and feel less needed by the children living away from them, so they make less of an attempt to contact them.

Number of Years of Being Noncustodial

Throughout this book, we have cited the finding that the number of years of being noncustodial did not affect the mothers in most areas. This conclusion was based on taking the number of years for the whole sample and seeing if with the individual cells the mean differed. We explored this issue a second way. Because we hypothesized that the first year was the hardest, we looked at all of the mothers (100) who had been noncustodial for a year or less and compared their responses with those of the other mothers. Of the fifteen key variables examined, four were significant at the .09 level. It was found that mothers who had been noncustodial for one year or less:

1. Were less satisfied with their children's progress ($z = -2.4246$; $p < .02$)

2. Were less satisfied with their relationship with their children ($z = -1.7921; p < .08$);

3. Felt less secure financially ($z = -1.8976; p < .06$)

4. Experienced fewer negative reactions from people because they were noncustodial ($z = 1.7209; p < .09$.)

Logically, the first year would seem to be harder for any divorced or separated person, whether custodial or noncustodial. Fairly consistently, though, even through the eyes of the newly noncustodial, the differences were not so great.

Statistical Tables

Table A–1
THE MOTHERS' AGES
(percentage)

Age Range	Adjusted Frequency
19–27	5
28–33	12
34–37	22
38–41	29
42–45	18
46–48	14

Mean = 38.9; mode = 36; median = 38.9.

Table A–2
FATHERS' (EX-HUSBANDS') AGES
(percentage)

Age Range	Adjusted Frequency
23–32	7
33–37	19
38–42	32
43–47	25
48–65	17

Mean = 41.8; mode = 40; median = 41.3.

Table A–3
YEAR OF MARRIAGE

(percentage)

Year	Adjusted Frequency
1948–57	7
1958–62	22
1963–67	41
1968–72	20
1973–80	10

Mean = 1965; mode = 1965; median = 1964.8.

Table A–4
YEAR OF SEPARATION OR DIVORCE

(percentage)

Year	Adjusted Frequency
1966–73	14
1974–77	25
1978–79	22
1980–81	22
1982–83	16

Mean = 1977.8; mode = 1982; median = 1978.5.

Table A–5
NUMBER OF YEARS OF BEING NONCUSTODIAL

(percentage)

Number of Years	Adjusted Frequency
1	20
2	21
3	16
4	10
5	9
6	4
7	9
8	3
9	2
10–17	6

Mean = 3.95; mode = 2; median = 3.

Table A–6
AGES OF CHILDREN LIVING
ELSEWHERE

(n = 798)

Age	Number (%)
2–5	43(5%)
6–10	143(18%)
11–15	375(47%)
16–18	237(30%)

Mean = 13; mode = 16 and 17.

Table A–7
NUMBER OF CHILDREN LIVING
AWAY FROM EACH MOTHER

Number of Children	Number (%) of Mothers
1	293(56.7%)
2	170(33%)
3	43(8.2%)
4 or more	11(2.1%)

Mean = 1.5; mode = 1.

Table A–8
SIX MOST COMMON
OCCUPATIONS OF MOTHERS

Occupation	Percentage of Mothers
Secretary	17.6
Office manager/salesmanager	10.0
Nurse/schoolteacher	8.5
Preschool teacher	8.0
Teacher's aide/clerk	4.5
Office machine operator	4.5

Note: The occupation coding system used combines occupations of similar status.

Table A–9
MOTHERS' INCOME, INCLUDING ALIMONY

Income	Percentage of Mothers
$3,000–$5,000	5.3
$5,200–$10,000	16.8
$10,100–$13,000	20.8
$13,200–$17,000	21.2
$17,500–$25,000	24.7
$26,000–$60,000	11.2

Mean = $16,298; median = $14,998; mode = $12,000.

Table A–10
AMOUNT OF CHILD SUPPORT PAID BY MOTHERS PER WEEK
(n = 71; 13.7%)

Amount	Percentage of Those Who Pay
$1–$10	7
$12–$20	22.6
$25–$30	16.9
$35–$40	11.2
$44–$50	21.2
$51–$75	12.6
$80–$125	8.5

Mean = $40.36; median = $36.75; mode = $50.

Table A–11
EDUCATION COMPLETED BY MOTHERS

Years of School	Percentage of Mothers
12 or less	34.5
Two years of college	26.2
College graduate	25.5
Postgraduate	13.8

Mean = 14.2; median = 13.8; mode = 12.

Table A–12
RELIGIOUS AFFILIATIONS OF
MOTHERS

Affiliation	Percentage of Mothers
Protestant	50.6
Catholic	28.7
Jewish	5.2
Other	6.0
None	9.4

Table A–13
GEOGRAPHIC DISTRIBUTION OF
MOTHERS: ELEVEN MOST
COMMON STATES

State	Percentage of Mothers
California	16.1
Ohio	7.7
Michigan	6.2
Texas	6.2
New York	5.8
New Jersey	5.0
Maryland	4.4
Illinois	3.9
Washington	3.3
Virginia	3.7
Florida	3.1

Notes

Chapter 1: "How Could a Mother Do that?"

1. U.S. Department of Commerce (1986b).
2. According to the U.S. Department of Commerce (1984a), from 1980 to 1983, women's salaries increased between 21 percent and 26 percent, depending upon their age bracket, while men's salaries incresed 8 percent to 18 percent.
3. See Fischer (1983) and Fulks (1984).
4. See Luepnitz (1982), Greif (1985a), Orthner et al. (1976), Katz (1979), and Goldner (1985).
5. See Eron et al. (1961).
6. See, for example, Polikoff (1982), Woods et al. (1982), and Atkinson (1984).
7. For more information on PWP, contact the national office at 8807 Colesville Road, Silver Spring, MD 20910.
8. For more information on MW/OC, contact Angela Mease, c/o Mothers Without Custody 10411 Grandin Road, Silver Spring, MD 20902.
9. For additional information on Greif's study of custodial fathers, see Greif (1983a,b; 1984; 1985a–d; 1987b; In Press) and Greif and Pabst (1986).
10. Some information from the study has been previously published see Greif (1986a; 1987a).
11. For more information on self-help groups, see, for example, Lemberg (1984) and Toseland and Hacker (1985).
12. Robert White (1974) discussed the importance of experiencing competence and mastery and how those experiences can help a person overcome other deficits.
13. For examples of Bowen's work, see chapters in Guerin (1976).
14. We have been influenced by a variety of writers in the social sciences. See, for example, Gilligan (1982), Carter (1986), Kaufman (1985), Berlin and Kravetz (1981), Goldner (1985), Sturdivant (1980), Collins (1986), and Hare-Mustin (1987).
15. See, for example, Kaufman (1985).
16. See Goldberg and Pepitone-Arreola-Rockwell (1986).
17. See Sturdivant (1980).
18. See Goldner (1985).

19. Systems theory has been explained in great detail in, for example, Minuchin et al. (1979), the early works of von Bertalanffy (1968), and Katz and Kahn (1969).
20. See Sarbin and Allen (1968).
21. See Van Sell, Brief and Shuler (1981), p. 44. Theories of deviance also could have been applied; that is, when someone goes against the norm, they are treated negatively (see Gibbs, 1968, for one view of deviance).
22. See Walsh (1982), Carter and McGoldrick (1980), and Rhodes (1977) for more on life cycle development.
23. See Nuta (1984) and U.S. Department of Commerce (1985).
24. See U.S. Department of Commerce (1984a).
25. Ibid.
26. Two types of information are available on mothers without custody: that published in professional journals and that published by the lay press. Readers who are interested in journal research should see Fischer and Cardea (1981; 1982), Fischer (1983); Greif (1986a; 1987a); Rosenblum (1986); and Todres (1978). Also see dissertations by Constantatos (1984) and Herrerias (1984a) and the master's thesis by Berke et al. (1979). Stoll (1985) and Koehler (1982) have also done some work in the area, writing from firsthand experience. For books and articles in the popular press, see Paskowicz (1982), Meyers and Lakin (1983), Chesler (1986), Cassady (1978), Doudna (1982), Lawrence (1985), and Greif and Pabst (1986). To get a view of the other side of the situation, see some of the research on single custodial fathers by Chang and Deinard (1982), DeFrain and Eirick (1981), Gasser and Taylor (1976), Greif (1983a,b; 1984; 1985a–d; 1987b), Hanson (1981), Katz (1979), Mendes (1976), Orthner et al. (1976), Risman (1986), Rosenthal and Keshet (1981), and Smith and Smith (1981). In addition, see Hanson and Bozett's (1987), review of research on fathering and McCant's (1987) discussion of the cultural discrimination against fathers.

Chapter 3: The Mothers' Own Childhoods and Family Backgrounds

1. See Kitson et al. (1985).
2. Also, these mothers grew up at a time when divorce was less common than it is now. In 1955, when many of the mothers were young, the divorce rate was 2.3 per 1,000, less than half of what it was in 1983, when the questionnaire was published. See U.S. Department of Commerce (1985).
3. A variety of circumstances might have led us to conclude that there was a correlation between childhood experiences and becoming noncustodial: (1) if a significant percentage of mothers had been raised by a custodial father; (2) if a significant percentage had been raised by an abusive or "rejecting" mother or had had extremely bad relationships with women; (3) if a significant percentage had an abnormal fear of men, which may have skewed their judgment in a custody dispute; and (4) if a significant percentage described themselves as being uninterested in dolls, baby-sitting, or other age-appropriate behavior for females growing up in the 1940s, 1950s, and 1960s.

Chapter 4: Marriage and Divorce

1. U.S. Department of Commerce (1985), p. 39.
2. Ibid., p. 57.
3. A number of theories concerning divorce have also been put forth. For example, social exchange theory has been used to show that when there is emotional profit in a relationship, the relationship improves. When that profit declines in terms of interaction costs, so does the quality of the relationship. Equity theory looks at the egalitarian nature of a relationship. If it is too unequal, the relationship does not last. See Price-Bonham and Balswick (1980).
4. Schorr (1982), for example, found a decrease in the income of single custodial mothers.
5. The noncustodial parent's adjustment and involvement also can influence the custodial parent. See Greif (1987b).
6. U.S. Department of Commerce (1985).
7. Goode (1956) and Zeiss et al. (1980).
8. See Lewis (1985).
9. See Lystad (1979).
10. See Greif (1985a).
11. This approach is limited because it excludes certain portions of the sample—those who gave more than one of our categorized reasons. However, it allows for a "cleaner" look at the reasons given by the mothers for the divorce and permits some comparisons to be made. Another way to use the reasons for the divorce for analysis as an independent variable is to take all those who gave reason 1, for example, and compare their characteristics with all those who did not give the reason. This allows the total sample to be used in some way but does not account for the overlap that develops when more than one reason appears in a response. This discussion is pursued further in the notes to chapter 5, where the same procedure is used.
12. The chi-square test for significance was used for points 1 through 10, with the following results:

    (1) $\chi^2 = 7.731; p < .06$
    (2) $\chi^2 = 16.063; p < .001$
    (3) $\chi^2 = 8.032; p < .05$
    (4) $\chi^2 = 28.166; p < .0001$
    (5) $\chi^2 = 20.342; p < .0001$
    (6) $\chi^2 = 23.881; p < .0001$
    (7) $\chi^2 = 11.541; p < .01$
    (8) $\chi^2 = 40.098; p < .0001$
    (9) $\chi^2 = 10.417; p < .02$
    (10) $\chi^2 = 36.305; p < .001$

Chapter 5: How the Custody Decisions Were Made

1. We had to decide how the different responses would be coded, and we consulted other answers on the questionnaire to get a more accurate reading of the meaning

if the written answer was difficult to interpret. To group them, we looked at conceptual similarities. It is important to remember that these answers were provided by a self-selected sample of mothers who had joined a self-help group.
2. See Greif (1985a).
3. Among a sample of maltreating mothers receiving AFDC, Greif and Zuravin (1987) found that 30 percent did not have custody of at least one child.
4. See Weiss (1984).
5. A high correlation was found between mothers who felt less competent according to this question and those who gave a similar reason for being non-custodial ($z = 4.3221; p < .0001$).
6. The same method was used here as was used to test the relationship between the reasons for divorce and later experiences. Responses that fell into two or more of the major groupings were excluded, as were those that did not appear in any of the groups. The result was an accurate measure of the impact of the custody decision for a smaller portion of the total sample. This approach resulted in groups of the following sizes for the analysis:

Mother's inability to parent—68
Children chose the father—67
Money—56
Best interests of the children—45
Court-related decision—29

The sixth category—the mother's desire to pursue a career—provided a discrete category of only 9 and was dropped from the analysis. As mentioned in note 11 of chapter 4, another method was attempted in the analysis of these data. Respondents who gave reason 1, for example, were compared with all those who did not give that reason. This approach permitted the use of the entire sample, but it resulted in a less clear delineation of the trajectory of mothers who gave any particular reason for the divorce or the custody decision.
7. $\chi^2 = 21.073; p < .05$.
8. The chi-squares for these were as follows:

(1) $\chi^2 = 42.212; p < .0001$
(2) $\chi^2 = 46.367; p < .0001$
(3) $\chi^2 = 19.752; p < .001$
(4) $\chi^2 = 19.117; p < .001$

9. $\chi^2 = 74.654; p < .0001$.
10. See Greif (1985a).

Chapter 6: The Mothers' Relationships with Their Children

1. See, for example, Jacobs (1982), Pichitino (1983), Tepp (1983), and Hetherington et al. (1976). Filial deprivation—a parent's feeling of being deprived by being away from a child—has been discussed by Jenkins and Norman (1972).

See Koch and Lowery (1984) and Wallerstein and Kelly (1980) for visitation patterns of noncustodial fathers.

2. See Greif (1985a). See also Lowery and Settle (1985) for a literature review of children and divorce and Santrock and Warshak (1979) for a comparison study of the adjustment of children living with single fathers and single mothers.

3. $\chi^2 = 11.192; p < .01.$
4. $\chi^2 = 8.761; p < .067.$
5. $\chi^2 = 19.109; p < .0001.$
6. $\chi^2 = 3.662; p < .056.$
7. $\chi^2 = 51.141; p < .0001.$
8. $\chi^2 = 96.950; p < .0001.$
9. $\chi^2 = 46.104; p < .0001.$
10. $\chi^2 = 17.324; p < .01.$
11. $\chi^2 = 26.846; p < .0001.$
12. $\chi^2 = 11.195; p < .05.$
13. $z = -3.2751; p < .01.$
14. $z = -4.2296; p < .0001.$
15. For more on the relationship between children and noncustodial parents, see Isaacs et al. (1987).

Chapter 7: Noncustodial Mothers and Their Ex-Husbands

1. Greif (1985a), p. 101.
2. Ibid.
3. A step-wise multiple regression equation was run that used all of the major demographic variables. Dummy variables were established for religion, the reasons given for custody, and the reasons given for divorce as these were nominal categories. The six categories cited in the text (voluntary nature of custody, the reasons for the divorce, the reasons for custody, the age of the children living elsewhere, the age of the mother, and the religion) proved to be the best predictors of the mothers' view of the father as a parent: Multiple $R = .39962$; Overall $F (7, 420) = 11.40256; p < .0001.$

   Some of the other variables that did not have a significant impact were the sex and age of the children living elsewhere, the number of the children living elsewhere, income, education, occupation, and whether a step-mother was involved in parenting.

4. The chi-squares for these four correlations were as follows:

   (1) $\chi^2 = 19.197; p < .001$
   (2) $\chi^2 = 26.846; p < .001$
   (3) $\chi^2 = 15.727; p < .01$
   (4) $\chi^2 = 77.297; p < .001$

5. The chi-squares for these four correlations were as follows:

   (1) $\chi^2 = 40.734 \, p < .001$

(2) $\chi^2 = 113.750; p < .001$
(3) $\chi^2 = 174.261; p < .0001$
(4) $\chi^2 = 147.403; p < .0001$

6. For a few of the mothers, a high rating of the father went hand-in-hand with a low level of involvement. These mothers tended to feel that their children were well taken care of, and they did not want to stay involved.

Chapter 8: What It's Like to Be a Noncustodial Mother

1. See Weitzman (1985) and Weiss (1984), who documented a drop in single mothers' income following divorce.
2. See U.S. Department of Commerce (1984).
3. Herrerias, (1984c) noted that the number of marriages also affects the mother's adjustment, because with each additional marriage comes the involvement of more people.
4. See Greif (1985a), p. 113.
5. See Greif (1987b).
6. $\chi^2 = 19.315; p < .001$
7. $\chi^2 = 7.091; p < .01$
8. $\chi^2 = 17.846; p < .001$
9. $\chi^2 = 16.934; p < .01$
10. The three chi-square correlations were:
    $\chi^2 = 106.556; p < .001; \chi^2 = 19.5657; p < .001; \chi^2 = 14.086; p < .01$
11. See U.S. Department of Commerce (1985), p. 399.
12. Ibid., p. 392.
13. Ibid., p. 396.
14. See Axxin and Levin (1975).
15. See Rexroat (1985).
16. See U.S. Department of Commerce (1985), p. 419.
17. See Greif (1985a).
18. Ibid.
19. Greif (1983b).
20. A multiple regression equation was run with all the antecedent variables that proved to be significantly related to the comfort the mother felt. Dummy variables were used where appropriate. If just the voluntary nature of the arrangement was used, the outcome was $R = .43056; F(1, 148) = 34.81812; p = .0001$. The next variable, the difficulty dealing with changed financial circumstances, added .048 to the multiple R. The stress at the time of the breakup added another .026, and the reason for the divorce, the reason given for custody, and the respondent's religion combined added another .01 (see table below).

MULTIPLE REGRESSION EQUATION OF
ANTECEDENTS OF COMFORT

Variables	Beta	Mult. R	Significance
Voluntarily gave custody	.26865	.43056	.0001
Financial difficulty	−.23007	.47897	.004
Stress at breakup	−.29954	.50479	.025
Divorce reasons	.91485E–01	.50961	.321
Custody reasons	.67502E–01	.51309	.397
Religion	−.40588E–01	.51455	.584

21. In a multiple regression equation, these three variables provided an outcome of $R = .61892$; $F(1, 439) = .90872$; $p = .0001$. When the next five variables were added in, the association value was pushed approximately .057 higher.

Chapter 9: Child Support

1. See also Horowitz (1985) and Dodson (1985).
2. See *Family Law Reporter* 12, 2, 1985, pp. 1016–17.
3. See *Family Law Reporter* 13, May 1986, pp. 1333–34. See also Corbett (1986) for information on the Wisconsin approach.
4. See Baker and Vishwanathan (1982) and Cassety (1982).
5. See National Women's Law Center (1986).
6. See *Family Law Reporter* 12, 8, 1985, p. 1095.
7. According to Nichols-Casebolt and Garfinkel (1987), Wisconsin is currently taking the lead by experimenting with a variety of approaches, including: withholding wages from the noncustodial parent, a "percent-of-income standard" that establishes the amount of support, and a "benefit to the child equal to the amount paid by the noncustodial parent or to an assured child support benefit" (p. 445).
8. See U.S. Department of Commerce (1985).
9. $t(479) = -2.50$; $p < .02$. There were minor or no significant differences between these groups in other areas; see Greif (1986a), where these findings were first published.
10. The differences were not statistically significant.
11. See U.S. Department of Commerce (1983).
12. See Nuta (1984).
13. $z = -3.3854$; $p < .001$
14. $\chi^2 = 3.5669$; $p < .001$
15. $z = -2.316$; $p < .03$
16. $z = -2.574$; $p < .02$.
17. See Greif (1985a).
18. This chapter was not intended as an exhaustive discussion of the issues surrounding child support. For more opinions and research on child support, see

Garfinkel and Uhr (1984), Robins and Dickinson (1984), Stuart (1986), and Wall-erstein and Corwin (1986). The Institute for Research on Poverty is also a source of relevant research, as are various publications of the Office of Child Support Enforcement.

Chapter 10: Experiences with the Court System

1. According to a Divorce Equity report, for example, there was almost a doubling of child custody contests in Cuyahoga County between 1968 and 1982.
2. For more information on joint custody, see Ahrons (1980), Elkin (1987), Luep-nitz (1982), Potash (1984), Schwartz (1984), Weitzman (1985), Irving et al. (1984), and Bowman and Ahrons (1985).
3. *Family Law Reporter* 12, 20, 1986, p. 1243; *Butternick v. Butternick.*
4. *Family Law Reporter* 12, 9, 1986, pp. 1108–9; *Carter v. Carter.*
5. Information from a personal interview with Dr. Alice Dvoscan (1986). See also Girdner (1985).
6. Wishik (1986), using data from four Vermont counties, conducted an in-depth study of divorce and its economic outcomes.
7. U.S. Department of Commerce (1985).
8. Weitzman's (1985) study of cases in San Francisco and Los Angeles in 1968 (before no-fault divorces) and 1972 (after no-fault) turned up custody decisions in which mothers won between 72 and 88 percent of the cases and fathers won between 5 and 8 percent, with joint custody covering the remainder (percentages of joint custody decisions went up in both cities over time). She also reported that the father's success rate in winning custody increased from 33 percent in 1968 to 63 percent in 1977. Our findings were significant at the .07 level.
9. Because we were preparing this book for publication, time did not permit a further analysis of the most recent cases, those from June 1987.
10. Since all data were gathered at the time of the divorce decree, we do not know whether the noncustodial parents who were not ordered to pay support at the time were subsequently ordered to pay at a later hearing designed to discuss child support.

Chapter 11: Noncustodial Mothers and Noncustodial Fathers: A Study in Contrasts

1. Another possible difficulty in comparisons could have been that the fathers were a regional sample, whereas the mothers were a national sample. However, region was not a significant variable in analyzing the mothers' responses.
2. See Greif (1985a).
3. Among 1,850 single parents polled—the 1,136 fathers with custody and the 150 mothers with custody sampled in Greif (1985a) and the 517 mothers without custody and 47 fathers without custody—most agreed that the wife is more likely to end the marriage.

4. See Greif (1985a). Furstenburg et al. (1983) found a much lower rate of visitation for noncustodial fathers and a higher rate of visitation for noncustodial mothers. See also Koch and Lowery (1984).
5. $t(554) = 3.265; p < .01$. (Only correlations that were significant at the .05 level are given in this chapter.)
6. $t(561) = -3.474; p < .01$.
7. $t(555) = 2.456; p < .05$.
8. $t(557) = 1.973; p < .05$.
9. $t(550) = -2.259; p < .01$.
10. See Santrock and Warshak (1979) and Ambert (1982; 1984) for differing findings on these points.
11. See Greif (1985a).
12. Weitzman (1985) also found a great deal of financial problems for single mothers. In our research the differences were $t(55) = 3.867; p < .01$.
13. $t(553) = 2.997; p < .01$.
14. For the fathers, $r^2 = .17212$; $F(44) = .41448$; Comfort also differs between custodial and noncustodial fathers. Stewart et al. (1986) found that divorced custodial fathers were less depressed than noncustodial fathers.

Chapter 12: Help for Noncustodial Mothers in Need

1. As Gilligan (1982) pointed out, these differences between men and women exist in their view of themselves as well as in their view of morality and have an impact on behavior. See also Gove and Tudor (1973), who found more mental illness among married women than among married men and less mental illness in single women than in single men.
2. See Sturdivant (1980).
3. See Goldner (1985), and Riché (1984).
4. Ibid.
5. See Simon (1984).
6. See Heineman and Chapman (1985) and Mills (1986).
7. See Pabst (1986), Yalom (1986), Rogers (1970), and Garvin (1981).
8. The Mothers Without Custody bylaws state that the group's first purpose is "to emotionally support mothers who do not have physical custody of their children." Other purposes cited are educating the public about noncustodial mothers and serving the public interest. See *Mothers Without Custody Newsletter* (1983), p. 1.
9. In a small study of mental health professionals, Lesser (1986) found that they tended to discount environmental factors in considering how mothers become noncustodial.
10. Many professional journals publish research and therapeutic approaches for working with children. See, for example, recent issues of *Journal of Marital and Family Therapy, Social Work, Social Casework, Family Process, Family Relations,* and *American Journal of Orthopsychiatry.* Some of the discussion in this chapter first appeared in Greif (1987a).

11. See the January 1986 issue of *Family Relations*, pp. 213–14 for a list of self-help groups for single parents. An updated list is also available from PWP.

Chapter 15: Follow-up, Conclusions, and a Look to the Future

1. See Blumstein and Schwartz (1983).
2. See Greif (in press).

References

Abelsohn, D. (1983). Dealing with the abdication dynamic in the post-divorce family: A context for adolescent crisis. *Family Process* 22(3): 359–83.

Ahrons, C.R. (1980). Joint custody arrangements in the post-divorce family. *Journal of Divorce* 3(3): 189–205.

Ambert, A.M. (1982). Differences in children's behavior toward custodial mothers and fathers. *Journal of Marriage and the Family* 44(1): 73–86.

———. (1984). Longitudinal changes in children's behavior toward custodial parents. *Journal of Marriage and the Family* 46(2): 463–67.

Atkinson, J. (1984). Criteria for deciding child custody in the trial and appellate courts. *Family Law Quarterly* 28(1): 1–42.

Axxin, J., and Levin, H. (1975). *Social welfare: A history of the American response to need.* New York:Dodd, Mead.

Baker, T., and Vishwanathan, N. (1982) *The use of organization theory in evaluating organizational performance in the public sector.* Paper presented at the Conference on Organization Theory and Public Policy, State University of New York at Albany, May.

Baldwin, W.H. (1972; originally published 1904). *Family desertion and non-support laws.* New York: Arno Press and New York Times.

Bartz, K.W., and Witcher, W.C. (1978). When father gets custody. *Children Today* 7(5): 2–6,35.

Bayes, M. (1981). The prevalence of gender role bias in mental health services. In E. Howell and M. Bayes, eds., *Women and mental health* (pp. 83–85). New York: Basic Books.

Beavers, R. (1985). *Successful marriage.* New York: Norton.

Berke, P.; Black, M.;' Byrne, M.; Fields, F.; Gallagher, B.; and Paley, N. (1979). *A study of natural mothers who terminated the primary parental role.* Unpublished master's thesis, University of Southern California School of Social Work, Los Angeles.

Berlin, S., and Kravetz, D. (1981). Women as victims: A feminist social work perspective. *Social Work* 26(6): 447–49.

Blumstein, P., and Schwartz, P. (1983). *American couples.* New York: Morrow.

Bowman, M.E., and Ahrons, C.R. (1985). Impact of legal custody status on fathers' parenting postdivorce. *Journal of Marriage and the Family* 47(2): 481–88.

Brandt, L. (1972; originally published 1904). *Five hundred and seventy-four deserters and their families.* New York: Arno Press and New York Times.

Broverman, I.K.; Broverman, D.M.; Clarkson, F.E.; Rosenkrantz, P.S.; and Vogel, S.R. (1981). Sex role stereotypes and clinical judgments of mental health. In E. Howell and M. Bayes, eds. *Women and Mental Health* (pp. 86–97). New York: Basic Books.

Carter, E. (1986). Lecture given as part of a presentation by the Women's Project in Family Therapy at the 44th Annual AAMFT conference, Orlando, Florida, October.

Carter, E., and McGoldrick, M. (1980). *The family life cycle: A framework for family therapy.* New York: Gardner Press.

Cassady, M. (1978). Runaway wives. *Psychology Today* 8(May): 42.

Cassety, J.H. (1982). Child support: New focus for social work practice. *Social Work* 27(6):504–8.

———. (1984). Child support: Emerging issues for practice. *Social Casework* 65(2): 74–80.

Chang, P., and Deinard, A.S. (1982). Single-father caretakers: Demographic characteristics and adjustment processes. *American Journal of Orthopsychiatry* 52(2): 236–42.

Chesler, P. (1986). *Mothers on trial.* New York: McGraw-Hill.

Clarke-Stewart, A. (1977). *Child care in the family.* New York: Academic Press.

Collier, H.V. (1982). *Counseling women.* New York: Free Press.

Collins, B.G. (1986). Defining feminist social work. *Social Work* 31(3): 214–19.

Constantatos, M. (1984). *Noncustodial versus custodial divorced mothers: Antecedents and consequences of custody choice.* Unpublished doctoral dissertation, The University of Texas Health Science Center at Dallas.

Corbett, T. (1986). Child support assurance: Wisconsin demonstration. *Focus* 9(1): 1–5.

DeFrain, J., and Eirick R. (1981). Coping as divorced single parents: A comparative study of fathers and mothers. *Family Relations* 30(2): 265–73.

Divorce Equity. (undated). *Research update of divorce statistics in Cuyahoga County.* Unpublished report, Cleveland.

Dodson, D.G. (1985). New remedies: Wage withholding gets tougher. *Family Advocate* 8(1): 2, 7–9.

Doudna, C. (1982). The weekend mother. *New York Times Magazine* (3 October): 72–75,84–88.

Elkin, M. (1987). Joint custody: Affirming that parents and families are forever. *Social Work* 32(1): 18–24.

Erikson, E. (1975). *Life history and the historical moment.* New York: Norton.

Eron, L.; Banta, T.; Walder, L.; and Laulicht, J.H. (1961). Comparison of data obtained from mothers and fathers on childrearing practices and their relation to child aggression. *Child Development* 32(3): 457–72.

Family Law Reporter. (1985–86 issues). The cases cited in the text are *Butternick v. Butternick* and *Carter v. Carter.*

Fischer, J.L. (1983). Mothers living apart from their children. *Family Relations* 32(3): 351–57.

Fischer J.L., and Cardea, J.M. (1981). Mothers living apart from their children. *Alternative Lifestyles* 4(2): 218–27.

———. (1982). Mother–child relationships of mothers living apart from their children. *Alternative Lifestyles* 5(1):42–53.

Fulks, N.J. (1984). Social perceptions of divorced parents; The effects of gender and custodial status (Doctoral dissertation, University of Kentucky, 1984). *Dissertation Abstracts International* 46: 946B.

Furstenberg, F.F.; Nord, C.W.; Peterson, J.L.; and Zill, N. (1983). The life course of children of divorce: Marital disruption and parental contact. *American Sociological Review* 48(5): 656–68.

Garfinkel, I., and Uhr, E. (1984). A new approach to child support. *Public Interest* 75(1): 111–20.

Garvin, C. (1981). *Contemporary group work*. Englewood Cliffs, N.J.: Prentice-Hall.

Gasser, R.D., and Taylor, C.M. (1976). Role adjustment of single parent fathers with dependent children. *Family Coordinator* 25(4): 397–401.

Gelles, R.J. (1980). Violence in the family: A review of research in the seventies. *Journal of Marriage and the Family* 42(4): 873–85.

Gibbs, J.B. (1968). Conceptions of deviant behavior: The old and the new. In M. Lefton, J.K. Skipper, and C.H. McCaghy, eds. *Approaches to deviance: Theories, concepts, and research findings*. New York: Appleton-Century-Crofts.

Gilligan, C. (1982). *In a different voice: Psychological theory and women's development*. Cambridge: Harvard University Press.

Girdner, L.K. (1985). Strategies of conflict: Custody litigation in the United States. *Journal of Divorce* 9(1): 1–15.

Goldberg, H., and Pepitone-Arreola-Rockwell, F. (1986). Foreword. *Psychotherapy* 23(2): iv.

Goldner, V. (1985). Feminism and family therapy. *Family Process* 24(1): 31–47.

Goode, W.S. (1956). *After divorce*. Glencoe, Ill.: Free Press.

Greif, G.L. (1983a). Widowers. *Single Parent* 26(6): 15–18.

———. (1983b). Single fathers: Findings from survey. *Single Dad's Lifestyle* 6(2): 7–8.

———. 1984. Custodial dads and their ex-wives. *Single Parent* 27(1): 17–20.

———. (1985a). *Single fathers*. Lexington, Mass.: Lexington Books.

———. (1985b). Single fathers rearing children. *Journal of Marriage and the Family* 47(1): 185–91.

———. (1985c). Children and housework in the single father family. *Family Relations* 34(3): 353–57.

———. (1985d). Practice with single fathers. *Social Work in Education* 7(4): 231–43.

———. (1986a). Mothers without custody and child support. *Family Relations* 35(1): 87–93.

———. (1986b). *Mothers without custody/Fathers with custody*. Paper presented at the 44th Annual AAMFT Conference, October. Orlando, Florida.

———. (1987a). Mothers without custody. *Social Work* 32(1):11—16.

————. (1987b). Single fathers and noncustodial mothers: The social worker's help-
ing role. *Journal of Independent Social Work* 1(3): 59–69.
Greif, G. (In press). A longitudinal examination of single custodial fathers: Impli-
cations for treatment. *American Journal of Family Therapy.*
Greif, G.L., and Pabst, M.S. (1986). Weekend mothers. *Single Parent* 24(4): 14–
17,46.
Greif, G.L., and Zuravin, S. (1987). Low-income maltreating mothers who do not
have custody. Unpublished manuscript.
Guerin, P.J., ed. (1976). *Family therapy: Theory and practice.* New York: Gardner
Press.
Hanson, S. (1981). Single custodial fathers and the parent-child relationship. *Nursing
Research* 30(4): 202–4.
Hanson, S., and Bozett, F. (1987). Fatherhood: A review and resources. *Family
Relations* 36(3): 333–39.
Hare-Mustin, R. (1981). A feminist approach to family therapy. In E. Howell and
M. Bayes, eds., *Women and mental health* (pp. 553–71). New York: Basic Books.
Hare-Mustin, R. (1987). The problem of gender in family therapy theory. *Family
Process* 26(1): 15–27.
Haskins, R.; Dobelstein, A.W.; Akin, J.S.; and Schwartz, J.B. (1985). *Estimates of
national child support collections potential and the income security of female-headed families.*
Washington, D.C.: Office of Child Support Enforcement.
Heineman, R., and Chapman, P. (1985). *The role of the adolescent in the remarried
family.* Paper presented at National Association of Social Workers Symposium,
Chicago, October.
Herrerias, C. (1984a). *Noncustodial mothers: A study of self-concept and social interactions.*
Unpublished doctoral dissertation, University of Texas at Austin.
————. (1984b). *Latinas as noncustodial mothers.* Paper presented at the Annual Meet-
ing of the National Coalition of Hispanic Mental Health and Human Services
Organizations, St. Louis, September.
————. (1984c). *Noncustodial mothers: Loving is leaving.* Paper presented at the Annual
Meeting of the Society for the Study of Social Problems, San Antonio, August.
Hetherington, E.M.; Cox, M.; and Cox, R. (1976). Divorced fathers. *Family Co-
ordinator* 25(4): 417–28.
Horowitz, R. (1985). New remedies: Congress gets tougher. *Family Advocate* 8(1):
2–6.
Horowitz, R., and Dodson, G.D. (1985). *Child support, custody and visitation: A report
to state child support commissions.* Washington, D.C.: American Bar Association and
National Legal Resource Center for Child Advocacy and Protection.
Howell, E. (1981). Women from Freud to the present. In E. Howell and M. Bayes,
eds., *Women and mental health* (pp. 3–25). New York: Basic Books.
Howell, E., and Bayes, M., eds. (1981). *Women and mental health.* New York: Basic
Books.
Irving, H.H.; Benjamin, M.; and Trocme, N. (1984). Shared parenting: An em-
pirical analysis utilizing a large data base. *Family Process* 23(4): 561–69.
Isaacs, M.; Leon, G.H.; and Kline, M. (1987). When is a parent out of the picture?
Different custody, different perceptions. *Family Process* 26(1): 101–10.

Jacobs, J.W. (1982). The effect of divorce on fathers: An overview of the literature. *American Journal of Psychiatry* 139(10): 1235–41.

———. (1983). Treatment of divorcing fathers: Social and psychotherapeutic considerations. *American Journal of Psychiatry* 140(10): 1294–99.

Jenkins, S., and Norman, E. (1972). *Filial deprivation and foster care.* New York: Columbia University Press.

Kagan, J. (1984). *The nature of the child.* New York: Basic Books.

Katz, A.J. (1979). Lone fathers: Perspectives and implications for family policy. *Family Coordinator* 28(4): 521–28.

Katz, D., and Kahn, R. (1969). Common characteristics of open systems. In F.E. Emery, ed., *Systems thinking: Selected readings.* Harmonsworth, Middlesex, England: Penguin.

Kaufman, D.R. (1985). Women who return to orthodox Judaism: A feminist analysis. *Journal of Marriage and the Family* 47(3): 543–51.

Kitson, G.C.; Babri, K.B.; and Roach, M.J. (1985). Who divorces and why: A review. *Journal of Family Issues* 6(3): 255–93.

Koch, M.A., and Lowery, C.R. (1984). Visitation and the noncustodial father. *Journal of Divorce* 8(2): 47–65.

Koehler, J.M. (1982). Mothers without custody. *Children Today* 11(2): 12–15,35.

Krause, H.D. (1983). Reflections on child support. *Family Law Quarterly* 27(2): 109–32.

Kravetz, D. (1976). Sexism in a woman's profession. *Social Work* 21(6): 421–26.

Lamb, M., and Lamb, J. (1978). The nature and importance of the father-infant relationship. *The Family Coordinator* 25(4): 379–85.

Lawrence, J. (1985). He got the kids. *Washington Post Magazine* (18 August): 10,11,13,17.

Lemberg, R. (1984). Ten ways for a self-help group to fail. *American Journal of Orthopsychiatry* 54(4): 648–50.

Lesser, E. (1986). *One of the last great crimes: Women who leave children.* Paper presented at the 44th Annual AAMFT Conference, Orlando, Florida, October.

Levinger, G. (1966). Sources of marital dissatisfaction among applicants for divorce. *American Journal of Orthopsychiatry* 36(5): 803–7.

Lewis, B. (1985). The wife abuse inventory: A screening device for the identification of abused women. *Social Work* 30(1): 32–35.

Lowery, C.R., and Settle, S.A. (1985). Effects of divorce on children: Differential impact of custody and visitation patterns. *Family Relations* 34(4): 455–63.

Luepnitz, D.A. (1982). *Child custody: A study of families after divorce.* Lexington, Mass.: Lexington Books.

Lystad, M.H. (1979). Violence at home: A review of the literature. In D. Gil, ed., *Child abuse* (pp. 387–412). New York: AMS Press.

McCant, J. (1987). The cultural contradiction of fathers as nonparents. *Family Law Quarterly* 21(1): 127–43.

Mendes, H.A. (1976). Single fatherhood. *Social Work* 21(4): 308–12.

Meyers, S., and Lakin, J. (1983). *Who will take the children? A new custody option for divorcing mothers—and fathers.* New York: Bobbs-Merrill.

Mills, D. (1986). *Differential diagnosis in non-traditional family structures.* Paper presented at the 44th Annual AAMFT Conference, November.

Minuchin, S.; Rosman, B.L.; and Baker, L. (1979). *Psychosomatic families: Anorexia nervosa in context.* Cambridge: Harvard University Press.

Mothers Without Custody Newsletter. (1983). Greenbelt, Md.: MW/OC.

National Women's Law Center. (1986). *Fact sheet: Child support enforcement amendments.* Washington, D.C.: National Women's Law Center.

Nichols-Casebolt, A. (1986). The economic impact of child support reform on the poverty status of custodial and noncustodial families. *Journal of Marriage and the Family* 48(4): 875–80.

Nichols-Casebolt, A., and Garfinkel, I. (1987). New child support assurance program: The Wisconsin demonstration. *Social Work* 32(5): 445–46.

Nuta, V.R. (1984). Single mothers hard hit financially in last four years. *Single Parent* 27(9): 7–8.

———. (1986). Emotional aspects of child support enforcement. *Family Relations* 35(1): 177–81.

Oellerich, T.D. (1984). The effect of potential child support transfers on Wisconsin AFDC costs, caseloads, and recipient well-being. *Social Work Research and Abstracts* 20(3): 66.

Office of Child Support Enforcement. (1984). *Child support enforcement: Ninth annual report to the Congress for the period ending September 30, 1984.* Washington, D.C.: U.S. Department of Health and Human Services.

Orthner, D.K.; Brown, T.; and Ferguson, D. (1976). Single parent fatherhood: An emerging lifestyle. *Family Coordinator* 25(4): 429–37.

Pabst, M. (1986). Support group setting for cognitive therapy. *International Cognitive Therapy Newsletter* 2(1): 2–5.

Parents Without Partners. (1986). *Fact sheet: What custodial parents should know about child support.* Silver Spring, Md.: PWP.

Paskowicz, P. (1982). *Absentee mothers.* Totowa, N.J.: Allanheld/Universe.

Pichitino, J.P. (1983). Profile of the single father: A thematic integration of the literature. *Personnel and Guidance Journal* 9(1): 295–99.

Pisano, D. (1986). *A look at mothers without custody.* Unpublished master's thesis, University of Maryland School of Social Work and Community Planning, Baltimore.

Polikoff, N. (1982). Why are mothers losing? A brief analysis used in child custody determinations. *Women's Rights Reporter* 7(3): 235–43.

Potash, M.S. (1984). Psychological support for a rebuttal presumption of joint custody. *Probate Law Journal* 4(3): 17–30.

Price-Bonham, S., and Balswick, J.O. (1980). The noninstitutions: Divorce, desertion, and remarriage. *Journal of Marriage and the Family* 47(1): 131–42.

Rhodes, S. (1977). A developmental approach to the life cycle of the family. *Social Casework* 58(5): 301–11.

Riché, M. (1984). The systemic therapist. *Family Therapy Networker* 8(3): 43–45.

Risman, B.J. (1986). Can men "mother?" Life as a single father. *Family Relations* 35(1): 95–102.

Robins, P., and Dickinson, K. (1984). Receipt of child support by single-parent families. *Social Service Review* 58(12): 622–41.

Rogers, C. (1970). *On encounter groups*. New York: Harper and Row.

Rosen, R. (1982). *The lost sisterhood: Prostitution in America, 1900–1918*. Baltimore: Johns Hopkins University Press.

Rosenblum, K.E. (1986). Leaving as a wife, leaving as a mother. *Journal of Family Issues* 7(2): 197–213.

Rosenthal, K.M., and Keshet, H.F. (1981). *Fathers without partners*. Totowa, N.J.: Rowman and Littlefield.

Rutter, M. (1972). *Maternal deprivation assessed*. Baltimore: Penguin.

Salts, C.J. (1979). Divorce process: Integration of theory. *Journal of Divorce* 2(1): 233–40.

Sametz, L. (1980). Children of incarcerated women. *Social Work* 25(4): 298–303.

Santrock, J.W., and Warshak, R.A. (1979). Father custody and social development in boys and girls. *Journal of Social Issues* 35(4): 112–25.

Sarbin, T.R., and Allen, V.L. (1968). Role theory. In G. Lindzey and E. Aronson, eds., *The handbook of social psychology*, Vol. 1 (2nd ed.). Reading, Mass.: Addison-Wesley.

Sarri, R.C. (1981). Federal policy changes and the formation of poverty. *Child Welfare* 64(3): 235–47.

Schorr, A.L. (1982). Single parents, women, and public policy. *Journal of the Institute for Socioeconomic Studies* 6(4): 100–113.

Schwartz, S.F.G. (1984). Toward a presumption of joint custody. *Family Law Quarterly* 28(2): 225–46.

Simon, R. (1984). From ideology to practice: An interview with the women's project in family therapy. *Family Therapy Networker* 8(3): 28–32,38–40.

Smith, R.M. and Smith, C.W. (1981). Child-rearing and single parent fathers. *Family Relations* 30(3): 411–17.

Stewart, J.R.; Schwebel, A.I.; and Fine, M.A. (1986). The impact of custodial arrangement on the adjustment of recently divorced fathers. *Journal of Divorce* 9(3): 55–65.

Stoll, K. (1985). Non-custodial mother. *Family Therapy Networker* 9(3): 53–57.

Sturdivant, S. (1980). *Therapy with women: A feminist philosophy of treatment*. New York: Springer.

Stuart, A. (1986). Rescuing children: Reforms in the child support payment system. *Social Service Review* 60(2): 207–17.

Tepp, A.V. (1983). Divorced fathers: Predictors of continued paternal involvement. *American Journal of Psychiatry* 140(11): 1465–69.

Todres, R. (1978). Runaway wives: An increasing North-American phenomenon. *Family Coordinator* 27(1): 17–21.

Toseland, R., and Hacker, L. (1985). Social workers' use of self-help groups as a resource for clients. *Social Work* 30(3): 232–37.

Tropf, W.D. (1984). An exploratory examination of the effect of remarriage on child support and personal contacts. *Journal of Divorce* 7(3): 57–73.

U.S. Department of Commerce, Bureau of the Census. (1983). *Marital Status and living arrangements: March 1982*. (Series P-20, no. 380). Washington, D.C.: U.S. Government Printing Office, May.

———. (1984a). *Statistical abstracts of the United States: 1985*. Washington, D.C.: U.S. Government Printing Office.

———. (1984b). *Earnings in 1981 of married-couple families, by selected characteristics of husbands and wives*. (Series P-23, no. 133). Washington, D.C.: U.S. Government Printing Office.

———. (1985). *Statistical abstracts of the United States: 1986*. Washington, D.C.: U.S. Government Printing Office.

——— (1986a). *Survey of income and program participation*. Unpublished data.

——— (1986b). *Household and family characteristics: March, 1985*. (Series P-20, no. 411). Washington, D.C.: U.S. Government Printing Office.

———. (1986c). *Child support and alimony: 1983* (Supplemental report, Series P-23, no. 148). Washington, D.C.: U.S. Government Printing Office.

Van Sell, M.; Brief, A.P.; and Shuler, R.S. (1981). Role conflict and ambiguity: Integration of the literature and directions for future research. *Human Relations* 34(1): 43–71.

von Bertalanffy, L. (1968). General systems theory in psychology and psychiatry. In *General systems theory: Foundations, developments, and applications*. New York: George Braziller.

Wallerstein, J. (1986). Women after divorce: Preliminary report from a ten-year follow-up. *American Journal of Orthopsychiatry* 56(1): 65–77.

Wallerstein, J., and Corbin, S.B. (1986). Father-child relationships after divorce: Child support and educational opportunities. *Family Law Quarterly* 20(2): 109–28.

Wallerstein, J., and Kelly, J. (1980). *Surviving the breakup: How children and parents cope with divorce.* New York: Basic Books.

Walsh, F., ed. (1982). *Normal family processes*. New York: Guilford Press.

Walters, M. (1985). Working with single-parent families. Workshop given at Family Institute of Philadelphia Annual Conference, Philadelphia, March.

Weiss, R.S. (1984). The impact of marital dissolution on income and consumption in single-parent households. *Journal of Marriage and the Family* 46(1): 115–27.

Weitzman, L. (1981). The economics of divorce: Social and economic consequences of property, alimony and child support awards. *UCLA Law Review* 28: 1181–1268.

———. (1985). *The divorce revolution: The unexpected social and economic consequences for women and children*. New York; Free Press.

White, R.W. (1974). Strategies of adaptation: An attempt at systemic description. In G.V. Coelho, D.A. Hamburg, and J.E. Adams, eds., *Coping and adaptation*. New York: Basic Books.

Wishik, H.R. (1986). Economics of divorce: An exploratory study. *Family Law Quarterly* 20(1): 79–107.

Woods, L.; Been, V.; and Shulman, J. (1982). *The use of sex and economic discriminatory criteria in child custody awards*. New York: National Center on Women and Family Law.

Wright, D.W., and Price, S.J. (1986). Court-ordered child support payment: The effect of the former-spouse relationship on compliance. *Journal of Marriage and the Family* 48(4): 869–74.

Yalom, I. (1985). *The theory and practice of group psychotherapy.* (3d ed.). New York: Basic Books.

Zeiss, A.; Ziess, R.; and Johnson, S. (1980). Sex differences in initiation of and adjustment to divorce. *Journal of Divorce* 4(2): 21–23.

Index

About the Authors

GEOFFREY L. GREIF received a master's degree from the University of Pennsylvania School of Social Work and a doctorate from the Columbia University School of Social Work. He is the author of *Single Fathers* (Lexington Books, 1985) and has written more than twenty articles about single parents. He serves on the professional advisory board of Parents Without Partners and is a contributing editor to *The Single Parent* magazine. He is currently an assistant professor in the School of Social Work and Community Planning, University of Maryland at Baltimore.

MARY S. PABST received a master's degree from the University of Maryland School of Social Work and Community Planning. She is currently a psychiatric social worker at The Sheppard and Enoch Pratt Hospital, Baltimore.